DEFIANCE
AT SEA

DEFIANCE AT SEA

DRAMATIC NAVAL WAR ACTION

JON GUTTMAN

CASSELL

To my father, Paul Guttman,
US Navy Rescue veteran of the Second World War in the Pacific,
to my brother Robert Guttman, US Merchant Marine
veteran of the 1991 Gulf War,
and to all those who fought on the seas and rivers.

First published by Arms and Armour Press 1995
This Cassell Military Classics edition 1998

Cassell Plc
Wellington House, 125 Strand, London WC2R 0BB

British Library Cataloguing in Publication Data: a catalogue
record for this book is available from the British Library

ISBN 0-304-35085-0

Designed and edited by DAG Publications Ltd,
Designed by David Gibbons; edited by Michael Boxall,
printed and bound in Great Britain by
Cox & Wyman Ltd., Reading, Berks.

Cassell Military Classics are available from all good bookshops
or from:
    Cassell C.S.
    Book Service By Post
    PO Box 29, Douglas I-O-M
    IM99   1BQ
    telephone: 01624 675137, fax: 01624 670923

Contents

Acknowledgements

The principal outside assistance I have had in researching this collection of naval actions came from three of the navies whose small-unit exploits are less well-documented in the English-speaking world. I wish to thank the *Musée de la Marine* in Paris and the French Naval Attaché in Washington, D.C., for their help in researching the battles of Beachy Head, Barfleur and La Hogue, and the Japanese Naval Attaché in Washington, DC, Captain Hiro Yokoyama, for his help and input with the battles of Tassafaronga, Samar and especially Badoeng Strait. The kind assistance of Lieutenant Bryn Owen, FMA, RN (ret.), curator of the Welsh Regiment Museum, is acknowledged for the additional information he provided on the 69th Regiment of Foot at Cape St. Vincent. Thanks also are extended to Lieutenant-Commander Julio E. Caravaglia, the Argentinean Naval Attaché in Washington, and to W. J. R. Gardner of the Naval Historical Branch in London for their help in piecing together the activities of the submarine ARA *San Luis* during the South Atlantic War.

Introduction

Last stands and grand gestures in the face of daunting odds have been around as long as organised warfare – with those at sea occurring only somewhat later than those on land. In the area of land warfare, much has been written of such desperate stands as those of Leonidas' 300 Spartans against King Xerxes' Persian host at the pass of Thermopylae in 480 BC, Colonel William Travis' Texans defying the Mexican army at the Alamo in 1836, or the 140 British troops who held off a 4,500-man Zulu corps at Rorke's Drift in 1879. Much-studied, too, have been the offensive actions of the élite few against the many, such as the advance of the unsupported British and Hanoverian infantry at Minden in 1759, the 'Death Ride' of Major-General Friedrich von Bredow's cavalry at Vionville in 1870, or just about any raid by Britain's Special Air Service during the Second World War. In equal measure, instances of outstanding valour and fortitude have taken place on the world's embattled oceans, seas, lakes and rivers, although the circumstances of the desperate situation and the manner in which it is handled vary widely.

A comprehensive study of unequal actions at sea would require a much larger volume than this microcosmic study, so examples – some well-known, some I hope less familiar – have been selected to illustrate various types of naval action in which daunting odds were challenged ... and often miraculously overcome. In so doing, the author accepts the likelihood that the actions selected might ignite some controversy among the history pundits – both regarding the eligibility of the cases chosen and those that were overlooked.

A case in point would concern the omission of what is arguably the earliest battle in which a naval force faced a significantly stronger opponent: Themistocles' Greek galleys and the vast floating host of Persian King Xerxes in Eleusis Bay off the Island of Salamis on 20 September 480 BC, with the fate of Greece – which to the Greek mind was to say the fate of Western civilisation – at stake. Salamis, however, also contained an element that often comes into play when evaluating the odds in a sea action: calculated risk. Although outnumbered, Themistocles knew that if he could goad Xerxes into sending his fleet into Eleusis Bay, its confines would cancel the Persians' numerical advantage. That, combined with the generally superior ship-handling skill of the Greek galley crews, turned Salamis into an unqualified Greek triumph, with an estimated 200 Persian ships sunk for the loss of 40 Greek vessels ... and, eventually, Xerxes' abandonment of his Greek invasion.

It might be argued that the small size of the English warship *Revenge* allowed Captain Richard Grenville and his crew to cancel the advantages of a succession of Spanish boarding-parties, who were forced to concentrate their numbers in a relatively narrow area in order to assault their opponent. The result was a series of bloody repulses for the Spaniards, but in the case of *Revenge* the overwhelming numbers and fire-power of the Spanish ships, the eventual attrition dealt to the English crew and the mortal wounding of their tenacious captain sealed the inevitable outcome.

The concept of using sheer aggression to counterbalance the advantages of a more powerful enemy force, exemplified herein by Jervis and Nelson at Cape St. Vincent, and by Captain Toshio Abe's two destroyers at Badoeng Strait, has figured in numerous other sea actions. At the Battle of Lissa on 20 July 1866 – the first engagement to involve ironclads at sea – the Austrian fleet soundly defeated an Italian fleet that had more armoured vessels, the three most powerful of which possessed more firepower than all the Austrian ironclads combined. In the case of Lissa, where the opposing crews were equally matched in terms of skill and courage, the difference was made by their leaders. While Italy's vac-illating Admiral Count Carlo Pellion di Persano shifted his flag from the ironclad *Re d'Italia* to the newer *Affondatore* without informing his cap-tains – thus completely forfeiting control of the battle – Austria's Admi-ral Wilhelm von Tegetthoff had his ships painted black and told his captains to 'ram everything painted grey'. A worthy disciple of Jervis and Nelson, Tegetthoff not only placed his flagship *Erzherzog Ferdinand Max* at the head of his three-vic formation when it slashed through Persano's untidy line, but personally rammed and sank the *Re d'Italia* and the corvette *Palestro*.

The use of an aggressive defence, exemplified by the defence of the Japanese troopship *Sasago Maru* in Badoeng Strait by the destroyers *Oshio* and *Asashio*, was far from unique. Perhaps the most significant such action was taken by Captain Robert St Vincent Sherbrooke (fittingly, a family descendant of John Jervis), who made aggressive use of his five destroyers to defend Convoy JW-51A from a German force consisting of the heavy cruiser *Admiral Hipper*, the *Panzerschiff Lützow* and six destroy-ers in the Barents Sea on New Year's Eve 1942. Although badly wounded, Sherbrooke survived to receive the Victoria Cross, while the disappoint-ing performance by his German opponents led to an order from an enraged Adolf Hitler for the scrapping of his entire High Seas Fleet, the resignation of Grand Admiral Erich Raeder and his replacement by Karl Dönitz.

A completely different form of daring comes into play when a lone ship operates deep in enemy-controlled waters, whether it be a commerce raider like *Constitution*, *Emden*, *Admiral Scheer* or *Stier*, or a small submarine such as *B.11* or *San Luis*. In either case, discovery by the enemy, followed by the concentration of his naval units against the raider, leaves its crew only two alternatives: to try to get away or to go down fighting. To effect her escape from the Sea of Marmara, *B.11* had to tackle the treacherous currents of the Dardanelles while running the gauntlet of Turkish shore batteries and mines; *San Luis*, by contrast, used patience and the ocean floor to survive hours of attack by state-of-the-art anti-submarine weaponry.

For ships such as *Constitution*, *Emden* and *Admiral Scheer*, the very nature of their mission – commerce raiding in waters controlled by the enemy – carried with it an extraordinary degree of risk. Paradoxically, while the distinctive appearance of *Constitution* (one of the world's largest frigates in 1812) and *Scheer* (one of only three pocket battleships in the world) made it difficult for them to keep a low profile, they were expected to damage, embarrass and confuse the British, while at the same time striving to elude discovery, entrapment and destruction, since neither of the small navies they served could afford their loss. So it was that *Emden* and *Scheer* played a tense cat-and-mouse game with the Royal Navy, relying on the wits of their captains to prolong the dangerous game they were playing for as long as possible.

Escape and evasion, too, tests the nerve, ingenuity and discipline of ship, officers and crew. In the case of *Scheer*'s most noteworthy cruise, successful evasion was achieved throughout, sometimes through what one of her British pursuers called '*Scheer* bad luck'. The most desperate moment of *Constitution*'s career did not involve the trading of broadsides, but the quest for speed on a windless sea, in one of the slowest sea chases in naval history. The light cruiser *Emden*'s destruction by a more powerful adversary would be the prototype for the finales of numerous other German warships in two world wars, but it was the aftermath that truly set *Emden* apart – as some fifty of her survivors had a defiant last laugh at the Allies by making their way home to Germany by means that could provide grist for several high-adventure novels.

However daring the forays of *Stier* and *Hokoku Maru* may have been, the honours in the actions in which both raiders met their ends rest strictly with their opponents.

The Confederate ironclad *Arkansas*, the only vessel in this volume not to operate at sea, was a unique case. The very fact that she was completed in the rustic backwaters of a poorly industrialised South whose resources were limited further by the Union blockade, was a remarkable achievement in itself. After having completed his fighting ship, Lieutenant Isaac N. Brown, like Count Tourville at Barfleur, was looking for a fight when he encountered two Union fleets near Vicksburg – but, while Tourville accepted odds of more than two to one, those faced by *Arkansas* were 33 to 1. At la Hougue, Tourville and his crew fought gallantly to stave off the fiery finish that befell their beached ships. The crew of *Arkansas*, when finally undone by her recalcitrant engines, scuttled her and defiantly consoled themselves that her decks 'had never been pressed by the foot of an enemy'.

The reader may draw his own conclusions as to the appropriateness of each of the following episodes. Whenever possible, I have striven to strike a balance between the 'big picture' of the battle and the 'little picture' of the individuals who ultimately determine their outcome. Other aspects of the tenuous thread that binds them will be explored in the postscript.

CHAPTER 1

Grenville's Lone *Revenge*
Flores, 31 August 1591

Centuries before Britannia ruled the waves, long before there even was a Britannia, the kingdom of England sat on an island on the fringe of Europe. Wales was part of her domain, but her control over Scotland to the north and the neighbouring island of Ireland to the west was tenuous at best. The year was 1591 and, notwithstanding its success in fending off an invasion attempt three years earlier, the upstart realm of Queen Elizabeth I was still engaged in a struggle for its very existence against the most powerful empire in the world – Spain.

The ill-conceived voyage of their Armada in the autumn of 1588 ended in disaster for the Spaniards, but King Philip II quickly set about rebuilding his fleet, a programme that included the introduction of a new type of galleon, the 'Apostle' class, that was about three times the size of the principal English warship of the time. Displacing 1,500 tons, the 'Apostles' shipped more than 60 guns and carried hundreds of naval infantrymen.

Queen Elizabeth, too, emerged from the Armada crisis with aroused ambitions for England to become a sea power in her own right. Two events in November 1577 had marked the serious beginnings of that process – the beginning of Francis Drake's globe-girdling expedition against the Spanish treasure routes and colonies, and the appointment of John Hawkins as Treasurer of the Navy Board. Cracking down on years of corruption among the royal officers, contractors and dockyard officials, Hawkins reformed the efficiency of the English ship-building industry to the point where Elizabeth was getting double the output for her money.

Hawkins also fostered an approach to warship design very different from that of the Spaniards. Based on his own experience as a sea-raider, he rejected the towering castellated carracks that had been the pride of Henry VIII's fleet, as well as Spain's, as being too vulnerable to Atlantic gales. In contrast to the Apostle class, which was just a larger variation on that theme, Hawkins' ideal ship was small and slim, with a waterline-to-beam ratio of 3.5 to 1 which offered less resistance to wind and presented a smaller target. It was also fast and manoeuvrable. Hawkins' personal choice for his own flagship, and as the model for future vessels, was the

Revenge, a 450-ton ship that had been laid down in 1575, and which was later enlarged to 500 tons.

While the English fleet was being expanded and upgraded, Elizabeth planned to field a commerce-raiding squadron of unprecedented size to prey upon the rich gold convoys coming from the Spanish colonies in the Americas.

Overall command of the squadron was given to Lord Thomas Howard, First Earl of Suffolk, a young cousin of Lord Admiral Charles Howard, Earl of Nottingham. Although only 30 years old, Thomas Howard had distinguished himself as captain of the *Golden Lion* during operations against the Armada. A logical choice for second in command could have been Sir Walter Raleigh, had he not been enjoying the status of queen's favourite at the time. Evidently unable to bear having him away from her Royal Person for any length of time, Elizabeth gave the post of vice-admiral of the squadron to Raleigh's cousin and business partner, Sir Richard Grenville.

Born in 1541, Sir Richard Grenville (also spelled Granville, Grenfell and Greenfield before Lord Alfred Tennyson's poem was presumed to settle the matter), claimed descent from a long line of Anglo-Norman warriors, dating back to William the Conqueror's invasion in 1066. His grandfather, also named Richard Grenville, had been the High Sheriff of Cornwall and a staunch supporter of King Henry VIII's break with the Papacy, although he revealed an ulterior motive for his Protestant conversion when he came to Prime Minister Sir Thomas Cromwell, asking to purchase some of the monastic lands that were put up for sale by the Crown between 1536 and 1553, 'that his heirs may be of the same mind for their own profit'. Grenville's father, Roger, was a seafarer who died when the pride of Henry's growing fleet, the *Mary Rose*, capsized in 1545. After his father's death, the care of the 4-year-old Richard was taken up by his grandfather. With the death of the elder Richard in 1550, Richard the younger fell heir to vast estates in Bideford, Stow, Kilhampton, Devon and Cornwall.

As he matured, Richard Grenville became discontent with supervising his far-flung fiefdoms and set out on a life of adventure. England was not engaged in any war at the time, but he found action aplenty as a soldier of fortune in the service of Emperor Maximilian II against the Turks in Hungary in 1566. In 1571, however, he returned to England, where he acquired a seat in Parliament, was knighted and was appointed to his grandfather's old position of High Sheriff of Cornwall. Later, he also became commissioner of works for Dover harbour.

In 1585, Grenville was approached by his cousin, Sir Walter Raleigh, with a seafaring proposition. Raleigh had sent a small expedition to the shores of the New World a year earlier, and now he proposed the establishment of an English colony on a section of the coast of North America that had not yet been claimed by Spain. With this in mind, he dispatched Grenville on a colonising expedition that eventually settled on Roanoke Island in what is now North Carolina. After landing 100 colonists with Ralph Lane as their governor, Grenville returned to England with his seven-ship convoy, stopping along the way to capture a Spanish ship.

When Grenville returned to Roanoke Island the next year, he found it deserted and later learned that Sir Francis Drake had evacuated the disheartened colonists. Raleigh made another attempt to colonise Roanoke Island in 1587, when John White brought 150 settlers there, including his own grandchild, Virginia Dare. The threat of a Spanish invasion in 1588 kept Raleigh and Grenville at home, commanding the land defences of Devon and Cornwall. It also delayed White's return until 1590, and when he did get there, he found that the colonists had vanished without a trace.

Meanwhile, Elizabeth prepared to flex England's growing naval muscle by waylaying a large convoy of ships carrying gold from the Spanish colonies. Assembling for that purpose in the early spring of 1591, Thomas Howard's squadron was centred around four 500-ton men-of-war, each carrying about 40 guns and 250 crewmen. *Defiance* served as Howard's flagship, while Grenville commanded the *Revenge*, which by that time had already gained her share of renown as Sir Francis Drake's flagship during the fight with the Armada. Of similar size were *Bonaventure*, commanded by Robert Crosse, and Edward Denny's *Nonpareil*. Also adding their guns to the squadron were two 250-ton men-of-war, *Crane* and *Bark Raleigh*. Six armed merchantmen accompanied the warships in anticipation of a profitable expedition, together with eight swift pinnaces to scout and overcome any poorly armed prizes they might encounter. In the event of any of his ships losing contact with the squadron, Thomas designated the Azores as a rendezvous.

About a month after Howard set sail, word reached London that a large convoy of treasure ships was scheduled to make its way to Spain – and that a mighty fleet of Spanish warships was being dispatched to the Azores to protect its anticipated route. As quickly as possible, an English vessel called the *Moonshine* was dispatched to warn Howard, while more warships were readied to reinforce his squadron: *Foresight*, captained by Thomas Vavasour, *Lion* under George Fenner and several more armed merchantmen.

In an age when transoceanic communication could only be achieved by means of sail and the direct delivery of messages, events took their course slowly. Lord Howard spent four months searching in vain for Spanish prizes, then put in at the island of Flores in the Azores for provisions and water. Besides their inability to find any Spanish merchantmen, Howard and his officers were frustrated by the outbreak of an incapacitating malady among their crews. Then, on 31 August, new trouble came to light when a pinnace arrived, reporting that the powerful Spanish escort fleet might be in the vicinity.

In fact, a 53-ship Spanish fleet had put into Terciera, another island in the Azores, in mid-August. Commanding the force was Don Alonzo de Bazan, younger brother of the Marquis de Santa Cruz, who had originally conceived of the Spanish Armada, but who had died shortly before it put to sea. Bazan's battle fleet boasted six of the new 'Apostles', as well as 20 smaller galleons and a number of armed merchantmen.

Just a few hours after Lord Howard learned of its presence, the vanguard of Bazan's fleet approached Flores. Wisely choosing the better part of valour, Howard's ships hastily slipped their cables and put to sea, exchanging a few broadsides with the Spanish vanguard as they made for open water. Howard had reason to feel relieved. There were sick men ashore, and according to some accounts it had fallen on Grenville to take them aboard his ship. Although delayed as he took on the convalescents from other ships, Grenville also managed to follow Howard's squadron out to sea.

Suddenly, however, Howard's relief was replaced by disbelief when he saw *Revenge* go about – not to take her place in his formation, but directly toward the fifteen ships of the Spanish vanguard.

Grenville's reasons for taking on the Spanish formation remain a mystery. Did he fear that the Spanish ships were capable of overtaking Howard's squadron, and so had chosen to engage them in a delaying action? Did the misinterpretation of a garbled order cause him to think that he would have to fight such an action? Did he mistake the powerfully armed Spanish warships for merchantmen? The answer was destined to perish with him.

If Grenville had ambitions of splitting the Spanish formation, that notion was foiled when the man-of-war *San Felipe* came up to meet him – and her massive bulk took the wind out of *Revenge*'s sails. Grenville replied by firing a broadside of cross-bar into the great galleon, which withdrew to repair leaks in her hull. *San Felipe*'s place was quickly taken by another warship, the *San Benardos*, whose crew brought their vessel close enough to secure *Revenge* with grappling hooks.

At this juncture, the outcome should have been a foregone conclusion. Bazan had a total of 7,000 fighting men aboard his ships, while Grenville had about 150 men on deck, with 90 others sick in the hold. Yet somehow *Revenge*'s desperate crew managed to repel the boarders – and company after company of Spanish troops that made subsequent attempts to take them by storm.

A few hours into the engagement, the shot-riddled *San Andrea*, flagship of the Spanish vanguard, sank. Her loss left a gap in the Spanish line through which an English victualler, the 150-ton *George Noble*, unexpectedly sailed and took station alongside *Revenge*. The supply vessel's captain, whose name is lost to history, is said to have offered his services, but Grenville ordered him to 'save thyself, my friend, and leave me to my fate!' *George Noble* then darted between two massive Spanish galleons and escaped to rejoin Howard's squadron.

Although *Revenge*'s gunners battered her larger opponents relentlessly, time was on the side of the Spaniards. Every time one of their ships withdrew because of damage, exhaustion of ammunition or the decimation of its boarding-party, another galleon would take its place. Round-shot filled the air as *Revenge* took on as many as five galleons at once. On more than one occasion, *Revenge* was grappled by two Spanish ships. Once, the *Asuncion* found another Spanish warship alongside, offering her own company of naval infantry to join *Asuncion*'s as both boarding-parties tried to overwhelm *Revenge*. Incredibly, they, too, were bloodily repulsed.

Sunset found *Revenge* dismasted and dead in the water. Dozens of her crew were dead, many more wounded and ammunition was low. Yet Grenville darted about over the broken spars, tangled rigging and torn canvas that littered her deck, urging his men to fight on. Here, then, was the source of the stirring verse by which Tennyson sealed *Revenge*'s place in literary, as well as naval, annals:

> 'Ship after ship, the whole night long,
>   their high-built galleons came,
> Ship after ship, the whole night long.
>   with her battle-thunder and flame,
> Ship after ship, the whole night long,
>   drew back with her dead and her shame.'

About an hour before midnight, Grenville was shot in the side and was taken below to have his wound dressed. Spanish shot continued to crash through the battered *Revenge*, killing the ship's surgeon and wounding Grenville again, this time in the side of the head.

Just before dawn, *Revenge* ceased fire at last – after sixteen hours of almost uninterrupted fighting. Bazan, who had unsuccessfully pursued Howard's squadron until nightfall, returned and circled his vanguard, observing its effort to subdue the lone English adversary.

It had been a hollow victory for the Spaniards, and Bazan knew it. *San Andrea* had sunk early in the fight. *Asuncion* began to founder at midnight and slipped under the waves at 3 a.m. Two other galleons were so badly damaged that one went down later, taking a large number of her crew with her, and the other was only saved from a similar fate by running herself aground. A Dutch observer later stated that the Spaniards had lost more than 2,000 seamen and soldiers.

A passing English ship, the *Pilgrim* under Captain Jacob Whiddon of Plymouth, ventured by the scene of the battle until driven off by a dozen Spanish vessels. He later reported, however, that he had seen the *Revenge* still afloat. What Whiddon did not see was the charnel-house that she had become. More than half her crew lay dead or dying. Among the latter was Grenville, yet he was reported to have spoken to the master gunner, ordering him to scuttle *Revenge*, to 'split her in twain', as Lord Tennyson later embellished it, and have her 'fall into the hands of God, not into the hands of Spain!'

Initially, Grenville's crew was ready to comply, but they soon had second thoughts. While some occupied him in conversation, a party took a small boat to Bazan's flagship, the *San Pablo*, to negotiate surrender terms. Bazan, who had lost enough in men and *matériel* trying to subdue *Revenge*, was willing to make reasonable terms for her surrender, but when Grenville learned of it, he tried to commit suicide with his own sword.

Grenville made a pathetic sight as he was carried aboard the *San Pablo* and saw a Spanish prize crew take charge of what was left of his ship. He died two days later, never to learn that an unexpected turn of events would rob the Spaniards of the *Revenge* after all. Soon after the battle, a massive earthquake erupted in the Azores, killing thousands of people and sinking dozens of Spanish ships – including their hard-won prize.

In addition to the eye-witnesses, Spanish and English, who testified to Grenville's last fight, it was given early publicity later in 1591 by his cousin, Sir Walter Raleigh, in a tract entitled 'A Report Of The Truth Of The fight about the Iles of Acores, this last Sommer.' Besides describing the engagement itself, Raleigh's account was a violent diatribe against Spain's world policies that raised his already lofty status in Elizabeth's court. Grenville's place in history for his valorous fight against hopeless odds was ultimately assured, however, by a well-known public-relations expert of a much later century named Lord Alfred Tennyson.

References

Bryant, Sir Arthur. *The Elizabethans' Deliverance*, St. Martins Press, New York, NY, 1981, p. 98.

Dixey, Graham. 'Sir Walter Raleigh', in *Sea Classic International*, winter, 1985, pp. 72–3.

Fleek, Sherman L. 'Inspiration for the Poet', in *Military History*, December, 1989, pp. 10-20.

Palliser, D. M. *The Age of Elizabeth*, Longman House, Harlow, Essex, 1992, p. 1.

CHAPTER 2

Had Barfleur Had No Morrow...
Barfleur and La Hogue, May – June 1692

The sea engagements that sporadically took place in the English Channel between the French navy and the combined fleets of Britain and the Netherlands from 1689 to 1697 constituted a mere side-show to the land conflict that was raging on the European continent. Nevertheless, they marked a subtle but significant watershed in maritime history. For a newly ascendant French fleet, they represented an opportunity lost; for the still-nascent Royal Navy, they signalled the beginning of what was to be more than two centuries of supremacy on the high seas. None of this could have been foreseen at the time of course; in fact the most illustrious name to emerge from the struggle was that of a Frenchman, Count Tourville.

The sea war was the by-product of the War of the League of Augsburg, itself the consequence of yet another of the French King Louis XIV's many violations of the balance of power in Europe. On 30 September 1681, Louis' army had seized the city of Strasburg from the German Empire and, on the same day, the Sun King had purchased the city of Casale from the Duke of Mantua. Unable to oppose the French alone, the German Emperor began a series of negotiations that resulted in the signing on 9 July 1686 of a secret compact between the Emperor and the kings of Sweden, Spain and several German principalities that came to be known as the League of Augsburg. The alliance did not remain secret for long, and Louis, anticipating its ultimate plan, declared war on the German Empire on 24 September 1688 and sent his armies marching toward the Rhine.

While France was thus occupied, an event of momentous importance was taking place to her west. On 15 November 1688, a Dutch fleet landed Prince William of Orange and his English wife, Mary, at Torbay to set in motion the overthrow of Mary's father, James II, the over-zealously Catholic Stuart King of England. Upon his coronation as King William III on 21 April 1689, the Prince of Orange reversed decades of bloody maritime rivalry between Britain and his native Dutch United Provinces, and united the two sea powers against what he regarded as the greatest threat to both countries – France.

Meanwhile, in January 1689 James Stuart had fled to France, which continued to recognise him as the rightful king – an attitude tantamount to a declaration of war against King William. Louis XIV expected to eliminate England as an enemy by restoring James to the throne and, consequently, he was to devote a considerable amount of time and ships toward achieving that goal.

In March 1689, James landed in Ireland, where he was warmly received – though not in the Protestant North. He established a capital in Dublin and, on 9 May, the first 3,000 reinforcements were being ferried to him at Bantry Bay by the French when they were intercepted by nineteen English ships of the line and eight smaller warships under the command of Admiral Arthur Herbert, Viscount Torrington. The escorting squadron engaged the English with such intense gunnery that, after four hours, they withdrew with two ships disabled and casualties double those suffered by the French.

Although the French fleet had won the first round, it failed to prevent the transport of English troops to Londonderry and Carrickfergus by Admiral Sir George Rooke, who was also able to blockade Scotland from any contact with Ireland by sea – thus preventing contact between James and the many Stuart sympathisers who resided in Scotland. After an attempt to burn shipping in Dublin harbour that was foiled only by lack of wind, Rooke landed an occupying force on an island commanding the harbour of Cork before returning to the Downs in October.

Louis XIV's response to Rooke's raid was to concentrate on luring the allied British and Dutch fleets into a decisive engagement in which his naval forces could destroy them in one master stroke.

In 1690, the French privateer Jean Bart proposed to Louis that if the fleet at Toulon and fifteen galleys patrolling the Mediterranean were combined with the warships based at Brest, the resulting concentration would drive the Anglo-Dutch fleet from the Channel – and very likely deal Britain a demoralising blow such as Bart himself had witnessed in June 1667, as a sailor aboard the flagship of the Dutch Admiral Michiel A. de Ruyter when he sailed up the Thames and raided the Medway. The Sun King agreed to the plan, as well as to Bart's enthusiastic suggestion that the man best qualified to command such an armada would be Count Tourville.

Born in 1642, Anne Hilarion de Costentin, Comte de Tourville had begun his naval career with the Knights of Malta at the age of 14. His first captain thought little of him when he came aboard; his fair hair, blue eyes and pretty-boy looks seemed to suit him better for charming ladies at the palace of Versailles than fighting Turks in the Mediterranean, and the crew in the lower deck promptly christened him 'the Milksop'. But a few weeks later Tourville saw his first action and proved his true mettle. Thereafter, the sneers – and the nickname – vanished.

At the age of 27, Tourville was captain of a French ship of the line, seeing action at Solebay, Augusta, Palermo, Algiers and Tripoli. At 33, he had command of a squadron. On 22 June 1690, aged 48, he was hoisting his pennant in *Soleil Royal* (Royal Sun), the magnificent 98-gun centrepiece of the Sun King's newly demonstrated mastery of the seas, as a fleet of 75 ships of the line, six frigates and twenty fireships – but minus the galleys, which had not yet arrived – sailed from Brest in the most splendid array of naval power France had ever seen.

A drop in the wind becalmed Tourville's force for three days, thus preventing him from interfering with the landing of William III and a major land force at Carrickfergus from 288 transport vessels, escorted by only six warships, on 24 June. After reaching and patrolling along the English coast, however, Tourville found what he was looking for on 8 July: 58 British and Dutch ships at anchor off Beachy Head near Pevensey (called Béveziers by the French).

Although surprised to learn of the arrival of the French, Admiral Torrington was keen for a fight, despite the entreaties of his Dutch commanders that he await reinforcements. While the French spent two days dragging their anchors against a light, adverse wind, Torrington had time to prepare and on 10 July, exploiting his advantage in wind and current, he came out to fight.

Tourville was ready and waiting, with his three squadrons hove-to in battle order – which turned out to be more than could be said for his opponents. Aboard the 72-gun *Hollandia* the commander of the Dutch squadron, Lieutenant-Admiral Cornelis Evertsen the younger, lived up to his nickname of '*Keesje de Duivel*' (Keesje the Devil) by rashly forging far ahead of the English and plunging full-tilt into the French van. A murderous close-range cannon duel ensued, with *Dauphin Royal*, flagship of squadron commander François Louis Rousselet, Marquis de Château-Renault, receiving special attention. Just astern of her, *Ardent* took such grievous damage that Château-Renault gave her captain permission to drift out of the fight before the wind, to effect repairs.

That, however, constituted the critical moment for the French, as the rest of their van and Tourville's main body worked their way around the Dutch line and caught it in a crossfire. Except for a few ships that escaped through the gap caused by *Ardent*'s withdrawal, the Dutch were badly mauled. Attacked from two sides, *Vriesland* had 230 men killed or wounded when ordered to surrender, but her captain, Philips van der Goes, refused to strike his colours while he had a gun left to fire. When she was finally taken, the officer in charge of the prize crew reported that 'there was not a foot of space above the water-line that had not been hit, and the deck was strewn with dead and dying'.

For most of that time, the rest of Torrington's fleet was out of range and unable to help the Dutch. When it finally arrived, it was given a suitably warm reception by the French. Admiral Sir John Ashby's flagship, *Sandwich*, was so badly chewed up by *Soleil Royal* that she had to sheer off. The French *Tonnant* was temporarily disabled, but so were four dismasted British warships, which had to abandon the fight.

While this was going on, Torrington, unwilling to pit his ships of the line against Tourville's, led his main body against the weaker ships at the French rear, none of which carried more than 60 guns. But the crews of *Content*, *Entreprenant* and *Apollon* fought their guns with unmatched speed, efficiency and courage, while the *Fougueux* brought her 58 guns to bear with such deadly accuracy that she forced Torrington's flagship, *Royal Sovereign*, to disengage. This was not to imply that the British gun crews were remiss in their duties – the French ship *Terrible* had half her stern blown away. Elsewhere, Torrington's Blue Squadron, commanded by Admiral Sir Ralph Delaval, attacked another French division under Admiral Jean Gabaret, only to have two of his ships dismasted and a 90-gun three-decker beaten off by the French 48-gun *Vaillant*.

Thus far, all had gone well for Tourville and, with the wind shifting west as darkness approached, he was confident that he could annihilate the Dutch and possibly deal the English a decisive blow. In desperation, the latter sent a fireship at the French line, but it was blown to pieces by gunfire before it could do any damage. Torrington then signalled a withdrawal and ordered his boats out to tow as many cripples as possible to safety. Just then, the wind again played Tourville false, dropping off while the tide turned, causing the French to drift away from the English who, upon Torrington's timely order, had dropped anchor.

Too late to do more, Tourville dispatched a corvette with his combat report: 'The enemy has fled, having sent out his pinnaces to tow his ships away, leaving ten disabled vessels which we could take if there were a breath of wind. We have captured one ship, dismasted eleven, sunk two, and three fireships, and sunk a fourth fireship that was bearing down on us.' That night, the burning *Gekroondt Burcht*, flagship of Vice-Admiral Karel van de Putte, cast an eerie glow over the scene, while another Dutch warship, *Noord Quartier*, went down.

Over the next two days, while Torrington's fleet found shelter, the French continued their pursuit of the battered Dutch. The wind continued to render it a slow chase, and Tourville's decision to keep his ships in line of battle, rather than breaking formation into a general mêlée, assured that his squadrons would go no faster than their slowest man-of-war. Even so, *Wapen van Utrecht* and *Tholen* were overtaken and sunk, and four other ships of the line and a fireship forced aground, to be destroyed by their crews to prevent their capture. When the remains of the Dutch van finally reached the shelter of Dover harbour, its numbers had been reduced by a total of seventeen ships. The French had not lost one.

Tourville's victory off Beachy Head, won mainly at the expense of the Dutch, caused great indignation in the United Provinces. King William imprisoned Torrington in the Tower for several months, then had him court-martialled at Sheerness on 10 November 1690. Although Torrington was acquitted, William remained unconvinced that he had not deliberately sacrificed the Dutch squadron, and dismissed him from further military service.

In England, the Trained Bands were mustered to face the French invasion that was logically to be expected, but several weeks of bad weather and scurvy accomplished what the Royal Navy could not. Tourville returned to Brest to put ashore 6,000 sick crewmen, after having already released 2,800 in Norman ports along the way. In sum, they represented roughly one-third of his manpower. The decisive blow against the allied fleet would have to wait. So would the restoration of James II to the English throne, for on 11 July, while the Battle of Beachy Head was in its second day, James's army was decisively beaten at the River Boyne and he was forced once more into French exile.

With William's kingship and the Anglo-Dutch alliance thus secured, the French navy could claim nothing more than a great tactical victory amidst a strategic defeat. Over the next year, while healthy commerce overseas allowed the English and Dutch to make good their losses, Tourville proposed to let their navies come to him. 'Let our enemies wear themselves out at sea,' he said, 'and then we will sail out and attack them off Ushant when they're tired from their long patrol and want to return to port.'

Louis XIV's new war minister, Louis, Comte de Pontchartrain, had other ideas. He felt it necessary that the French fleet 'maintain our sense of superiority' in the Channel and in the summer of 1691, when he learned of a sizeable convoy bound from Smyrna to England, he ordered Tourville to sea after it – to deny its cargo to England, and to help reduce France's own growing war deficit. Leading 69 ships between Ushant and the Scilly Isles for seven weeks, Tourville failed to make contact with the Smyrna convoy, although he did catch another from Jamaica, capturing a few merchantmen and their two escorts.

Impatient to conclude the Channel war so that he could concentrate on his continental war against the League of Augsburg, Louis XIV again turned to the exiled James, whose hopes of regaining his crown waxed anew with a proposal to land in the south of England. James's rationale was based on the probability that many Royal Navy officers, who had served under him when he had been Duke of York and Lord High Admiral, might still harbour personal loyalties towards him. Among them was Torrington's successor as the Royal Navy's commander-in-chief, Admiral Sir Edward Russell, and Queen Mary in fact decided it prudent to summon Russell and his senior officers to London and order them to sign an address of loyalty to her as their English-born sovereign, if not to their Dutch-born king.

On 12 May 1692, while James and a French invasion force commanded by Marshal Bernardin Gigault, Marquis de Bellefonds, camped at St. Vaast-la-Hogue on the east coast of the Cherbourg peninsula, Admiral Tourville was ordered to sea to secure them a safe passage. He left Brest with only 39 ships this time, leaving a score behind because of a shortage of sailors to man them. Twelve more ships under the command of Victor-Marie d'Estrées were *en route* to join him from Toulon, but adverse winds prevented them from doing so. Likewise, of a squadron out of Rochefort, only five overtook Tourville's task force, bringing his total strength to 44.

More limiting than his numbers were the orders Tourville received, dated 26 March 1692, under the king's seal: 'His Majesty definitely desires him to leave Brest on the said day, April 25th, even should he have information that the enemy is at sea with a force superior to that in readiness to sail with him ... Should he meet with enemy ships he is to chase them back to their ports, whatever number they may be ... If, having escorted the troopships to the landing area or the landing being in progress, the enemy attacks with a number of ships greater than he had under his command, His Majesty desires him to engage them and to persevere, so that even should he be at a disadvantage the enemy is unable to prevent the landing. But, when the landing has been completed and the troopships are on the return journey, should the enemy then attack him, His Majesty does not permit him to engage unless the enemy is superior to his own by no more than ten vessels; but His Majesty desires him to approach close enough to discover for himself, when that should oblige him to fight.'

The superfluous last line of the order, with its implications of doubt regarding Tourville's courage, smacked more of Pontchartrain than of King Louis. Tourville's suspicions of that seemed to be confirmed by a letter he received from Pontchartrain on 20 May: 'It is not your place to query the King's orders, but to carry them out and sail up the Channel; write and tell me if you intend doing so, if not the King will replace you with someone more obedient and less circumspect than you.'

While Tourville beat against the wind for three days, Admiral Russell was leading 63 British ships into the Channel. On 9 May he was joined by Admiral Philips Van Almonde aboard the 92-gun *Prins*, at the head of 35 other Dutch warships, bringing Allied strength up to 99 warships against Tourville's 44; 6,756 guns to the Frenchman's 3,240, and 53,463 men against 20,900.

On 27 May, the wind shifted south-west and the French fleet made better progress, dropping anchor against the ebb tide to stay close to the coast. At daybreak on 29 May two of Tourville's frigates, *Perle* and *Henry*, were scouting beyond the Cherbourg peninsula when they encountered Admiral Russell's fleet. Breaking off contact, they hurried back to alert Tourville. By signal flag and gunfire, Captain Roche Allard of the *Henry* reported a veritable forest of masts and sails about seven leagues north-east of Barfleur Point. But if Tourville possessed any advantage to compensate the disparity in numbers, it did not lie in intelligence. At the same time that his scouts spotted the Allies, his own fleet was discovered by the English frigates *Chester* and *Charles Galley*, which reported forthwith to Russell.

Russell deployed his ships in line north to south, with Van Almonde's White Squadron making up the van, followed by the Red Squadron under Russell's direct command, seconded by Vice-Admiral Sir Ralph Delaval and Rear-Admiral Sir Cloudesley Shovel. Their main body comprised 31 ships in three divisions. In the rear were the 32 ships of the Blue Squadron under Admiral Sir John Ashby, Vice-Admiral Sir George Rooke and Rear-Admiral Richard Carter. The French, too, were deployed in three squadrons of three divisions each, line abreast. To the north was the Blue Squadron with fourteen ships under Jean Gabaret, in the centre, Tourville led the White with sixteen ships, and to its south the Blue and White with fourteen under François David, Marquis d'Amfreville.

With a faint south-west wind in his favour, Tourville had the option of slowly approaching this overwhelming enemy force or dropping anchor and refusing combat. His orders, however, left him no such option, nor would his affronted sense of honour allow him to take any other than the course of action specified. Signal flags were hoisted in *Soleil Royal*'s rigging: 'Make ready', followed by the order to advance. Keeping his ships in close formation, Tourville aimed his flagship directly at Russell's *Britannia*, hoping to achieve the miracle he needed by eliminating the flagship of the Allied force.

To the Dutch in the Allied van, the steady approach of the outnumbered French appeared suicidal. Survivors of the débâcle off Beachy Head began to have misgivings – were the English going to abandon them again? Had Russell struck a secret deal with the French and the deposed James? They would soon learn the contrary. Treachery or cowardice were the last things on the minds of Russell and his captains, eager to allay the doubts of their new rulers, William and Mary.

Just as the opposing fleets approached cannon range, the wind died, leaving them embarrassingly becalmed 'within musket-shot of each other', as one survivor observed. The French *Foudroyant* lowered a pinnace, whose crew strained at their oars to tow her into battle. Most of the other ships followed suit, and soon the first fighting broke out between the small craft of the opposing fleets.

So far, neither commander had given the order to open fire, nor was either destined to do so. The first broadside was fired at *St. Louis* at extreme range by a nervous Dutch ship; seconds later, both battle lines commenced firing.

Tourville's only hope now lay in the discipline and close co-operation of his subordinates ... and he got it. When a dangerous gap developed between his van and main body, the commander of the Blue and White Squadron, the Marquis d'Amfreville, in *Merveilleux*, took a few of his ships and filled it. When the Dutch tried to encircle the French right, *Bourbon* held them up until the 92-gun *Monarque*, flagship of Admiral André Nesmond, and three other ships of his division could arrive to 'double' around Van Almonde's own flank.

In the centre of the mêlée, *Soleil Royal* came under attack from three sides, by *Britannia*, *London* and *St. Andrew*, each of which mounted 100 guns. Having been herself upgunned to 106 cannon, Tourville's flagship fought off several attempts by the English to board her and twice forced them to break off action, while the French admiral simultaneously directed both her defence and the manoeuvres of his fleet. At 1 p.m., *Soleil Royal* was still in fighting condition, but her rigging was badly torn and Tourville ordered her towed clear of the fight by his oarsmen so that repairs could be made. With a brisk wind now coming in from north-north-west, d'Amfreville led five ships to take *Soleil Royal*'s place and keep up the pressure against Russell's main body.

That same wind shift allowed Ashby's Blue Squadron to drive into the French left wing, cutting off the three ships of Admiral François Panitié's division from the French line. Panitié wisely withdrew to the south-west rather than be drawn into an impossible fight and had the satisfaction of seeing Ashby unwisely following him with all 32 ships – thereby taking a lot of pressure off Tourville.

Even so, by 4 p.m. Russell's force had encircled the French, whose attack on his centre now took on a desperate intensity. The little frigate *Perle* under Captain Claude Gardanne, Chevalier de Forbin, lost a third of her crew while engaging enemy ships of the line. True to her name, *Ambitieux* took on – and badly battered – Sir Ralph Delaval's *Royal Sovereign*, while the English frigate *Chester* withdrew with her sails and rigging in tatters and *Eagle* backed off with her bowsprit and foremast shattered, and 70 of her crew dead and twice as many wounded. On the French side, *Henry* and *Fort* were disabled and had to be towed out of line by their boats. Back in the fray again, *Soleil Royal* was hard-pressed, but Tourville's plight was noticed by Admiral Alain Emmanuel, Marquis de Coëtlogon aboard *Magnifique*, who declared, 'We'll save this brave man or die with him!' *Magnifique* and *Prince* left formation to assist the flagship, their places in line taken by other attentive French vessels.

Soleil Royal's position was still critical. Sir Cloudesley Shovel had worked his Red Squadron around her when a thick mist came down, rendering visibility almost nil and giving Tourville a needed respite. When the wind picked up and cleared the mist, the tide also turned, so that when Tourville's ships dropped anchor, the majority of their opponents were drawn eastward. Ashby, however, was still to the west of the French, and his ships also dropped anchor, thus keeping Tourville's main body caught between his Blue Squadron and the Allied main body.

Again the wind shifted, this time to the north-east, and Russell resorted to his fireships. Five were sent bearing down on *Soleil Royal*, but by adroit manoeuvring and with the help of her small boats, she managed to avoid them all. *Ambitieux* also dodged three of the burning juggernauts.

As darkness fell, the English began drawing off to the east – first the Red Squadron, then Van Almonde's Dutchmen. Farther to the west, Ashby's ships had to sail with the current through gaps in the French line, thus running a gauntlet of musketry and cannon. His flagship, *Royal William*, took successive broadsides in turn from *Soleil Royal*, *Magnifique* and *St. Philippe*, and was disabled. Rear-Admiral Carter in the *Duke* was mortally wounded in the deadly crossfire, but – giving the lie to Queen Mary's suspicions regarding his loyalty – his last order to *Duke's* captain was, 'Fight on as long as the ship floats!' When *Duke* limped clear of the inferno, her captain was also among her dead.

As night finally brought fifteen hours of battle to an end, all 44 of Tourville's ships were still afloat, although *Soleil Royal* was battered and leaking, and her decks awash with blood. The French had lost a total of 1,700 dead or wounded. But the English had sustained even greater damage, a score of ships having to be towed to port, too badly holed to conduct repairs at sea and carry on the fight on the morrow. The Dutch got off more lightly this time because they were not as closely engaged as the English; their worst-hit vessel, the *Zeven Provincien*, had lost only nineteen men dead and fourteen wounded. Total Anglo-Dutch losses came to 2,000 dead – including two admirals – and 3,000 wounded.

Up to this point, Tourville had exceeded even his own wildest expectations. He had carried out his king's orders to the letter, and inflicted a stinging defeat on an enemy force more than double the size of his own. Even an English chronicler of the time admitted that, '... Had Barfleur had no morrow, the action would have been a French triumph.' But the morrow was coming, and seamen on both sides got little rest as they patched up holes and sealed broken seams with oakum and melted pitch, while topside, masts, rigging and sails were being repaired.

Tourville's force was far from the shelter of any fortified port – Cherbourg and Le Havre had yet to be developed so as to accommodate a fleet such as his – and, despite its losses, the Allied fleet still outnumbered his. Exploiting a thick mist that aided his withdrawal in the night, Tourville ordered his units to retire westward. At 8 a.m. on 30 May the mist cleared, leaving seven French vessels under Admiral Nesmond unaccounted for. Nesmond released the two most badly damaged ships of his squadron at La Hogue, and later sent two others into Le Havre. Nesmond's *Monarque* and her remaining two consorts, reversing the round-about route taken by the Spanish Armada in 1588, made for the North Sea via Scotland, eventually returning safely to Brest.

The receding morning mist also revealed the 35 vessels still in Tourville's formation to be Van Almonde's White Squadron. The Dutch relayed the news to Admiral Russell, who ordered his ships to resume pursuit. A wind shift from north-east to south-west at the end of the morning again slowed the chase, and by 4 p.m. both fleets were anchoring off Cherbourg to keep from losing headway in the ebb tide.

Although he was about two miles ahead of the Dutch van, Tourville's unwillingness to abandon *Soleil Royal*, which for all her battle-scarred grandeur was wallowing badly, hindered the progress of the rest of his fleet. During the night, the 22 ships of Tourville's van, now led by Panitié aboard *Grand*, broke away and sailed south, between the Cherbourg peninsula and the Channel Islands, to make safe anchorage at St. Malô. Sometime after midnight, Admiral Russell's flagship *Britannia* lost her foremast, which had been damaged in the earlier battle, and she dropped out of line while repair crews worked feverishly to restore her to operational status. Ashby's and Van Almonde's squadrons continued after Tourville's main force, closing the distance between them thanks to the painfully slow progress being made by *Soleil Royal*. West of Alderney, the French ships missed the tide and then lost their anchors, which left the more damaged among them almost helpless. Reluctantly, Admiral Tourville transferred his flag to *Ambitieux* and, soon after that, *Soleil Royal*, *Triomphant* and *Admirable* ran aground in quick succession near Cherbourg.

The morning of 31 May found Tourville's remaining twelve ships anchored off St. Vaast-la-Hogue, seeking the protection of a few shore batteries and James's army. There might have been more support available, had not the construction of two forts at Cherbourg and St. Vaast, begun in 1688 by Louis XIV's great military engineer, Sébastién le Prestre Vauban, been cancelled at the suggestion of Louis' secretary of war, François-Michel le Tellier, Marquis de Louvois. With uncharacteristic short-sightedness, Tourville himself doubted that the forts would be of much use in any engagements he would have against the English between Ushant and the Lizard, and so he did not protest the king's decision to terminate the projects. In his present precarious circumstances, however, Tourville probably wished he had pressed the matter more vigorously.

Back at Cherbourg, Sir Ralph Delaval's division came upon the three beached men-of-war and attempted to finish them off, only to be driven back by *Soleil Royal*'s gunners and the six cannon of a local makeshift fort. Changing tactics, Delaval ordered out his boats to escort four fireships against the stranded but still dangerous warships. One of the fireships was blown up and a second struck a reef, but two got through the maelstrom of cannon fire. Captain Thomas Heath sailed the fireship *Blaze* up to the towering *Soleil Royal* and, with her guns still firing above him, managed to secure his sacrificial vessel to her stern. Moments later, the pride of the Sun King's fleet was enshrouded in flames that soon found their way to her still amply stocked magazine. The resulting explosion tossed many of her crew skyward. In like manner, the fireship *Wolf* came alongside *Triomphant*, making her last triumph one of pyrotechnics, while the crews of the small boats managed to turn *Admirable* into an admirable bonfire.

While these fireworks were livening up Cherbourg, Russell had taken position off La Hogue, to find Tourville moored in the shelter of Le Crocq de Quinéville, a long, narrow sand bank which jutted out to sea from La Hogue. Tourville's royal instructions now placed him at the disposal of James and Marshal Bellefonds. After a day of discussion, it was decided on 1 June to beach six of Tourville's ships behind La Hogue and the other six at the neighbouring islet of Tatihou, then quickly unload them of all useful *matériel* and cargo. The operation was carried out with such disorder as to bear more of a resemblance to looting than salvage work, and of the 150 boatloads of troops promised by Bellefonds to protect the ships, barely a dozen arrived.

Early on the morning of 2 June, Vice-Admiral Rooke resorted to Delaval's tactic of launching an attack by fireships and longboats. Virtually no support was given to the stranded warships by the garrison on Tatihou, nor from the French army at St. Vaast, from which James and Bellefonds watched the six vessels burn. The exiled ex-king and former Lord High Admiral of the British fleet is said to have been unable to resist remarking to his French companions: 'Who but brave English tars could do such a thing?' – thereby displaying just the tact that had got him deposed in the first place.

Tourville and his naval officers, disgusted by the army's lack of initiative, took the defence of the last six ships at La Hogue into their own hands. When Rooke's fireships and boats came at them next morning, they and their sailors threw them back, while a gun hurriedly mounted on a barbette sank several boats and killed a number of their crews. But the British numbers prevailed, and soon their fireships were sending the last six ships of Tourville's division – and his triumph at Barfleur – up in smoke. With the Channel now completely theirs, the allied ships laid into the French transport vessels, burning several before the turn of the tide forced them to retire.

After having virtually ordered Tourville's fleet into a death ride, Louis XIV was relieved to learn that his greatest admiral had escaped alive from the débâcle, exclaiming: 'More ships can be found, but not another Tourville.' The Sun King was not the only one who had praise for him; Admiral Russell, later Lord Orford, wrote a letter to his antagonist, graciously complimenting him 'on the great valour he had shown by attacking in such a dauntless manner, and by fighting so valiantly although having an unequal force'.

The Battle of La Hogue has been cited as the decisive naval action of the Channel war. Certainly from the material standpoint, it was no such thing – the fifteen French ships destroyed there barely made up for the losses they had inflicted on the allies at Beachy Head. What made La Hogue a French fiasco was that it occurred where it did, in plain sight of the invasion force and French civilians in the vicinity. James Stuart, for one, made no further attempts to invade England. And while the morale of the French sailors themselves was undiminished – they knew that they had done their best and more – defeatism began to creep into the Naval Ministry in Paris.

The War of the League of Augsburg continued for another five years, during which the French navy engaged mainly in privateering and commerce raiding. On 27 June 1693, Tourville caught 400 Mediterranean-bound merchant vessels, escorted by 23 warships under Admiral Sir George Rooke, off Lagos in southern Portugal and, over the next two days, destroyed 92 merchantmen and two fighting ships before Rooke could extricate the convoy. Despite that and further successes, however, Tourville, Jean Bart and their distinguished colleagues failed to weaken England's overall naval superiority.

The Peace signed at Ryswick in 1697 was disadvantageous to France, Louis XIV losing most of his gains of the past twenty years, with the important exception of Strasburg. Among his concessions was the recognition of William III as King of England. The Sun King's ambitions were far from being squelched, nor had the Royal Navy by any means faced its last challenge from the French fleet. But it might fairly be said that never again would the French come so tantalisingly close to victory over the British at sea as they did when Tourville led them to hell and back – at Beachy Head, Barfleur and La Hogue.

References

Mordal, Jacques. *Twenty-five Centuries of Sea Warfare*, Abbey Library, London, 1970.
Mahan, Alfred Thayer. *The Influence of Sea Power Upon History, 1660-1805*.

CHAPTER 3

Nelson's Patent Boarding Device
Cape St. Vincent, 14 February 1797

For Captain Horatio Nelson, the year 1796 began with great promise. On 19 January, Admiral Sir John Jervis arrived at the Italian port of San Fiorenzo to take command of the Mediterranean Squadron, of which Nelson and his ship, the 64-gun *Agamemnon*, were part.

In Nelson's opinion, his last two commanders, Vice-Admiral William Hotham and Hotham's temporary replacement, Sir Hyde Parker, had been too cautious. The most galling case in point had come in March 1795, when Hotham's fourteen ships gave chase to seventeen French warships leaving Toulon to escort a troop convoy bound for Corsica. The French commander, Rear-Admiral Pierre Martin, chose flight rather than battle, but off Genoa two of his ships, the 84-gun *Ça Ira* and 74-gun *Jean Bart*, collided and *Ça Ira* fell behind with damaged rigging. On the morning of 13 March Nelson's *Agamemnon* and the frigate *Inconstant* under Captain Thomas Fremantle, caught up with and took *Ça Ira*. Hotham subsequently managed to capture a second French ship, the 74-gun *Censeur*, but then called off further pursuit of Martin's retiring squadron. 'We must be contented,' he said. 'We have done very well.' But Nelson was anything but content. In a letter to his brother, William, he complained, 'Had our good Admiral followed the blow, we should probably have done more.'

On meeting Jervis, Nelson realised that he had found the leader under whom he would prefer to serve. In contrast to a good many Royal Navy officers who had got their commissions through family connections, Jervis had started out at the age of fourteen with nothing more than a gift of twenty pounds from his father. He had worked his way up through the ranks to become Admiral of the Blue in June 1795.

At the age of 60, Jervis was a stern but just disciplinarian whose stated dictum was, 'Responsibility is the test of a man's courage.' He was also known, however, for instituting such improvements in the average sailor's living conditions as enforcing cleanliness and ventilation below decks, and seeing to it that all his men received doses of citrus juice to prevent scurvy. Militarily, Jervis had a reputation for getting results. In February 1794, he and General Sir Charles Grey invaded the French West Indian island of Martinique and, through an outstanding showing of co-operation between army and naval forces, forced its surrender on 20 March.

A perceptive judge of character, Jervis knew something of Nelson, whom he had briefly met in the House of Commons in London, while representing Yarmouth some years before. Barely five foot seven inches tall and weighing no more than 130 pounds, Nelson hardly cut an imposing figure – especially when viewed alongside the bullish-looking Jervis, with his head set low on his broad shoulders. Nelson was as sickly as he was frail-looking, prone to coughing fits as a result of many cold nights spent on deck, combined with the recurring effects of malaria that he had contracted in the Far East. Nervous anxiety caused him sleepless nights and a loss of appetite. On top of all this, he often suffered from seasickness. While convalescing from a bout of fever, however, Nelson claimed that 'a sudden glow of patriotism was kindled within me, and presented my King and my country as my patron; my mind exulted in the idea. "Very well," I exclaimed, "I will be a hero, and confiding in providence, I will brave every danger."' His subsequent actions had already lent ample credence to his convictions.

Born the son of a Norfolk parson in 1758, Horatio Nelson lost his mother when he was nine and spent some years in boarding-schools before he first went to sea in March 1771. Since then, he had sailed Arctic, Indian and American waters. As he was leaving the frigate *Lowestoft* to take command of the brig *Badger* in December 1778, Nelson received a parting scrap of advice from his friend and mentor Captain William Locker: 'Always lay a Frenchman close and you will beat him.' Those words forged a credo which Nelson put into practice when he engaged the *Ça Ira*, outmanoeuvring her while his well-drilled gunners blasted her into submission at point-blank range, killing 110 of her crew at a cost of only seven English wounded

During their first meeting aboard his new flagship, the veteran 100-gun ship of the line *Victory*, Jervis quizzed Nelson about the Mediterranean Fleet, its station, the men's morale and the enemy's capabilities. He also asked Nelson for his ideas on prospects for the future and the best means of achieving a satisfactory conclusion to the campaign against Revolutionary France. Nelson's answers were optimistic, but also frank and realistic.

Satisfied that he and Nelson were of like mind, Jervis asked him if he would object to serving under him as a rear-admiral, to which Nelson replied that he would be proud to do so. For the moment, Nelson was only promoted to commodore, but Jervis did give him an independent command. In June, Nelson shifted his pennant from the war-weary *Agamemnon* to the 76-gun third-rate ship of the line *Captain*. He took some of his old crew with him, including the detachment of the 69th Regiment of

Foot who served as the ship's sea soldiers in place of Royal Marines. Commanded by Lieutenant Charles Pierson and comprising three sergeants, two corporals, one drummer and 57 privates, the 69th contingent was frequently referred to by Nelson thereafter as 'my old Agamemnons'.

Thus far, then, 1796 had seemed a fair year for the Mediterranean Fleet, but on 8 September things took an abrupt turn for the worse. Spain, once part of the international coalition against France, changed sides. Informing Sir Gilbert Elliott, the viceroy of British-occupied Corsica, of Spain's declaration of war, Jervis announced: 'I have orders to attack ships of war of that nation, in fleets, or singly, wherever I meet them.' Such orders would have suited the aggressive Jervis down to the ground, but his fleet had had its hands full in dealing with the French. The entry of Spain's powerful Armada into the contest threatened the Royal Navy's supply lines through the Strait of Gibraltar, making Britain's position in the Mediterranean untenable.

On 29 September, Commodore Nelson marked his 38th birthday as he arrived at Bastia, to be greeted with the shocking news that Corsica was to be abandoned, and that he was to be in charge of the evacuation. Nelson had taken part in the original occupation of Corsica in the summer of 1794, during which he had been detached with a party of seamen and Royal Marines to construct artillery batteries on the nearby islands of Bastia and Calvi. On 12 July his fortifications at Calvi had come under a French artillery barrage and a near miss threw sand into his right eye, damaging the pupil. Only later did Nelson come to realise the permanency of the injury, noting: 'I can distinguish light from dark, but no object.'

Having sacrificed half his sight and many slain friends for Corsica, he wrote bitterly to his wife: 'I lament our present orders in sackcloth and ashes.' Nevertheless, on 15 October he began to remove the viceroy, his family, British troops and civilians, and about 600 French and Corsican royalists from the island. Republican French forces landed on 18 October, but by dawn of the 20th the evacuation was complete.

By the end of 1796, Jervis' fleet had been driven father east in the Mediterranean, where it maintained its watch on the French naval base at Toulon. Meanwhile, encouraged by the recent successes of General Napoleon Bonaparte in Italy and by its recent alliance with Spain, the Directory that ruled Revolutionary France decided to launch an expedition to Ireland, where French troops would aid disaffected Irish in a revolt against the British. As had been the case in 1691, sea power would be the key to the success of any such undertaking. This time, however, Spanish ships, including some of the largest in the world, would add the weight of their mighty broadsides to those of France's own sizeable fleet.

On 1 December, five French ships of the line and three frigates, led by Admiral Pierre Charles de Villeneuve, left Toulon for Brest, accompanied by a fleet of 26 Spanish ships of the line and ten frigates that had been in Toulon since October. On 6 December, Spanish Admiral Don Juan de Langara put in at Cartagena, leaving Villeneuve to pass through the Straits of Gibraltar alone. He did so on 10 December, in full view of the British. An easterly gale aided the French by speeding them on their way, while doing so much damage to Jervis' fleet that he was unable to pursue them. Of three British ships driven ashore in the storm, two were damaged and one, *Courageux*, was a total loss, with 464 of her 593 crewmen killed. Despite his good fortune, however, Villeneuve did not arrive at Brest in time to support the intended Irish invasion, which was postponed.

Langara spent two months in Cartagena, until Admiral Jose de Cordoba arrived to take over command of his fleet. Then, under urgent orders from the Directory to rejoin Villeneuve, the Spaniards – their strength now up to 27 ships of the line – set sail again on 1 February 1797, passing through the Straits on the 5th, again driven by strong easterly winds.

Since Villeneuve's audacious run past Gibraltar, Jervis' 10-ship squadron had left Lisbon on 18 January, escorting some Portuguese merchant ships bound for Brazil. Once the convoy was clear of European waters and the threat of enemy attack, Jervis returned to his regular patrol station off Cape St. Vincent, where he was reinforced by five more ships on 6 February.

Meanwhile Nelson had been detached aboard a captured French frigate, the *Minerve*, accompanied by the frigate *Blanche*, to evacuate the British naval garrison from the isle of Elba. Along the way, Nelson's two ships encountered two Spanish frigates and captured both after a spirited three-hour fight. The captain of one of the prizes, *Santa Sabrina*, was Don Jacobo Stuart, grandson of England's deposed King James II. During an encounter with a larger Spanish force next morning, *Santa Sabrina* was recaptured together with her 40-man British prize crew, led by Lieutenant Thomas Masterman Hardy.

As soon as he was able, Nelson sent a letter to the Spanish Captain General of Cartagena, requesting the return of Hardy and his men in exchange for Stuart and his crew. After removing Elba's Royal Navy personnel on 29 January 1797, Nelson passed by Cartagena to reconnoitre the Spanish fleet – only to observe that it was no longer there. Arriving at Gibraltar on 11 February, he found that Jervis' fleet had also departed, but he was pleasantly surprised to find Hardy and his prize crew waiting for him – the Spaniards had agreed to his proposal for a prisoner exchange, after all.

Hastening out of Gibraltar to rejoin Jervis, Nelson's two frigates passed the nearby Spanish port of Algeciras, from which two ships of the line and a frigate emerged in pursuit. During the ensuing chase, a man fell overboard and Lieutenant Hardy joined the crew of a longboat to go after him. By the time it was determined that the crewman had already drowned, the rescue boat was being overhauled by the Spaniards and was unable to make headway against the current. 'By God,' cried Nelson, 'I'll not lose Hardy! Back the mizzen topsail.'

With *Minerve*'s speed thus decreased, Hardy was able to catch up with her – but so were the Spaniards. On seeing their quarry slow to take on their overwhelming broadsides, however, the Spaniards surmised that the frigate must have sighted the larger British squadron to which it was attached over the far horizon, and therefore prudently backed their own sails. As a result of this miraculous reprieve, Nelson escaped in the gathering dusk, having saved Hardy from becoming a guest of the Spaniards twice within one month.

An even stranger adventure lay ahead for *Minerve*'s crew that night, as one by one a multitude of vague mammoth shapes appeared in the fog. After speculating as to whether these were a Spanish convoy bound for the West Indies or Cordoba's force, Nelson determined that they were the latter. Through a remarkable combination of skill and luck, *Minerve*'s Captain George Cockburn navigated her through the very middle of the Spanish fleet without being challenged. On the morning of 13 February, the frigate reached Jervis' fleet off Cape St. Vincent where, after imparting his information to Jervis at dinner aboard *Victorious*, Nelson was transferred back to *Captain* for the confrontation to come.

And there would be a fight, notwithstanding the larger number and heavier firepower of the Spanish ships. Jervis, like Nelson, counted on the greater experience and discipline of his officers and crewmen to even the odds. He had also been keeping a weather eye on the situation at home. France dominated Continental Europe. British commerce was suffering to the brink of bankruptcy. The Irish remained restive and only bad weather had prevented the Brest-based French fleet, now reinforced by a Dutch fleet, from attempting a landing in Ireland. The reunion of Villeneuve and Cordoba's fleets in the Atlantic or the Channel might provide the decisive incentive for an all-out Irish rising. Jervis was overheard summing up his motives succinctly: 'A victory is very essential to England at this moment.'

At 5 a.m. on 14 February the frigate *Niger*, which had been shadowing Cordoba's fleet for some days, broke contact and sailed ahead to inform Jervis that the Spaniards were 10 to 12 miles southward and westward, and coming his way. The wind, after having been a strong southeasterly for days, had finally shifted to south by west, greatly easing the Spaniards' progress westward to Cadiz.

Because of hazy weather with occasional patches of fog, it was not until 9 a.m. that the approaching fleets could see each other. The first man on a ship of the line to spot them was the signal lieutenant in *Barfleur*, who exclaimed: 'By my soul, they are thumpers! They loom like Beachy Head in a fog.' Aboard his flagship, Jervis and Ben Hallowell, the

Canadian-born captain of the wrecked *Courageux*, listened as *Victory*'s
Captain Robert Calder reported the number of enemy ships he could see
approaching.

'There are eight sail of the line, Sir John.'
'Very well, Sir,' Jervis acknowledged.
'There are twenty sail of the line, Sir John.'
'Very well, Sir.'
'There are twenty-five sail of the line, Sir John.'
'Very well, Sir."
'There are twenty-seven sail of the line, Sir John – near
double our own.'
'Enough, Sir, no more of that! The die is cast, and if there
are fifty sail, I will go through them.'
'That's right, Sir John, that's right,' cried Hallowell,
gleefully slapping his commander on the back, 'And, by
God, we'll give them a damned good licking!'

At 9.30 a.m., Jervis dispatched three of his ships ahead to chase, followed a
few minutes later by three more. At about 10 o'clock the fog lifted and both
sides had a more accurate grasp of their respective situations. Jervis hauled
his squadron close on the starboard tack, steering south to south by west,
to intercept the Spaniards, who were coming on east-south-east. Jervis ran
a tight squadron, and it showed in the formation he had placed them in
the night before – two columns of eight and seven ships, which even their
hard-nosed commander commended 'for their admirable close order'.

The Spaniards, in contrast, had been intent only on reaching Cadiz
and had been thrown into confusion by the wind shift of the previous
night. Even after Jervis' force appeared, they had not yet formed a line of
battle and were bunched in two groups – a van of six, with the main force
of 21 ships following more than eight miles behind. Compounding the inef-
ficiency of the Spanish officers and their commander was faulty intelligence;
a neutral ship they had encountered earlier had informed them that there
were only nine British men-of-war in the area, rather than fifteen.

The six ships of the Spanish van, having seen Jervis' two columns
heading for the gap between them and the main force, were close on the
wind on the port tack, heading about north-north-west in hopes of rejoin-
ing their main body. Jervis, meanwhile, signalled his ships to form into a
single column – the line of battle – and pass through the enemy's line.

Jervis' order flew in the face of the Royal Navy's Fighting Instructions, which prescribed a simple slugging match between two parallel,
opposing lines of warships. Despite the Admiralty's strict insistence on
adhering to the Fighting Instructions, however, Jervis' gambit was not

unprecedented. Edward Hawke had done it against a Franco–Spanish fleet off Toulon in 1744 and George Brydges Rodney had done it to the French in the Battle of the Saints in 1782. 'Hawke, when he ran out of the line, sickened me of tactics,' Jervis said, but he also knew that his prospects of success were far better if he took advantage of the Spaniards' already divided state than if he waited for them to join their components and form a single, devastatingly powerful line of their own.

As it moved closed on the larger Spanish formation, Captain Thomas Troubridge's *Culloden* led the British line, followed by *Blenheim, Prince George, Orion, Colossus, Irresistible, Victory, Egmont, Goliath, Barfleur, Britannia, Namur, Captain, Diadem* and *Excellent*, the last commanded by Cuthbert Collingwood.

It was soon apparent that the Spanish van would not be able to cross the British bows in time. For a moment, the leading Spaniards wavered in their determination, bearing up to south-east; then, five of the six ships resumed their north-westerly course, with the intention of breaking through the British battle line. The sixth ship continued on a south-easterly course and disappeared.

As the 74-gun *Culloden* neared the Spanish main body, Troubridge's first lieutenant notified him that a collision with the nearest enemy ship was imminent. 'Can't help that, Griffiths,' replied the captain, 'Let the weakest fend off.' *Culloden* blasted her way through, without colliding.

'We flew at them like a hawk to his prey,' Collingwood wrote to his wife afterwards, 'passed through them .... and then tacked upon their largest division'. Plunging between the two groups, the British poured broadside after withering broadside into the main Spanish force. But Cordoba, flying his pennant in the mammoth 132-gun *Santissima Trinidad*, had gauged Jervis' intentions and had ordered his main body to sail opposite and parallel to the British line. Jervis responded by ordering his ships to tack in succession, reversing course to close in once more and rake Cordoba's formation. The British were slow in making the reverse turn, however, forming a wide V-shape while Cordoba endeavoured to sail around the tail end of Jervis' line and join up with his own vanguard, after which his ships would be able to bring their full number to bear.

From the quarter-deck of *Captain*, sailing third from last in Jervis' line, Nelson sized up the situation and gave a fateful order to his ship's American-born captain, Ralph Miller. 'At 12.50 p.m.', *Captain*'s log recorded, 'the Commodore ordered the ship to be wore (altering course by bringing the stern, rather than the bow, toward the wind) when she was immediately engaged with the *Santissima Trinidad* and two other 3-decked ships.' In disobedience of Jervis' order to turn in succession, Nelson had broken out of line and thrown his ship across the bows of the eighteen oncoming Spaniards.

One minute later, however, Nelson's flagrant act of insubordination was transformed into a case of pre-empting his commander's own change of plan. At 12.51, *Victory*'s signal flags announced: 'General Signal: Take suitable stations and engage enemy as arriving up in succession.' Nelson and Jervis were indeed of like mind.

On seeing *Captain* tack about, Collingwood ordered his own ship, *Excellent*, to do likewise. Troubridge, too, was turning *Culloden* about, with *Blenheim* following suit, when he saw Jervis' general order confirm the validity of his manoeuvre. Observing him, Jervis commented: 'Look at Troubridge! He tacks his ship as if the eyes of all England were upon him!' Noting that *Captain* and *Excellent* were at risk of being cut off and destroyed by Cordoba's fleet, Calder asked Jervis if they should be recalled back into line. 'No,' replied Jervis, 'I will not have them recalled. I put faith in those ships. It is a disgrace they are not supported.'

At first, *Captain* was alone as she closed to gunnery range with seven Spanish vessels. One was the gigantic *Santissima Trinidad* – of which Collingwood wrote: 'Four complete decks, such a ship as I never saw before' – as well as *San Salvador del Mundo* and *San Josef*, each mounting 112 guns. A total of 512 cannon raked *Captain*, carrying away her foretopmast and her wheel, and leaving her unable to manoeuvre. Nevertheless, Nelson managed to navigate his riddled ship into the midst of the disorganised Spanish throng, while his gunners kept up a higher rate of fire than their Spanish counterparts – 'We gave them their Valentines in style,' remarked one British gunner.

Captain did not go 'unsupported' for long, as *Culloden* joined her and *Excellent* took on two Spaniards. Within fifteen minutes, a report noted, 'the engagement became close and general'. Blazing away at *San Salvador del Mundo* at a range 'not farther from her when we began than the length of our garden', Collingwood managed to compel her to surrender, then promptly turned on *San Ysidro*, 'so close alongside that a man might jump from one ship to the other'.

'Our fire carried all before it, and in ten minutes she hauled down her colours,' Collingwood continued, 'then making all sail, passing between our line and the enemy, we came up with the *San Nicolas* of 80 guns, which happened at the time to be abreast of the *San Josef*, of 112 guns; we did not touch sides, but you could not put a bodkin between us.' While Collingwood may have exaggerated somewhat, the range was close enough for some of *Excellent*'s shot to go clear through one of the Spanish ships and into the next.

Turning to escape the punishment that *Excellent* was dishing out, *San Nicolas* and *San Josef* got their rigging hopelessly entangled. They also drifted toward the disabled *Captain*, on which, according to Nelson, there was 'not a sail, shroud or rope standing'. *Culloden*, too, had been crippled and had fallen behind. With the two Spanish warships coming at him, however, Nelson saw an irresistible opportunity. Calling on Lieutenant Pierson's 69th Regiment of Marines and additional boarders to make ready, he ordered Captain Miller to put the helm to starboard, deliberately putting *Captain* on a collision course with the Spaniards. Moments later, she, like *San Josef*, became entwined with *San Nicolas* – aided, in this case, by grappling hooks.

The first aboard *San Nicolas* was Edward Berry, Nelson's first lieutenant, recently promoted to commodore but yet to be assigned a ship of his own. Hot at his heels came Pierson and his 'Old Agamemnons'. Miller tried to go next, but Nelson prevented him, saying, 'No, Miller, I must have that honour.' Nelson himself described what happened next:

'A soldier of the 69th Regiment [Private Matthew Stevens] having broken the upper quarter-gallery window, I jumped in myself, and was followed by others as fast as was possible. I found the cabin doors fastened, and some Spanish officers fired their pistols; but having broke open the doors, the soldiers fired ... I pushed immediately onwards for the quarter-deck, where I found Captain Berry in possession of the poop, and the Spanish ensign hauling down. I passed with my people, and Lieutenant Pierson, on the larboard gangway, to the forecastle, where I met two or three Spanish officers, prisoners to my seamen; they delivered me their swords.'

So far, Nelson had taken one of his opponents for the loss of seven dead and a few wounded of his boarding-party, while the Spaniards had sustained twenty casualties in the mêlée. But the fight was not over yet. Berry was still hauling down *San Nicolas*' colours when a fusillade of small-arms fire rattled from the stern of the second, even larger Spanish warship still entangled alongside. Nelson ordered his Marines to return the volley, then reorganised them for a new assault while Miller brought reinforcements aboard *San Nicolas*. Clambering up the main chains of the *San Josef*, Nelson grabbed the quarter-deck rail and found himself face to face with an armed Spanish officer.

The Spaniard could have killed him, but he did not, and Nelson swiftly bounded over the rail and on to the deck. At that point, the Spanish officer knelt and presented his sword, hilt first, in token of surrender. Identifying himself as the flag captain, he explained to an elated but still rather suspicious Nelson that his commander, Admiral Don Xavier Winthuysen, lay below decks, mortally wounded.

'I gave him my hand,' continued Nelson in his account, 'and desired him to call to his officers and ship's company that the ship had surrendered which he did; and on the quarter-deck of a Spanish first-rate, extravagant as the story may seem, did I receive the swords of the vanquished Spaniards, which as I received I gave to William Fearney, one of my bargemen, who placed them with the greatest sang-froid under his arm.'

Nelson's boarding and capture of two ships of the line in rapid succession created an instant legend. He recalled 'a sailor's taking me by the hand on board the *San Josef*, saying he might not soon have another place to do it in and assuring me he was heartily glad to see me'. Word of the feat had already reached *Victory*; as she passed by in her pursuit of Cordoba's retiring fleet, her crew lined the deck and Jervis led them in cheering Nelson and his men.

Soon, too, the jokes sprang up. Nelson's favourite was a reference to the *San Nicolas* as 'Nelson's Patent Bridge for Boarding First-rates'. Another, more elaborate bit of drollery was 'Commodore Nelson's receipt for making an Olla Podrida', which among other things involved 'battering and basting' the two Spaniards for an hour until they were perceived to be 'well stewed and blended together', then board each one in turn until they were 'completely dished and fit to be set before His Majesty'.

As Jervis had inferred earlier, the Battle of Cape St. Vincent was every inch the victory that Britain needed. The Spaniards were scattered and four of their ships captured – two by Collingwood's *Excellent* and the other two by Nelson's single audacious boarding-party. The remainder of Cordoba's fleet reached Cadiz, but was too demoralised to attempt a breakout for Brest. Not one British vessel had been lost, and Jervis' fleet now blockaded Cadiz as once it had blockaded Toulon. Apart from the strategic reward of keeping the French, Dutch and Spanish navies from pooling their resources against Britain, the battle gave an incalculable boost to the morale of the Royal Navy and the British public in general.

For routing an enemy fleet nearly twice the size of his own, Jervis was made Earl St. Vincent and given an annual pension of £3,000, but he was more than generous in his praise for the man he recognised as the chief architect of his victory. In consequence, Nelson was promoted to Rear-Admiral of the Blue and made a Knight of the Bath. Jervis' two seconds in command, Vice-Admiral Charles Thompson and Rear-Admiral William Parker, were made baronets and all flag officers and captains involved in the action were awarded a gold medal. One sour note amid the general revelry was sounded by Calder who, although himself knighted for his part in the battle, was envious of Nelson and reminded Jervis that Nelson's breakout of line on his own initiative was 'an unauthorised departure from the prescribed mode of attack'. 'It certainly was so,' Jervis replied, 'and if you ever commit such a breach in your orders, I will forgive you also.'

Another distinction stemming from the Battle of Cape St. Vincent lay in store for the 69th Regiment, albeit many decades in the future. In June 1891, the unit was granted a Battle Honour for its role in the action. Later renamed the Welsh Regiment, the former 69th received another Battle Honour for its role in the Battle of the Saints on 12 April 1782. The re-organised, present-day Royal Regiment of Wales (24th/41st Foot) inherited the old 69th's unique laurels as the only such unit in the British Army with two naval battle honours.

More adventures lay ahead for Nelson, although the next was nearly his last. On the night of 24 July, he led a force to capture Santa Cruz de Tenerife in the Canary Islands, where it was rumoured a Spanish treasure ship lay anchored. Bad weather threw the landing-party into disarray and, as the Spanish garrison repulsed the assault, a musket ball shattered Nelson's right arm, which subsequently had to be amputated. After a painful convalescence, the despondent Nelson wrote to Jervis that 'a left-handed admiral will never again be considered useful'.

Jervis disagreed. So did George, 2nd Earl Spencer, First Lord of the Admiralty. Nelson eventually recovered and was in command of HMS *Vanguard* when a French fleet was reported to be building up at Toulon in the spring of 1798. On 2 May, at Lord Spencer's recommendation, Jervis dispatched Nelson to investigate. The eventual result, on 1 August, was an audacious night attack by Nelson on the French fleet that had carried General Bonaparte's army to Egypt. Of thirteen French ships of the line found in Aboukir Bay, ten were captured, one blown up and two escaped, leaving Bonaparte's army stranded in the Sinai Desert and Britain's navy again in control of the Mediterranean.

The Battle of the Nile, won without the loss of one British ship, was strategically and tactically the greatest naval victory of the 18th century. But it was not long into the 19th before Nelson added another triumph to his growing collection. By 1801, Britain was the only nation still at war with France when the neutral nations of Russia, Prussia, Sweden and Denmark formed the Northern Convention and barred the Baltic Sea to 'belligerent' ships – which was to say, in practice, British ships. On 2 April, when Admiral Sir Hyde Parker led a fleet of twenty ships into Copenhagen harbour and delivered an ultimatum to Crown Prince Frederick, regent to the mentally ill Christian VII, King of Denmark and Norway, Danish shore batteries opened fire. Parker ordered a withdrawal, but his second in command, Admiral Nelson, literally turned his blind eye to the signal and pressed his attack, silencing the batteries and disabling ten Danish ships.

Following the assassination of Tsar Paul I and the accession of Alexander I to the Russian throne, the Northern Convention dissolved and with it the threat to the Royal Navy in the Baltic. In 1803, Nelson, in the scrawl of a right-handed man learning to write with his left, sardonically summed up his sufferings in a letter to an admirer:

'Wounds received by Lord Nelson
His eye in Corsica
His belly off Cape St. Vincent

> His arm at Teneriffe (*sic*)
> His head in Egypt.
> Tolerable for one war.'

But the war was not over yet. Nelson's last occasion to 'lay a Frenchman close' came on 19 October 1805, when Admiral Villeneuve slipped out of Cadiz with eighteen French and fifteen Spanish ships of the line and headed for the Strait of Gibraltar. On the 21st, Nelson, now commanding a 27-ship fleet from the quarter-deck of the same *Victory* from which Jervis had commanded him at Cape St. Vincent, sighted the enemy force off Cape Trafalgar, to which Villeneuve reacted by turning north. Raising the signal, 'England expects that every man will do his duty', Nelson attacked in a manner that was the direct opposite of that used by Jervis at Cape St. Vincent – he divided his line in two, leading twelve of his ships against Villeneuve's van and centre, while his second in command, Vice-Admiral Collingwood in *Royal Sovereign*, led the rest into the tail-end of the Franco–Spanish line. The ultimate result was the destruction or surrender of eighteen French and Spanish ships, including Villeneuve's flagship, *Bucentaure*, while four of those that fled back toward Cadiz were subsequently captured off La Coruña. Again, no British ships were lost, but 1,500 of their crewmen were killed or wounded – including Nelson, mortally struck by a sniper from the French 74-gun *Redoutable*.

Nelson died with the consoling knowledge that he had won his last battle, although he could not have realised its full magnitude. At Trafalgar, Nelson eliminated France as a naval threat for the remaining ten years of the Napoleonic conflict and established Britain as the world's undisputed premier naval power for more than a century.

The Battle of Cape St. Vincent assured Horatio Nelson of an honoured niche in the annals of naval history, but it was just the pattern-setting prelude for a succession of greater achievements, the last of which, Trafalgar, firmly established him as a hero for the ages.

References

Fregosi, Paul. *Dreams of Empire: Napoleon and the First World War 1792-1815*, Birch Lane Press, New York, NY, 1990.

Hough, Richard. *The Great Admirals*, William Morrow & Co. Inc., New York, NY, 1977.

Howarth, David, and Howarth, Stephen. *Lord Nelson: The Immortal Memory*, Viking Penguin Inc., New York, NY, 1977.

Mahan, Alfred Thayer. *The Influence of Sea Power upon History 1660-1805*, Presidio Press, Novato, CA, 1980.

Pocock, Tom. *Horatio Nelson*, Alfred A. Knopf, New York, NY, 1988.

Preston, Anthony. *History of the Royal Navy*, Greenwich House, New York, NY, 1983.

Whipple, A. B. C. *Fighting Sail*, Time-Life Books, Alexandria, VA, 1976.

CHAPTER 4

The One That Got Away
USS *Constitution*, 1812–1815

Isaac Hull, captain of the US frigate *Constitution*, strained to ascertain the identities of the ships he could see on the horizon. A state of war existed between America and Great Britain, and *Constitution* had been ordered to join a squadron commanded by Commodore John Rodgers in the Atlantic Ocean. Making her way north from Annapolis, Maryland, *Constitution* was about twelve miles off Cape Barnegat, New Jersey at 2 o'clock in the afternoon of 16 July 1812, when her lookout spotted the sails of four ships on the horizon to the north-west, while a frigate was observed approaching from the north-east.

Hull knew that Rodgers' squadron consisted of five ships – the frigates *President*, *United States* and *Congress*, the sloop of war *Hornet* and the brig *Argus* – but his elation at the almost too timely encounter was tempered by caution. Until he was sure that the ships were indeed American, Hull deemed it prudent to keep his distance.

A fresh breeze was blowing from the north-east, but at 3 o'clock Hull decided that he was getting too near the coast and therefore took an opposite tack, sailing due east, the other frigate following in distant attendance. At 10 o'clock that night, the unidentified frigate closed to signalling distance – six to eight miles – and Hull ran up a pre-arranged sequence of lights that would identify his ship to Rodgers. When no reply was forthcoming, Hull realised that his misgivings were justified; whatever those five ships were, they were not Rodgers' squadron.

Constitution and the unknown frigate maintained their guarded, parallel courses until daybreak, when a visual sighting confirmed Hull's suspicions. All the unidentified ships – a ship of the line and four frigates accompanied by a brig and a schooner – were flying British colours.

The principal warships in the far group were, in fact, the 64-gun man-of-war *Africa* and three frigates – the 32-gun *Aeolis*, the 36-gun *Belvidera* and the 38-gun *Shannon*, flagship of Captain Philip Bowes Vere Broke. One of the smaller ships was the *Nautilus*, an American 14-gun brig that had been captured by Broke's squadron. As for the nearer frigate that had been shadowing *Constitution* all night, she was the 38-gun *Guerrière*, a former French ship that had been captured by the British in 1806

41

and which, since 1811, had been under the command of Captain James Richard Dacres.

At this point, the serendipity of the encounter was Broke's, not Hull's. As a prize, *Nautilus* was small fry to the British commander; but now, the 44-gun *Constitution*, one of the three most powerful ships in the US Navy, was his for the taking.

But now, too, fate took the most inopportune turn imaginable in that age of sail – the wind, which had been faint all night, died away entirely. With their primary means of propulsion lost, *Constitution* and her British adversaries were about to engage in one of the strangest, most exhausting and agonisingly slow sea chases in history.

Constitution's birth had coincided with that of the United States Navy itself. The naval phase of the War of American Independence had been carried out by a combination of state fleets, privateers and a relatively small Continental navy. Notwithstanding some noteworthy successes, the Americans suffered near-crippling losses at the hands of Britain's Royal Navy. In 1785, the last of the few surviving warships were sold off, leaving the new-born United States with no navy at all.

While President George Washington and most congressmen favoured a policy of non-involvement in world affairs, it soon became clear that the world would not co-operate. Pirates, operating from the North African Barbary states, such as Tripoli and Algiers, regularly intercepted American merchant ships plying the Mediterranean and demanded tribute (i.e., extortion money) from their crews, with seizure of their ships and cargoes as the alternative. In the Atlantic, British warships stopped American ships and searched them for deserters from the Royal Navy – often impressing American citizens into service along with the legitimate fugitives.

After years of enduring such humiliations, in March 1794 a reluctant US Congress authorised the construction of six large frigates as the nucleus of a new navy. Like light cruisers or destroyers of a later century, frigates served as fast scouts and versatile utility vessels for the fleets of such major sea powers as Britain, France or Spain. Ill-disposed to expenditure on larger vessels, the Americans settled for compensating as best they could with frigates that would be somewhat larger, faster and more heavily armed than their foreign counterparts – in essence, ships capable of outgunning whatever enemy they could not outrun and outrunning any that they could not outgun.

The basic design of the new frigates was conceived by Joshua Humphreys, an experienced Quaker shipbuilder from Philadelphia. Construction was carried out at different seaports throughout the country. Two of the ships, *Chesapeake* and *Congress*, were to carry 36 guns and were built in Norfolk and Portsmouth, respectively. A third, the 38-gun *Con-*

stellation, was built in Baltimore. The heavy hitters of the new fleet, however, were the three frigates of the *President* class, each displacing 1,576 tons and mounting 44 guns. Of these, *President* was built in New York, *United States* in Philadelphia and *Constitution* in Boston.

Launched in October 1797 and completed in the following summer, *Constitution* was soon put to work, patrolling the West Indies against French commerce raiders during an undeclared 'quasi war' between America and Revolutionary France. From 1800 to 1803, *Constitution* and her sisters were recalled to port and held 'in ordinary', in accordance with the isolationist policy fostered by President Thomas Jefferson. On 12 September 1803, however, *Constitution* arrived off the Barbary Coast to confront the Tripolitanian pirates. That war ultimately ended with a treaty, signed aboard *Constitution* on 10 June 1805, granting American ships passage through the Mediterranean without further payments of tribute. The conflict's outcome set a precedent for similar free passage for other nations, and served notice that America was prepared to fight to protect its interests abroad, as well as at home, if necessary..

Meanwhile, relations between the USA and Great Britain were deteriorating. On 22 June 1807, the British 50-gun frigate *Leopard* accosted the *Chesapeake* off Hampton Roads, Virginia, demanding to 'stop and inspect' the American frigate for deserters. When *Chesapeake*'s captain, Commodore Samuel Barron, refused, *Leopard* fired a broadside, inflicting 23 casualties. Barron struck his colours and, without even acknowledging the surrender, *Leopard*'s captain boarded *Chesapeake* and interned four of her crew. Two of the men were indeed deserters, one of whom, William Ware was left to die of his injuries; the other, Jenkin Ratford, was hanged. The other two prisoners, Americans Daniel Martin and John Strachen, were sentenced to receive 500 lashes, but a strong appeal from President Jefferson persuaded the British to return them to their ship with a token apology.

The *Chesapeake* affair marked the start of a downward spiral to war. On 1 May 1811, the British frigate *Guerrière* stopped and boarded the American brig *Spitfire* off Sandy Hook, NJ, and made off with an American passenger named John Deguyo. America responded by dispatching the frigate *President*, commanded by Captain John Rodgers, to intercept *Guerrière* and recover Deguyo. On the night of 16 May Rodgers encountered what appeared to be his quarry. It is not certain who fired the first shot, but an exchange of cannon fire broke out and, several minutes later, the British ship was disabled. At daybreak, *President*'s victim was seen to be the 22-gun sloop *Little Belt*, which had lost eleven men dead and 21 wounded in the unequal fight. Whether or not Rodgers apologised for the error is unknown, but he did offer assistance to *Little Belt*, which her captain angrily refused.

As *Little Belt* limped home, it was the turn of the British public to be outraged, especially when it became clear that Rodgers was being viewed by his own people as more hero than blunderer. By the autumn of 1811, a total of more than 6,000 cases of American citizens being impressed had been registered in Washington, of which number the British themselves admitted to 3,000.

While American and British diplomats negotiated, relations between the USA and Napoleon Bonaparte's French Empire improved and American merchant ships defied Britain's blockade to trade in French ports. In Washington, a growing faction of 'young war hawks' called for war with Britain and even the invasion and assimilation of Canada into the United States. Finally, on 19 June 1812, Congress declared war against Great Britain.

The conflict that the Americans would call the War of 1812 found the US Navy pitting a total of seventeen sea-going warships against the 219 ships of the line and 296 frigates at the Royal Navy's disposal. For the British, the American War, as they called it, represented no more than a quaint side-show to their global struggle against Napoleon. Just a relative handful of their warships, the British reasoned, would suffice to sweep the upstart Yankees from the seas.

Constitution was made operational just days before war was declared. In mid-June 1810, she returned from Mediterranean service and Isaac Hull, a portly seadog from Derby, Connecticut, who had worked his way up from cabin boy to captain, took command of the big frigate. Soon afterwards, Hull noticed that *Constitution's* speed and handling were not all that he expected and had divers go below to investigate. What they found was an estimated ten wagon-loads of oysters, mussels, barnacles and weeds hanging off her coppered bottom 'like bunches of grapes', as Hull described it. Hull sailed *Constitution* to Chesapeake Bay, hoping the fresh water would kill some of the Mediterranean organisms, then removed the rest by dragging an iron scraper of his own invention back and forth along her bottom. In April 1812, he laid her up in the Washington Navy Yard to have her bottom recoppered, only to learn that there was only enough metal available to patch it partially. Satisfied that his frigate had at least been restored to a semblance of competitive performance, Hull took the additional step of replacing a number of the 42-pound carronades on her spar deck with lighter, less potent but longer-range 32-pound cannon.

On 18 June, *Constitution* was out of the yard and taking on stores in Alexandria, Virginia, when Hull received a message from Secretary of the Navy Paul Hamilton, advising him of the imminence of war, and instructing him to join Commodore Rodgers' five-ship squadron in the Atlantic. Sailing to Annapolis, Hull prepared his ship for a long voyage and took on new recruits, carefully assessing each man's experience. He also took some time out on 4 July to mark his country's Independence Day with a salute from *Constitution*'s guns before departing Annapolis the next morning for New York, where Rodgers' squadron was supposed to be.

While *Constitution* was being made ready to join him, Rodgers had already left New York, hoping to intercept a 100-ship merchant convoy reported to be *en route* from Jamaica to England. Rodgers never found the convoy, but on 23 June he encountered the British frigate *Belvidera*. As she fled to the north-east, Rodgers fired the first cannon shot of the war from *President*'s bow chaser. Three hits inflicted nine casualties in *Belvidera*, but when a cannon on the main deck was fired once more, it burst and ignited the 'passing box' used for bringing gunpowder up from the magazine. Among the sixteen Americans killed or injured by the resulting blast was Rodgers, who was blown skyward off the forecastle deck and came down with a broken leg.

Supported by his officers, Rodgers ignored the pain of his injury and continued to direct the pursuit, but with *President*'s bow demolished it was necessary to yaw the ship to bring her broadsides into play against *Belvidera*. That evening, *Belvidera*'s Captain, Richard Byron, ordered his ship's anchors, many of her boats, and most of her food and water cast overboard. Thus lightened, *Belvidera* was able to leave *President* behind.

Three days later, *Belvidera* reached Halifax, Nova Scotia, the principal British naval base in North America, and Byron reported his close brush with Rodgers to Captain Broke. Reacting to the news that the Americans were operating in squadron strength, three lone British warships patrolling the American coast were recalled and, on 5 July (the same day that *Constitution* left Annapolis), Broke led his squadron out of Halifax to help establish a blockade of American coastal waters and, if possible, engage Rodgers' force. After taking *Nautilus* on 15 July, Broke was approaching Cape Barnegat next day when his lookouts spotted *Constitution* on her eastward tack. *Guerrière*'s arrival only added to the hopeless odds against the American frigate.

Judging discretion the better part of valour under the circumstances, Hull headed *Constitution* south as fast as the feeble wind would carry her. *Guerrière* wasted 10 to 15 minutes wearing and tacking, allowing *Constitution* to slip out of the range of her guns and put some precious distance between herself and her pursuers before the hunt began in earnest.

Constitution was now involved in a race for survival, although it would not have seemed so to an outside observer, if he judged it on speed alone. The weather was clear, but the wind remained slight all day and throughout the night. At 5 o'clock next morning, even that breeze died, fixing *Constitution* in a state of limbo while her enemies slowly began to overtake her. At 5.15 Hull lowered a cutter and soon had his other boats engaged in towing his ship forward. As the prospect of contact became imminent, he had a 24-pounder brought up from the main deck to the quarter-deck, and an 18-pounder was brought aft from the forecastle, while a portion of the taffrail was cut away to accommodate it. Two more guns were run out of the stern window, giving *Constitution* a total of four stern chasers. The frigate then set her topgallant studding sails and stay-sails, while hammocks were removed from their nettings and any cloth other than the sails was rolled up to streamline the ship as much as pos-sible in the event of the wind returning.

By now the British, too, were becalmed. At 5.45, *Belvidera's* Captain Byron saw *Constitution* slowly drawing away and figured out what Hull was up to. He, too, sent his boats ahead to tow, and soon the other British ships were doing the same. The pursuit of *Constitution* now became a strenuous rowing and towing match; one for which Broke's frigates held the advantage, since they were lighter than the 'overbuilt' *Constitution*, and their hulls produced less drag for their crewmen to overcome as they strained at the oars. Moreover, at 8 o'clock Broke ordered most, if not all, of the other ships' boats to be put at *Shannon's* disposal and had all the sails of his flagship furled.

With her speed raised to as much as three knots, *Shannon* soon lay off *Constitution's* port bow, tantalisingly close to gun range, but just then a light breeze arose. Hull, who had taken the trouble to have buckets of sea water hoisted and poured over his sails to render them less porous, was able to take the greater advantage of it, leaving *Shannon* behind while *Constitution's* own boats rowed frantically to keep up with her.

In thirty minutes, *Constitution* increased her lead on Broke's ships by a few hundred yards, but then the wind failed again. Soon, *Shannon's* straining boatmen had drawn her back within striking range and she was taking a few test shots with her bow chasers. Some of the projectiles passed over *Constitution*.

At this critical juncture, one of Hull's officers, Lieutenant Charles Morris, suggested a technique that he had used in the past to make his way out of windless harbours – kedging, which involved rowing an anchor ahead of the ship, dropping it and then having the crew haul the ship along by the hawser. Hull sounded the water and, on finding it to be 26 fathoms (156 feet) deep, agreed to give Morris' idea a try. All non-essential ropes were spliced into a line nearly a mile long. One end was tied to a small, sharp-fluked kedging anchor, which was then rowed ahead in the ship's cutter.

When the anchor was dropped, *Constitution's* crew grabbed the hawser and walked aft – slowly and gingerly at first, then gradually increasing the pace as the ship began to move. Each crewman who reached the stern let go of the line and raced forward to pull anew. Mean-while, more rope was spliced and another anchor attached, so that while

Constitution was being kedged along on one anchor, the second could be hauled ahead. Hull lost some distance on the British while improvising his kedging arrangements, but once the laborious process got under way, he found *Constitution* beginning to leave *Shannon* behind again. In what for him was a rare fit of overconfidence, Hull ordered his ship's colours hoisted high and a stern chaser fired a cocky farewell salute to his would-be captors. It did not take long, however, before Captain Byron again figured out how the Americans had increased their speed and reported it to Broke. Soon, British crews were hauling away at their own kedging lines.

At 9.09, a light breeze sprang up from the south and Hull skilfully caught it on the port tack. At the same time, Hull pulled his boats up on davits, or on temporary tackles rigged to various spars, with the crews still in them, ready to be lowered and take to their oars at minimum notice. As Hull had anticipated, at 10 o'clock the wind died again and the boats were lowered. Gripping the kedging hawsers, the crews of both ships, hunters and hunted, plodded their way aft silently, their purpose too earnest to warrant the rhythmic shanties that normally accompanied their labours.

On the British side, it was now *Belvidera* that was given the extra boats, advancing by both kedging and the continued towing efforts of her boats' crews. As she slowly but visibly advanced on *Constitution*, Hull endeavoured to lighten his ship by pumping 2,335 gallons of fresh water overboard. At 1.35 p.m., Byron thought he had narrowed the range enough to fire, to which *Constitution* answered with a volley from her stern chasers. All shots fell short of their targets, however, and both ships subsequently curtailed the futile gunplay.

For the rest of the afternoon and early evening of July 18, the bizarre chase continued. At 7 p.m., Hull lowered three boats to give his ship a complementary tow while the kedging proceeded. At 10.53, a fresh southerly breeze arose and *Constitution* set her fore topmast staysail and main topgallant studding sail to catch it. At the same time, Hull hastily picked up his boats to prevent their falling behind and into the hands of the British – and to give his crew a much-needed rest.

At midnight, the breeze died again but this time, almost by unspoken mutual agreement, Hull and his British counterparts decided to give their exhausted crews some additional time to regain their strength. A few optimists caught some snatches of sleep, though none strayed far from their assigned posts. At 2 a.m. on 19 July, the towing and kedging resumed and the ships glided silently on at their snail's pace through the darkness.

By sunrise, *Belvidera* had advanced to a threatening position off *Constitution*'s lee beam when a renewal of the wind offered the Yankees another reprieve. Hull tacked away from *Belvidera*, only to find himself coming within firing range of *Aeolis*, which had also managed to narrow the distance from the opposite side of the American frigate. Much to Hull's relief, however, *Aeolis* did not fire a shot and *Constitution* was again able to make her way out of danger. At noon the morning breeze slackened, but remained sufficient for *Constitution* to increase the distance between herself and the leading British vessel, *Belvidera*, to four miles.

At 6.30 p.m. Hull noticed a summer rain squall approaching. Although a heavy squall was capable of tearing away a yard or a topmast, Hull judged the coming storm to be relatively light – and therein, he thought, lay a stratagem. Recalling that the British had copied every trick he had employed to stay ahead of them up to that time, he decided on a feigned tactic. As the storm closed in, Hull ordered his heavy canvas secured, a double reef put in the mizzen topsail and his light canvas taken in. As Hull expected, the British observed his precautions and followed suit, also turning their ships in the opposite direction of *Constitution*'s flight in order to face the coming blow bows-on.

When the rain squall finally overtook his ship, obscuring it from the eyes of the British, Hull ordered as many sails set as possible with all the speed his tired crew could muster. His calculated risk paid off; the storm was not heavy enough to damage his sails or rigging, but its winds were brisk enough to propel *Constitution* ahead at 11 knots before blowing over 45 minutes later.

By the time that the British realised that they had been hoodwinked, *Constitution* lay close to the horizon and was making steady progress away from them. Unfurling all sails, Broke's ships tenaciously kept up their pursuit through the night, but by 8 a.m. on the 20th, *Constitution*'s sails could barely be seen as she slipped away to the south-west. Ordering his crews to stand down, Broke finally gave up the chase after 66 hours and 30 minutes of tense pursuit.

Hull was probably congratulating himself on having had *Constitution*'s bottom cleaned, but he made no secret of what a near thing it had been, noting: '... had they taken advantage of their early proximity and crippled me when in gunshot range, the outcome might have been different'.

As it was, *Constitution*'s hairbreadth escape represented a remarkable achievement of resourcefulness, coolness and discipline by a crew that had only mustered five days before she put to sea. That she had managed to outwit and outrun an entire squadron of His Majesty's ships was a sobering blow to British pride. And Broke's squadron could not have let a more troublesome adversary escape, as subsequent events would prove.

After doubling back north and arriving in Boston on 26 July, *Constitution* left her home port on 2 August and patrolled off Halifax, during which time she captured two British merchant brigs on 10 and 11 August. On the 15th, she encountered the *Adeline*, an American brig that had been captured by a British sloop and placed under a prize crew. Following *Adeline*'s recapture by *Constitution*, Hull learned from her crew that Broke's squadron was in the vicinity and prudently set course south for Bermuda. On the night of 17 August, *Constitution* met the privateer *Decatur* whose captain, William Nichols, told Hull of a lone British man-of-war not far to the south. Shortly afterwards, off Sandy Hook, New Jersey, *Constitution* encountered the enemy ship, which turned out to be one of her pursuers of the previous month – *Guerrière*, whose Captain Dacres had reportedly challenged Captain Rodgers in *President* 'or any other American frigate' to meet him for 'a few minutes *tête-à-tête*'. Dacres had *Guerrière*'s topsails painted with a slogan referring to *President*'s victim of 1811 – 'THIS IS NOT THE LITTLE BELT' when *Constitution* closed to accept the challenge.

Dacres got the duel he wanted, but not the outcome he expected. After 45 minutes of manoeuvring for position, combat commenced, with *Guerrière*'s guns volleying relentlessly at the American's rigging while Hull held his fire and closed bows-on to present the smallest target possible. Finally, as *Constitution* drew abreast of her opponent at a range of 25 yards, Hull cried: 'Now, boys, pour it into them!' The portly American captain's trousers split with the force of his abrupt command while his gunners hurled a full broadside of double shot and grape into the British frigate. *Guerrière*'s crew never recovered from the shock of that first, crippling salvo and after half an hour their ship was a battered and dismasted hulk. When *Guerrière* fired a gun to leeward as a signal of surrender, Hull backed off for half an hour to effect repairs to his own damaged spars and rigging before returning to accept Dacres' formal surrender.

The officer whom Hull sent aboard *Guerrière*, Lieutenant George Read, found her beyond salvaging, with thirty holes below the water-line and her decks already awash. Of her crew of 302, there were 101 casualties including Dacres, wounded in the back by a musket ball while urging his crew to fight on. Dacres accepted Read's offer to put *Constitution*'s surgeon at his disposal, but added that he might be too busy with his own patients. 'Oh, no,' replied Read. 'We have only seven wounded, and they were tended to long ago.' In addition, *Constitution* had suffered only seven dead out of her 456-man crew.

Hull and Dacres had met several times before the war, and after helping the wounded British captain aboard, Hull gently declined the token of his sword in surrender, saying: 'No, no, I will not take the sword from one who knows so well how to use it.' Before having *Guerrière* blown up, Hull saw to it that Dacres' mother's Bible was recovered for him. 'The conduct of Captain Hull and his officers to our men has been that of a brave enemy,' Dacres later reported. 'The greatest care being taken to prevent our men losing the smallest trifle, and the greatest attention being paid to the wounded.' But then, Dacres had been no less chivalrous, allowing ten impressed American seamen serving in *Guerrière*'s crew to shelter below decks rather than force them to fight their own countrymen. After the war was over, Hull and Dacres became life-long friends.

If *Constitution*'s escape from Broke's squadron had been a source of mild humiliation to the Royal Navy, news of her victory over *Guerrière* came as an unqualified shock to the British. 'It is not merely that an English frigate has been taken, after what we are free to express, may be called a brave resistance,' noted *The Times* of London, 'but that it has been taken by a new enemy, an enemy unaccustomed to such triumphs, likely to be rendered insolent and confident by them.' Apparently forgetting some American successes from the War of Independence, *The Times* added: 'Never in the history of the world did an English frigate strike to an American.'

Paroled from captivity by the Americans, on 2 October Captain Dacres faced a court-martial for the loss of his ship, but was exonerated, largely because of the revelation that *Guerrière*'s masts were rotten at the time of the fight. That disadvantage aside, the British frigate had been outgunned and outclassed by her larger American opponent. As for his confidence that British experience, seamanship and fighting élan would prevail over *Constitution*'s greater firepower, after having witnessed the cool-headed discipline of Hull's crew during the earlier sea chase, Dacres should have known better.

For the Americans, the victorious outcome of the war's first naval engagement provided an immeasurable boost to morale – and a natural foundation for legend. The words of a young crewman as he watched one of *Guerrière*'s round shot glance harmlessly off the triple-layered live oak superstructure of his ship – 'Good God, her sides are made of iron!' – became a fixture in American folklore and the source of the nickname by which *Constitution* was known thereafter: 'Old Ironsides'.

Constitution's first success would not be her last. Shortly afterwards, Hull relinquished command to Captain William Bainbridge and *Constitution* was made flagship of a squadron comprised of herself, the 36-gun frigate *Essex* and the sloop-of-war *Hornet*. Sailing from Boston on 26 October, *Constitution* and *Hornet* had to proceed without *Essex*, which was still fitting out in Philadelphia, and they too later parted company off Bahia, Brazil.

Three days later, *Constitution* encountered HMS *Java*, a new French frigate captured eighteen months earlier and pressed into British service, which was escorting the *William*, an American merchantman which she had recently captured. *Java* dispatched her prize to Bahia, then turned to square off with *Constitution*.

Although *Java* was the faster ship, after an hour of manoeuvring *Constitution* managed to score a hit on *Java*'s head rig, bowsprit and jib-boom, depriving the British ship of her headsails and much of her control. Bainbridge, though struck in the leg by a musket ball and wounded in the hip by a copper bolt when his wheel was shattered by a shot from *Java*, closed in to press his advantage and dismasted her with two more raking broadsides.

Even in this helpless state, *Java* put up a gallant fight. Her captain, Henry Lambert, was shot in the chest by a Marine while attempting to lead a boarding-party on to the American vessel and his first lieutenant, Henry Ducie Chads, kept up the fight for a time thereafter. But finally, when *Constitution* took position off *Java*'s bow for a final broadside, Chads decided that 'it would be wasting lives to resist any longer' and struck his colours.

Compared to the fifteen minutes it had taken to disable *Guerrière*, *Constitution*'s slogging match with *Java* had taken nearly four hours. Too badly holed to take as a prize, she was burned. Only her wheel was salvaged and used to replace *Constitution*'s. The 360 survivors of her crew, including about 100 wounded, were put ashore at Bahia, where Captain Lambert died of his wound soon afterwards.

Java's destruction marked the third British loss in less than a year; in addition to *Constitution*'s two victories, her sister, *United States*, commanded by Captain Stephen Decatur, had dismasted the 35-gun *Macedonian* off the Canary Islands and, after spending two weeks restoring the prize to sailing condition, brought her back to New York after a return voyage of nearly 4,000 miles.

After undergoing a complete yard overhaul in Boston, *Constitution* returned to sea in December 1813. By now the British blockade was tightening all along the Eastern seaboard and the Royal Navy, having acquired a new respect for the big American frigates, was making it a policy for its own frigates to operate in units of two or more, so that in the event of an encounter they could team up to overpower their larger opponent. In the course of running in and out of Boston for what proved to be ineffective commerce-raiding sorties, *Constitution* had a few more close brushes with superior forces, avoiding combat on each occasion. During one such encounter, on 3 April 1814, *Constitution* ran foul of HM frigates *Juno* and *Tenedos* off Cape Ann, Massachusetts, and was only able to outrun them by the use of every inch of canvas, including the royal studding sails, taking temporary shelter in Gloucester Harbour before making her way back to Boston.

On 17 December 1814, 'Old Ironsides', now under the command of Captain Charles Stewart, managed to slip past the Boston blockade and resumed her commerce-raiding activities. She managed to seize a merchantman off the Portuguese coast but, shortly afterwards, on 22 February 1815, she encountered the light frigate *Cyane* (34 guns), under Captain Gordon Falcon, and the corvette *Levant* (22 guns, mostly 32-pound carronades), captained by the Hon. Sir George Douglass. Although they were individually outgunned by the big American frigate, the two British ships might have overpowered *Constitution* by a skilful team effort (which had helped the British frigate *Phoebe* and sloop *Cherub* to capture the USS *Essex* in Valparaiso Bay on 28 March 1814 – and, in a later century, would allow the Allied cruisers *Exeter*, *Ajax* and *Achilles* to foil the German pocket battleship ship *Graf Spee* off the River Plate on 13 December 1939). Indeed, by the time action commenced at 6 p.m. the captains of *Cyane* and *Levant* were prepared to work together to corner *Constitution* in their collective crossfire – aided, they hoped, by the gathering darkness.

Captain Stewart, however, understood exactly what the British were trying to do and was not about to let them succeed. Using the skill and discipline of his now well-seasoned crew to advantage, he put *Constitution* through some extraordinary manoeuvres to keep the British vessels separated and deal with them in turn. At one point, a broadside of double-shot had disabled *Levant* when Stewart saw *Cyane* coming up astern and positioning herself to rake his ship. He reacted by having *Constitution*'s headsails cast loose and the main and mizzen topsails backed, with the incredible result of stopping and backing his ship out of danger and positioning himself to give *Cyane* a murderous diagonal raking broadside.

After an hour of punishment from *Constitution*'s guns, *Cyane* surrendered. *Levant* fled to effect emergency repairs, then bravely returned to resume the fight. By that time, however, *Constitution* had turned the odds decisively in her favour and one last murderous broadside forced *Levant* to strike her colours as well.

Of a collective total of 313 men, the two British ships lost 35 killed and 46 wounded. The virtuoso seamanship of *Constitution*'s captain and crew had kept her casualties down to four dead and ten wounded. In Stewart's cabin, Captains Falcon and Douglass got into an argument over who had been responsible for losing the battle until Stewart intervened: 'Gentlemen, there is no use in getting warm about it; it would have been the same whatever you might have done. If you doubt that, I will put you all on board and you can try it over.'

Given a prize crew, *Levant* was later recaptured by three frigates of the Boston blockade that had been hunting for *Constitution* since her breakout. *Constitution* and *Cyane* managed to reach Puerto Rico, where Stewart learned that the war had ended. Signed on Christmas Eve, the Treaty of Ghent was officially ratified on 18 February, with a 30-day grace period to allow for the time needed to convey the news to the United States and to the combatants' ships at sea. Under these circumstances, *Constitution*'s victory over *Cyane* and *Levant* was regarded as the excusable result of slow communications, rather than an embarrassing breach of the treaty. On 15 May, Stewart returned to a gala reception in New York, having won *Constitution* her third naval victory.

In the course of the War of 1812, *Constitution* had successfully defied the odds on several occasions, her escape from Broke's squadron being undoubtedly the most suspenseful. After serving in the peacetime navy, she was returned to Boston on 4 July 1828 and left to rot until the autumn of 1830, when she was declared unseaworthy and condemned.

Constitution's final struggle for survival was won against her own navy. A public outcry of patriotic fervour, spurred on by Oliver Wendell Holmes' poem 'Old Ironsides', prevailed over the Navy Department to save the 'eagle of the sea' from the 'harpies of the shore', as the poet himself put it. In February 1831, the first of a number of restorations restored *Constitution* to seaworthiness. As a diplomatic ship, she paid goodwill visits to ports all over the world. From August 1853 to June 1855, she patrolled the African coast to enforce the 1807 law banning the slave trade, taking her last prize in September 1953 when she caught the American schooner *Gambril* in the act of trying to smuggle slaves to the USA. From 1860 to 1871 she served as a school ship, then was retired once and for all from any duties other than that of an historic relic of the Age of Sail. Preserved by the US Navy in the Charlestown Navy Yard unit of the Boston National Historical Park, *Constitution* is the oldest warship still in commission on the Navy's rolls. About 20 per cent of the ship is original.

In September 1992, *Constitution* was placed in the Quincy Adams Dry-dock – where she had undergone her first major overhaul in 1833. There, sailors and civilian employees working for the Navy, aided by ultrasonic testing and X-rays, gave her 5 million dollars' worth of inspection and repairs, including the reinstallation of key structural supports. Even while such maintenance was being carried out, on-board tours of the ship continued, together with tours of the nearby USS *Constitution* Museum and the World War II-vintage destroyer *Cassin*. It is expected that the historic frigate will be fully rigged and back at Pier No. 1 by March 1996 – well in time for the bicentennial of her maiden launching.

References

Gilmer, Thomas C. *Old Ironsides: The Rise, Decline and Resurrection of the USS Constitution*, International Marine, Camden, ME, 1993.

Gruppe, Henry E. *The Frigates*, Time-Life Books, Amsterdam, VA, 1970, pp. 65–7, 78–90.

Maclay, Edgar Stanton. *A History of the United States Navy*, 1893.

CHAPTER 5

Terror from the Yazoo
CSS *Arkansas*, July – August 1862

Fought from 1861 to 1865, the American Civil War saw a number of naval actions involving the defiance of overwhelming odds. For the most part, the outnumbered naval units doing the defying belonged to the Confederate Navy, which from the beginning was even more disproportionately outmatched by its Union counterpart than was the case with the contending armies. While the North drew on its vast industrial capacity to build up a vast fleet of modern, often inventive warships, the South had to rely on ingenuity to create a fleet from scratch – supplemented by a measure of skullduggery in purchasing commerce-raiding ships overseas, particularly in Britain. With almost naive determination, the Confederate Navy's officers and sailors hoped to make up the numerical disparity by skill and daring, sometimes with astonishing success, more often with inevitable failure.

As Union forces moved to eliminate the Southern seaports one by one, their Rebel garrisons tried to counter the threat with a variety of 'equalisers', including 'torpedoes' (underwater mines), semi-submerged boats called '*Davids*' that were designed to sink their Union opponents with torpedoes extending in front of them on spars, and even a man-powered submarine christened *H. L. Hunley* after its late designer, whose spar torpedo succeeded in sinking the Union sloop *Housatonic* in Charleston Harbour, South Carolina, on 17 February 1864, but at the cost of itself being swamped and lost with its entire 16-man crew.

The most common vessel on which Confederate ports pinned their hopes, however, was the casemate ram, an armoured vessel designed to be impervious to cannon fire while sinking its Union opponents either with its own broadsides or with an iron ram on the bow – a steam-powered throwback to ancient galley warfare. A number of Confederate coastal cities built one or more such ironclads for their own defence, and several of them gained fame for the spirited fights they put up when the Union fleet arrived.

It is doubtful, however, if the exploits of such renowned Confederate sea-raiders as the *Alabama*, or armoured rams like the *Virginia*, could compare with those of a rusty, scratch built ironclad that operated far from the sea, along the Yazoo and Mississippi Rivers. For sheer determination in the face of impossible odds, the very genesis of the CS Ship *Arkansas*, let alone her subsequent fighting record, was in a class by itself.

On paper, *Arkansas* was typical of Confederate ironclad designs – a steam-powered, screw-driven floating casemate, with a ram bow. In practice, however, she was more primitive than most, being cobbled together under the constraints of limited resources, characteristic of the Mississippi region. Nevertheless, *Arkansas* put up a one-ship fight against the entire Union river fleet around the besieged Mississippi port of Vicksburg that made her a nautical legend – and proved that Rebel ships, as well as men, knew how to 'die game'.

Construction of *Arkansas* and a sister, the *Tennessee*, commenced on October 1861 at Fort Pickering, just below Memphis, Tennessee. The two rams were to be 165 feet long, with a beam of 35 feet and a draft of 11 feet, 6 inches. They were to be propelled by two screws, each powered by a 900hp horizontal direct-acting non-condensing, low-pressure steam engine, with two boilers each. Crews would number 200 men. In addition to the ram, *Arkansas* was to be armed with ten guns.

Despite entreaties by Lieutenant General P. G. T. Beauregard, commander of the Confederate Army of the Mississippi, that the ironclads be completed as soon as possible, construction languished. In March 1862, *Arkansas*' assigned executive officer, Lieutenant Henry Kennedy Stevens, wrote to his wife: 'Our work goes on very slowly, and it seems impossible to get it done faster.' He also revealed just what he thought of the vessel itself, stating that 'she is a humbug, and badly constructed'.

Arkansas was launched on 25 April 1862, and her builder, John Shirley, intended to complete her before concentrating on *Tennessee*. On that same day, however, New Orleans fell to a 13 ship Union invasion fleet commanded by Flag Officer David Glasgow Farragut. Memphis' access to the outside world via the Mississippi River had been effectively cut off. Moreover, it was learned that a second Union force, Captain Charles H. Davis's Western Gunboat Flotilla, made up of seventeen riverine gunboats and rams, was coming down the Mississippi from the north and closing rapidly on Memphis itself. Therefore the senior naval officer at Memphis ordered *Arkansas* evacuated to 'some swamp until she can be completed'. On 26 April she was towed by the steamboat *Capitol* south to Greenwood, Mississippi, on the Yazoo River. The unfinished *Tennessee* remained in Memphis, where she was destroyed before Union forces finally captured the city on 5 June 1861

At the time of her move, *Arkansas*' woodwork and deck armour were in place, but her engines, guns and casemate armour had not yet been installed; in fact, the scow carrying some of the latter material sank near Greenwood. Although *Arkansas* was officially commissioned on 25 May, her commander, Lieutenant Charles H. McBlair, had done practically nothing to make her battleworthy during the previous month. Then, at the urging of General Beauregard, a new commander, Isaac Brown, arrived in Greenwood to take charge of the derelict warship.

The son of a Kentucky Presbyterian minister, 45-year-old Isaac Newton Brown had been raised on the river, but left home at the age of 23 to seek the excitement of a naval career. Over the next 22 years, he fought in the Mexican War (1846–8), sailed around the world twice and served on the staff of the Naval Observatory. When the Civil War broke out, Brown took a secessionist stand and laid plans for mining the Mississippi channel at Columbus, Kentucky, and for equipping gunboats on the Cumberland River. Both schemes were undone by Kentucky's decision to remain in the Union, a choice soon sealed by the entry of Federal forces into the state. Brown, like thousands of other staunchly secessionist Kentuckians, became an 'orphan' – an exile from a Union state, fighting for the Confederacy.

Arkansas was Brown's first ship command. Desperate to redress the deteriorating situation on the Mississippi, the Confederate navy ordered him to render the uncompleted vessel battleworthy 'without regard to expenditure of men or money'.

'It being the season of overflow,' Brown reported, 'I found my new command four miles from dry land. Her condition was not encouraging. The vessel was a mere hull, without armour; the engines were apart; guns without carriages were lying about the deck; a portion of the railroad iron intended as armour was at the bottom of the river, and the other and far greater part was to be sought for in the interior of the country.' He found McBlair to be indolent and inept, yet so ill-disposed toward relinquishing his command that Brown later claimed that 'I came near shooting him, and would have done so had he not consented and got out of my way.'

Discouraging though the whole situation was, Brown was not the sort of officer to walk away from a challenge – as one of his officers put it, 'Brown is a pushing man'. Commandeering the *Capitol*, he used her derricks to fish the sunken railroad iron from the river and place it on a barge. He then towed *Arkansas* 110 miles to Yazoo City, a once bustling cotton-shipping port that had fallen into decline since the war began, but which still had a repair yard with mechanics, machinery and 'the possibility of equipment', as Brown put it. After arriving on 4 June, he converted the *Capitol* into a floating dock, complete with living-quarters for the workers, lashed her alongside *Arkansas* and drafted 200 men from a nearby army detachment to provide the raw manpower he would need. Despite summer temperatures that averaged 100 degrees Fahrenheit, work proceeded day and night – lit by lanterns and pine flares. When workers were overcome by the heat or by malaria, they were replaced by others. Stevens, who had once complained of how slowly work had gone, now wrote to his wife: 'I have not much time for writing now, as my whole day from five in the morning until seven in the evening is taken up, and I am then pretty tired.'

The building of the *Arkansas* itself was an epic of ingenuity and determination. Iron rails were gathered from all over the state to complete her armour. Since the nearest railroad terminal was 25 miles from Yazoo City, the iron had to be dragged the rest of the way. Fourteen blacksmiths' forges were appropriated from local plantations. Drilling machines, powered by the *Capitol*'s steam engine, were improvised to drill holes in the armour so that it could be bolted on to a wooden frame and the panel thus created attached to the vessel itself. A special forge was required to bend the rails to conform to the curve of the bow and stern, but no such item could be found. Undaunted, Brown nailed boiler plate over those areas 'for appearance's sake'. After much searching he found a manufacturer in Jackson, Mississippi, that would construct carriages for the ship's ten guns.

Although the original design of the *Arkansas* class was similar in configuration to that of the famous *Virginia*, which had been built on the hull of the partially burned Union sailing ship *Merrimack*, the circumstances of *Arkansas'* completion necessitated some alterations. Because of the shortage of iron rails, the armour was laid at a 35-degree angle on timber walls that were thicker than originally planned; between the wood and the iron, the total thickness came to eighteen inches at the bow and stern, and twelve inches at the sides. The insides of the walls were lined with compressed cotton. The small pilot house, situated in front of the ship's single smokestack, was imperfectly covered with a double thickness of 1-inch iron bars.

With the Union fleet only fifty miles away, Brown and his work force managed to bring *Arkansas* to a rude state of readiness in five weeks. But in mid-June, a new problem arose: the Yazoo's water level was dropping and, given *Arkansas'* draft of 13 feet, Brown realised that unless he moved her to deeper water soon, his new ironclad would be left stranded at her docks. On 20 June he set out for Liverpool Landing, 25 miles downstream, and soon discovered his ship's Achilles' heel: her balky engines had a tendency to stall at the most inopportune moments. When one screw stopped, the other would drive the boat around in a circle until both could be restored to working order.

Once *Arkansas* was safely out of the shallows, Brown gathered a crew of 232. About 100 of his men, including Lieutenant Charles W. Read, were veterans of the River Defense Fleet that had been defeated by Farragut at New Orleans, experienced and eager for a chance to even the score. The balance was a mixed bag of artillery and infantrymen from Missouri – tough fighters on land, but most of whom had never been on a boat before.

The cannon armament of what Brown called his 'box of guns' consisted of two 8-inch 64-pounders in the bow, two 32-pound rifled cannon in the stern and two 100-pound Columbiads and a 6-inch naval gun to each broadside. Six of the weapons had been obtained from Memphis, the others appropriated from two old gunboats. The total cost of building and arming the ironclad was $76,920.

Brown's first idea for using *Arkansas* was to stage a surprise attack on Memphis, in hopes of liberating the city. On 24 June, however, Confederate Major General Earl Van Dorn notified him that powerful Union naval forces were approaching Vicksburg, the last major Mississippi port still in Rebel hands.

On 18 May, a 7-ship flotilla from Farragut's fleet, commanded by Captain S. Lee Phillips, had steamed north to Vicksburg and demanded its surrender. The mayor, Laz Lindsay, refused, to which Colonel James L. Autry added: 'Mississippians don't know how, and refuse to learn, how to surrender. If Commodore Farragut or Brigadier General [Benjamin] Butler can teach them, let them come and try.'

Farragut did come up to try, subjecting the city to a rather ineffective bombardment on 26 and 27 May. After withdrawing to New Orleans to gather reinforcements, he returned on 25 June. At that same time, he learned that Commodore Davis had taken Memphis and was just twenty miles north of Vicksburg. On 28 June, Farragut ran all but three of his eleven warships past Vicksburg's shore batteries and was joined by four ironclads and six mortar boats from Davis's Western Gunboat Flotilla.

Despite the stubborn refusal of its garrison to surrender, there was now a serious likelihood that Vicksburg would fall to a combined onslaught of Union naval and land forces, in the same way as had such Rebel river bastions as Fort Henry, Fort Donelson, New Orleans, Island Number 10, Fort Pillow, Memphis and Baton Rouge. Once Vicksburg was taken, Federal control of the Mississippi, as well as over American coastal waters, would be absolute.

Desperate for a means of redressing the situation, Van Dorn, like a good many other Confederates, pinned his last hopes on a mighty ironclad to cancel the Union's superior numbers. *Arkansas* being the only such floating champion available, he suggested to Brown that she come out of the Yazoo and run past the Union river force, inflicting as much damage as possible. Brown concurred, but then learned, much to his disgust, that the only Confederate vessels then capable of supporting him, the ram-equipped wooden steamboats *General Earl Van Dorn, Polk* and *Livingston*, had been burned to avoid capture when two Union rams of similar design ventured up the Yazoo on 27 June. Convinced that he stood no chance of success, but duty-bound to try his best, a bitter Brown wired Van Dorn: 'I trust we shall use our vessel creditably, and if the army will attack against the same odds as that which awaits me, the war will soon be over.'

On 12 July, Brown judged *Arkansas* ready for a 'shakedown cruise' and steamed her to Satartia, a Yazoo port 65 miles north of the Mississippi. There Brown took an extra day to drill the 'backwoodsmen' of his crew in shipboard gunnery while Lieutenant Read rode ahead on horseback to scout the enemy fleet. On his return, Read reported at least 80 Union ships and 129 guns around Vicksburg.

On the morning of 14 July, Brown resumed his riverine trek, but had only gone fifteen miles when one of *Arkansas'* boilers developed a leak, spraying hot water into the forward magazine. The ironclad stopped at a deserted sawmill where the wet gunpowder was spread out on tarpaulins to dry in the sun, while lookouts kept a tense watch for approaching Union forces. *Arkansas* got under way again later that day, but during the night low-hanging trees almost knocked over her smokestack, after which she ran aground, requiring an hour to work herself free.

Sometime after midnight, Brown dropped anchor at Haines Bluff, about ten miles above the Mississippi, and let his men get three hours of sleep, reckoning that they'd probably need it. Read described the scene aboard her at daybreak on 15 July, as her crew awoke and prepared for the coming fight:

'The morning was warm and perfectly calm. The dense volume of smoke from our funnel rose high above the trees, and we knew that the enemy would soon be on the lookout for us. The men of the *Arkansas* were now all at their stations, the guns were loaded and cast loose, their tackles in the hands of willing seamen ready to train; primers in the vents, locks thrown back and the lanyards in the hands of the gun captain; the decks sprinkled with sand and tourniquets and bandages at hand; tubs filled with fresh water were between the guns, and down in the berth deck were the surgeons with their bright instruments, stimulants and lint, while along the passageways stood rows of men to pass powder, shell, and shot, and all was quiet save the dull thump, thump, of the propellers.'

Gathering his officers, Brown gave them final instructions: 'Should I fall, whoever succeeds to the command will do so with the resolution to go through the enemy's fleet, or go to the bottom. Should they carry us by boarding, the *Arkansas* must be blown up; on no account must she fall into the hands of the enemy.'

The Union forces around Vicksburg already had some knowledge of the mysterious ironclad lying somewhere up the Yazoo, though Farragut did not regard her as much of a threat, remarking in a letter to Union Secretary of the Navy Gideon Welles on 10 July: 'I do not think she will ever come forth.' During the night of 14 July, two of *Arkansas'* crew deserted and came aboard the ironclad gunboat *Essex*, reporting Brown's intent to attack. Farragut and Davis still found it hard to believe the enemy capable of building a serious piece of floating weaponry given the primitive technology at his disposal, but at the urging of the Confederate deserters they sent three vessels up the river with orders 'to procure correct information concerning obstructions and defenses of the river, and ascertain if possible the whereabouts of the ram *Arkansas*'.

At about 5 a.m. the ironclad gunboat *Carondelet*, wooden gunboat *Tyler* and wooden ram *Queen of the West* steamed up to meet the crude-looking monster, which their crews described as 'chocolate coloured' because *Arkansas*' iron sides were utterly coated with rust.

Tyler, which was in the lead, was first to sight the smoke of the approaching vessel at about 7 a.m., but her skipper, Lieutenant Commander William Gwin, apparently mistook *Arkansas*' rusty iron for wood and dismissed her as a commercial packet coming to surrender – an opinion reinforced by the fact that *Arkansas* was not yet flying a flag of any sort. After instructing his crew to prepare to fire a warning shot, Gwin returned to his breakfast. But a salvo from *Carondelet*, followed by two shots from the unknown vessel ahead, brought him back on deck, ordering his men to battle stations. *Tyler* fired an ineffective salvo, then Gwin shouted to *Queen of the West*'s Captain Hunter, ordering him to ram the Rebel vessel. The Union ram had only begun to comply when a Confederate shell burst over her. *Queen of the West* slewed to a halt, then reversed direction. Gwin swore as he realised that the *Queen*'s captain had lost his nerve, then backed *Tyler* down the river also, keeping her bow guns in action. Hunter later offered the excuse that he had merely been following standing orders to rejoin the fleet and report if he saw the dreaded Confederate ironclad.

Ignoring *Tyler*, Brown decided to deal first with his most potent adversary – *Carondelet*, whose captain, Henry Walke, had been a long-time friend of Brown's in pre-war days. Running down the river's current in order to increase her modest speed, *Arkansas* bore down on *Carondelet*, engaging her with her bow guns while keeping the other Federal vessels at bay with her broadside battery. Walke responded by executing a clumsy turn and retiring, later answering critics of his decision by saying: 'Being a stern-wheel boat, the *Carondelet* required room and time to turn around ... If I had continued bows-on, in that narrow river, a collision, which the enemy desired, would have been inevitable, and would have sunk the *Carondelet* in a few minutes.' In presenting her stern to *Arkansas*, however, *Carondelet* was also exposing the side with the thinnest armour to the Confederate's guns.

Arkansas lost the use of her starboard bow gun when the recoil of its first shot threw it completely off its chassis. Despite this inauspicious start, Brown turned *Arkansas* on an oblique course to bring her broadsides into play and soon her remaining guns were shattering *Carondelet*'s armour, while the latter's return fire was having little effect on *Arkansas*' thick, well-angled shell. Brown later wrote: 'While our shot seemed always to hit his stern and disappear, his missiles, striking our ironclad shield, were deflected over my head and lost in the air.'

For the next hour, Brown conducted a running fight at a snail's pace with *Carondelet*, steering *Arkansas* on a zigzag course to minimise exposure of his imperfect bow armour, which was most vulnerable to Federal cannon fire. As he closed in, one of *Arkansas'* gunners peered out of his embrasure to get a better look at what was going on. Seconds later, his body fell back inside, decapitated by a shell, while his brother looked on aghast. Another shell struck *Arkansas'* pilot house, mortally wounding Chief Pilot John Hodges and disabling his assistant. A sailor volunteered to take over the wheel. Brown himself was stunned by a shell, then a Minié ball from one of *Tyler's* sharpshooters grazed his temple and he fell down a hatchway. Even in Brown's absence, however, his officers and crew fought on as he would have wished.

By now, *Carondelet* was in trouble. Her water pipes were riddled, her gauges shot away and her steam escape pipes had collapsed on to the deck, blasting the after compartment with live steam. Another shot severed her steering ropes and she careened out of control, finally running aground in a muddy shallows.

Meanwhile, some of Brown's crewmen were laying him among the dead and wounded when he suddenly came to his senses and, to their astonishment, sprang to his feet and hastened topside to resume command. Bringing *Arkansas* as close as he dared to the grounded *Carondelet*, Brown gave her a parting broadside that almost capsized her. Holed below the waterline, *Carondelet* listed in a cloud of steam, while members of her crew leaped overboard and swam for shore. The Federal ironclad did not sink, but she was out of the fight with five crewmen dead and twenty wounded.

Arkansas' crew gave three hearty cheers as they passed the crippled *Carondelet*, then went for the *Tyler*, which turned and fled downstream, desperately covering her retirement with cannon and small arms from her contingent of sharpshooters from the 4th Wisconsin Infantry. 'We were fighting for existence, and we knew it,' a Yankee crewman recalled of the uneven exchange, as Rebel shells ravaged *Tyler's* wooden stern. Finally, *Tyler* managed to outdistance her pursuer, giving both vessels a 30-minute respite. Gwin counted fourteen hits in his boat, which had killed eight men and wounded twice that number.

Lined up at anchor twelve miles north of Vicksburg, with fighting vessels generally near the city and transports on the opposite, Louisiana, side of the river, the two Union fleets could hear firing from upriver as early as 6 o'clock, but, as Davis later wrote, 'most of us came to the conclusion that the firing was upon guerrilla parties'. As the sound of shooting drew nearer, the captain of Davis's flagship, the giant ironclad gunboat *Benton*, asked Davis's permission to raise steam, while on their own initiative gunners on Farragut's flagship *Hartford* began casting loose the gun tackles.

At 7.15 *Arkansas*, now flying the Confederate naval ensign, followed *Tyler* into the main channel of the Mississippi and advanced steadily toward the Union fleet lying twelve miles above Vicksburg: 33 vessels – as Brown described it, 'a forest of masts and smokestacks, sloops, rams, ironclads and other gunboats on the left side, and ordinary river steamboats and bomb-vessels on the right'. It seemed to be impossible odds, but Brown had his orders. Besides, it was unlikely that *Arkansas'* engine would be able to generate enough power for her to outrun the Yankees if she were to try withdrawing upriver – Brown's engineers reported that steam pressure in the engine room had dropped from 120 pounds to a dangerously low 20 in the course of the earlier fight. Regretting his inability to ram any one of the Yankee vessels, Brown ordered his helmsman to 'shave that line of men-of-war as close as you can, so that the rams will not have room to gather headway in coming out to strike us'. And with that, on through the Union fleet *Arkansas* charged, firing broadsides at targets of opportunity while shot and shell from the outraged Federals clanged against her iron sides.

Among the first Union vessels to fire were the gunboat *Kineo* and Farragut's flagship *Hartford* while the flag officer rushed on to the latter's quarter-deck clad only in his night-gown and, in the words of a crewman, 'seemed much surprised'. Most of the Federal shells glanced off *Arkansas'* railroad iron sides, but one of *Hartford*'s managed to penetrate the armour, a bale of cotton and twenty inches of wood before exploding, killing four of the crewmen at the 32-pounder. The gunnery officer recalled: 'The Captain of the gun standing at my right was knocked down by the concussion and the shock was so great that he lost his mind and never recovered.'

The first vessel with which the passing *Arkansas* was able to trade broadsides was Gunboat Number 6 from Farragut's fleet, armed with an 11-inch Dahlgren gun and two 12-pounders in the bows. *Arkansas* struck the gunboat with several shots, to which she replied with a blast from her big gun. The shot missed, and *Arkansas* chugged on to fire at the Federal warship *Louisville*. The wooden ram *Lancaster*, a sister of *Queen of the West*, got under way and tried to ram the Rebel ironclad until a shot penetrated her boilers and stopped her dead in the water. Frantic crew members, some trying to tear off their scalding clothing, jumped overboard to get away from the escaping steam. Eighteen less fortunate crewmen lay dead – including three fatally scalded – and another ten injured as the disabled *Lancaster* drifted away on the current.

Next, *Arkansas* drew up to the gunboat *Kineo* and a Confederate lieutenant notified Lieutenant Read. He knew that Read had lost a friend during the Battle of New Orleans – Lieutenant Thomas B. Huger, commander of the Confederate gunboat *McRae* – and that Read regarded the *Kineo* as being responsible for Huger's death (an incorrect notion, since Huger's mortal wound was actually inflicted by another Union gunboat, the *Iroquois*). Read's brother officer noted that he came forward 'leisurely and carelessly, swinging a primer lanyard ... I have never looked at a person displaying such coolness and self-possession'. After identifying the object of his revenge, Read returned to the two stern 6-inch rifles, over which he had personal charge, and waited his turn. *Arkansas* put a shell through *Kineo* with her bow guns, then subjected her to a broadside from her port battery. Finally, as *Arkansas* left the damaged Federal gunboat behind, Read gave her a last dose of punishment with his own guns.

Caught in a crossfire of Federal guns, *Arkansas* could only withstand so much punishment herself. Federal shot riddled her sheet iron smokestack. Repeated hits weakened her armour and the concussion caused furnace connections to come loose, reducing steam pressure while her firemen strove just to keep her under way. At one point Brown's executive officer told him that the temperature in the inadequately vented engine room was up to 130 degrees and that the firemen would not be able to perform their duties if they were not relieved every ten minutes.

Inside the ironclad's casemate, a round shot struck a shield over a port gun, knocking a gunner down. Miraculously, he found that he had merely been bruised and returned to his position – only to be killed moments later when another shell came through the same hole. Cotton partitions caught fire, filling the gun deck with smoke. A shot penetrated the forward armour, felled the entire crew of one gun, caromed around the smokestack and rolled to the opposite gun, crushing eight more crewmen. When yet another shot brought down *Arkansas*' colours, Midshipman Dabney Scales emerged from her iron casemate and scrambled up the ladder to replace them. Despite his exposure to enemy fire, he succeeded in re-installing the Rebel colours – only to see them carried away by another Yankee shell shortly afterwards.

At this point, *Arkansas*' speed was reduced to a crawl, but to her adversaries she seemed to be unstoppable as Brown steered her toward Farragut's flagship *Hartford*, and fired a few hasty shots her way. Another of Farragut's sailing ships, *Richmond*, gave the ironclad a 13-gun broadside of 100-pound balls at a range of no more than 80 yards. 'But it was only a waste of shot,' wrote *Richmond*'s deck officer. 'Most of them struck her plated sides and glancing, bounded up in the air 50 feet.'

In addition to *Richmond*, *Arkansas* fired at the wooden warship *Iroquois*, then approached two of Commander Davis's ironclad gunboats, *Essex* and *Benton*. Although unable to move because her engines were under repair, *Essex* got off two shots at the passing Confederate. Aboard *Benton*, firemen had managed to stoke her boilers enough to get her engines up to operational pressure, and the giant gunboat steamed out across *Arkansas'* path. Spotting Davis's pennant flying from *Benton's* staff, Brown ordered his pilot to ram the Yankee flagship on the port beam. *Benton's* momentum carried her out of harm's way at the last moment, *Arkansas* nearly shearing off her stern as she cut across her opponent's wake.

After firing a parting broadside at *Benton* – scoring six hits, killing one Federal crewman and wounding three – *Arkansas'* captain and crew found themselves clear of the line of Union ships and, with Vicksburg finally in sight, made for the sanctuary of that friendly port. *Benton* made a cautious pursuit, but turned back when she came within range of Vicksburg's shore batteries.

It had taken *Arkansas* thirty minutes to pass through the Yankee line, a spectacle that was observed by Van Dorn and Major General John C. Breckenridge from the dome of Vicksburg's courthouse, as well as thousands of cheering city residents.

Safe at last, but with barely enough steam left to turn her propellers, *Arkansas* had to drift the final mile to Vicksburg landing, where 20,000 people crowded the shores to greet the battered ironclad that had defied two Union fleets. Rowing out to meet the vessel in a small boat, General Van Dorn came aboard and embraced Brown in front of the cheering throng. But the festive mood evaporated when some of the civilians entered the gun deck to assist the wounded. 'Her deck was bloody from one end to the other,' recalled one horrified soldier, 'and the walls were besmeared with brains and blood, as though it had been thrown by hand from a sausage mill.' Acting Master's Mate J. A. Wilson reported that 'blood and brains bespattered everything, whilst arms, legs and several headless trunks were strewn about'. Besides injuries to some of the officers, twelve of *Arkansas'* crewmen had been killed and eighteen wounded.

Taking stock of the damage to *Arkansas* herself, Lieutenant Read found that 'the iron on her port side ... had been so often struck with heavy projectiles that it was very much loosened'. An artillery inspector reported that 'there is but one gun out of the ten in working order, Their carriages were shattered .... the embrasures, or portholes, were splintered, and some were nearly twice the original size.'

Arkansas had already fought two battles that day, but she would have to fight a third before midnight. Aboard *Hartford*, Flag Officer Farragut grieved over the 42 dead and 69 wounded inflicted on his and Davis's men by the Rebel ironclad, and fumed at the war correspondents who swarmed around him. 'What will be said of us?' he lamented. 'Let a little boat like that escape a whole fleet!' He soon found out after reporting the action to Navy Secretary Welles: 'It is with deep mortification that I announce to the Department that notwithstanding my prediction to the contrary, the ironclad ram *Arkansas* has at length made her appearance and took us all by surprise.' Welles, who referred to the action in his diary as 'the most disreputable naval affair of the war', telegraphed Farragut that: 'It is an absolute necessity that the neglect or apparent neglect of the squadron should be wiped out by the destruction of the *Arkansas*.'

Farragut needed no such prompting. Within hours of *Arkansas*' attack, he laid plans to run his ships past Vicksburg a second time, placing them back down river from the Rebel fortress and, at the same time, having another crack at *Arkansas*. His instructions to his officers paraphrased Nelson's credo: 'No one will do wrong who lays his vessel alongside of the enemy or tackles the ram. The ram must be destroyed!'

Shortly before nightfall, as storm clouds gathered over Vicksburg, Union scouts placed a range light on the shore opposite *Arkansas*' mooring site, giving Farragut's gunners a reference point. At 9 p.m., just before sunset, fourteen Union ships came down the river in two columns, exchanging shots with Vicksburg's shore batteries. As they approached the high bluff where the battered *Arkansas* lay, they also came abreast of the range light and used it to guide their broadsides at the enemy vessel's mooring. For the most part, however, it was wasted effort. Brown and his crew had spotted the light and let *Arkansas* drift a few hundred yards downstream to a new mooring.

As Farragut's ships engaged their phantom target, Brown, still eager to fight another round with the Yankees, prepared *Arkansas* to come out and engage them once more. Before she could get under way, however, a 160-pound bolt, fired from the Union warship *Sumter*, crashed through her makeshift armour and entered the engine room. Immobilised, the Rebel ram was forced to spend the rest of the skirmish at anchor, although she did loose one broadside at the passing Union vessels. Farragut's ships scored no more hits on their weakened adversary; the river current carried them past at a faster speed than expected, and *Arkansas*' rusty brown patina, combined with the shadows and red clay of the bluff, made her a difficult target to see, let alone aim at. *Sumter*'s one lucky hit had been bad enough, though. After the Union ships had gone, another burial party had to be sent ashore to bury two more of *Arkansas*' crew, while three more wounded had to be cared for.

Farragut had not got off Scot-free either. Five of his sailors were killed and eleven wounded by Vicksburg's batteries, and the gunboat *Winona* was so badly damaged that she had to be run ashore to prevent her from sinking.

Over the next week, Federal mortar boats lobbed 13-inch shells in the general direction of the Vicksburg waterfront in an attempt to hit *Arkansas*. A direct hit or an overhead explosion would have eliminated the ironclad, which had no roof armour, but while big shells fell all around her, sometimes dousing the repair crews with geysers of spray, none succeeded in striking her a telling blow. Even while undergoing a steady bombardment, *Arkansas* constituted a threat-in-being that Farragut acknowledged in a letter to Davis: 'The continued existence of the rebel gunboat *Arkansas* so near us is exercising a very pernicious influence upon the confidence of our crews, and even upon the commanders of our boats.'

Just before dawn on 22 July, both Farragut's and Davis's flotillas returned to Vicksburg in force. While the combined fleets shelled the town and its waterfront for half an hour, *Essex* came around the upper bend of the river to bombard the *Arkansas*, followed by *Queen of the West*, whose new commander, Army Lieutenant Colonel Alfred E. Ellet, had orders to administer the *coup de grâce* with a ramming attack.

Although partially repaired, *Arkansas* still had trouble getting up enough steam even to manoeuvre, and most of her crew had either been hospitalised or, in the case of many of the Missouri volunteers, pressed into service on land again. Brown, who by now had been promoted to the rank of commander, deployed his forty available men to the batteries. Racing from the magazine to whichever gun happened to be pointing at the enemy at a given moment, they fought back with as many as they could load and fire at a time.

Braving cannon fire from the shore as well as from *Arkansas*, Commander William Porter, commanding *Essex*, brought his vessel within five feet of his quarry. One of his point-blank shots passed through one of *Arkansas'* gun ports and another bored a new hole in her armour; 'We could distinctly hear the groans of her wounded,' he later recalled. Forty-two Rebel shells hit *Essex*, failing to cause serious damage but killing one man and wounding three – including her captain, who suffered a small gash in the head from a shell fragment – and convincing Porter to call off his attack. One of *Arkansas'* officers described *Essex*'s attack from the receiving end:

'On she came like a mad bull, nothing daunted or overawed. As soon as Captain Brown got a fair view of her ... he divined her intent, and seeing that she was as square across the bow as a flat boat or scow, and we were as sharp as a wedge, he determined at once to foil her tactics. Slacking off the hawser which held our head to the bank, he went ahead on the starboard screw, and thus our sharp prow was turned directly to her to hit against. This disconcerted the enemy and destroyed his plan. A collision would surely cut him down and leave us uninjured. All this time we had not been idle spectators. The two Columbiads had been ringing on his front and piercing him every shot; to which he did not reply until he found that the shoving game was out of the question; then, and when not more than fifty yards distant, he triced up his three bow port shutters and poured out his fire. A 9-inch shot struck our armour a few inches forward of the unlucky forward port, and crawling along the side entered. Seven men were killed outright and six wounded. Splinters flew in all directions. In an instant the enemy was alongside, and his momentum was so great that he ran aground a short distance astern of us. As we passed, we poured out our port broadside, and as soon as the stern rifles could be cleared ... we went ahead on our port screw and turned our stern guns on him, every man – we had but seventeen left – and officer went to them. As he passed he did not fire; nor did he whilst we were riddling him close aboard. His only effort was to get away from us ... But our troubles were not over. We had scarcely shook this fellow off before we were called to the other end of the ship – we ran from one gun to another to get ready for a second attack. The *Queen* was now close to us, evidently determined to ram us. The guns had been fired and were now empty and inboard. Somehow we got them loaded and run out, and by the time she commenced to round to ... we struck her with the Columbiads as she came down ... Capt. Brown adopted the plan of turning his head to her also, and thus received her blow glancing. She came into us going at ... fifteen miles an hour ... His bow, through glancing, was a heavy one. His prow ... made a hole through our side and caused the ship to career and roll heavily, but we all knew in an instant that no serious damage had been done ... He ran into the bank astern of us and got the contents of the stern battery, but [*Queen of the West*] was soon off into deep water ... Beating off their two vessels, under the circumstances, was the best achievement of the *Arkansas*.'

Only when it was too late did the Union sailors learn how near a thing it had been for *Arkansas* that morning. Had they known how small a crew she had left to man her two remaining operational guns, *Essex* could have pounded her into submission or captured her with a boarding-party, rather than make a fruitless attempt to ram her – an endeavour rendered the more difficult by the fact that *Essex* was steaming across the current, rather than with it. *Queen of the West*, too, might have penetrated *Arkansas*' hull, had she not been bucking the current, and had Brown not turned *Arkansas*' prow towards her so that she only struck his ship a glancing blow.

On 24 July, with the river's depth dropping to a dangerous level, Farragut had to shelve any further plans for dealing with Vicksburg or *Arkansas*. Leaving two ships under Commander Davis to keep an eye on the enemy ironclad, he withdrew the rest of his fleet south. Four days later, Davis took his small flotilla north to Helena, Arkansas. For the time being, Vicksburg was safe and would remain Confederate for nearly a year thereafter, finally surrendering on 4 July 1863 to a Union commander even more tenacious than Farragut: Major General Ulysses S. Grant.

Lauded for his part in defending Vicksburg from the riverine Union threat, Isaac Brown was exhausted. Leaving *Arkansas* and the supervision of her repairs in the hands of his executive officer, Lieutenant Stevens, Brown went on a well-earned leave to rest with friends at Granada, Mississippi. While there, however, he fell ill and had to stay longer than he had intended. Meanwhile, General Von Dorn made plans for *Arkansas* to go south to assist a 3,000-man Confederate army, led by General Breckenridge, in an attempt to retake Baton Rouge from its Union occupiers. While Breckenridge's troops engaged a Union force of similar size led by Major General Thomas Williams, *Arkansas* would deal with the Federal gunboats *Essex*, *Cayuga*, *Kineo* and *Katahdin*.

With only nine days' worth of refitting done on *Arkansas*, Stevens protested that the vessel was not ready, nor were his engineers up to the task of keeping her creaky engines operational during another battle. Brown backed Stevens' appraisal and ordered him to remain in port, but Van Dorn obtained confirming orders from Brown's superiors that nullified Brown's instructions. Assembling what remained of *Arkansas'* crew, including several of the walking wounded, supplemented by volunteer gunners from Vicksburg's garrison, Stevens left Vicksburg at 2 a.m. on 3 August – 30 hours in advance of Breckenridge's scheduled assault on Baton Rouge.

Brown was furious when he heard that *Arkansas* had left without him, insisting that he was the only one who knew how to handle her quirky machinery. He may have been right, for Stevens pushed her engines too hard as he rushed down river. On several occasions they showed signs of strain and Stevens prudently ordered her stopped for adjustments and maintenance.

As *Arkansas* approached the mouth of the Red River, Stevens questioned his chief engineer, an army volunteer named E. Brown, as to the wisdom of continuing. The engineer replied that he felt the engines would hold up, provided that he was given time for one last inspection. Stevens agreed and, during the pre-dawn hours of 4 August, paused to give his engineer the time he needed. The voyage resumed at 8 a.m., and for the next twenty miles, *Arkansas'* engines ran smoothly. As she came within sight of Baton Rouge, the sound of gunfire from shore indicated that the fight for the city had already begun. Stevens ordered his crew to battle stations and had just concluded a planning session with his pilot when *Arkansas* gave an abrupt lurch. Her ever-troublesome starboard engine had stalled again and, while soldiers in blue uniforms fought opponents dressed in gray or butternut, *Arkansas* spent the day on the sidelines.

At nightfall, mechanics repaired the recalcitrant engine and Stevens withdrew a short distance upstream to replenish *Arkansas'* fuel from a coal yard. In the process, the starboard engine broke down again and the ship's blacksmith spent the night forging a replacement crank pin.

At 9 o'clock the next morning, *Arkansas* arrived five miles south of Baton Rouge. She was in full view of Union forces there, and waiting between her and the port was an old enemy, the *Essex*, accompanied by the wooden ships *Cayuga* and *Sumter*. *Essex* had just fired her opening shots and *Arkansas* had advanced about 150 yards when her port engine gave out, followed about a minute later by the starboard. This time, Engineer Brown reported the situation to be hopeless. Unable to return *Essex*'s fire, Stevens saw no choice but to withdraw to the nearest river bank and order his crew ashore. His officers loaded all *Arkansas*' guns and then, with tears in his eyes, Stevens set fire to the berth deck. The last to abandon ship, he jumped off the stern and swam for shore to witness his ship's last minutes.

Cast adrift, the burning *Arkansas* drifted with the current toward *Essex* – much in accordance with Stevens' last forlorn hope. The heat of the fire touched off *Arkansas*' cannon, failing to damage the Union vessels but sufficient to drive them back, leaving the abandoned Confederate vessel to drift on downstream. At about noon, as her crew watched silently from the shore, the flames reached her magazine and, as one of them recalled, 'with colours flying, the gallant *Arkansas*, whose decks had never been pressed by the foot of an enemy, was blown into the air'.

On land, Breckenridge's troops managed to drive the Federal forces from Baton Rouge, but were unable to hold the city themselves. He withdrew north to Port Hudson, while the Union army retired to New Orleans on 15 August.

On hearing of *Arkansas*' departure from Vicksburg, the still-ailing Commander Brown tried to rejoin her by taking the train to Tangipahoa, Louisiana, but only arrived in time to gather her crew and bring them back to Mississippi. Having thus lost his ship – and with no others left to take her place Brown re-applied his ingenuity to the defence of the Yazoo by other means. He improvised two torpedoes by filling two 5-gallon glass demijohns with gunpowder, anchoring them to the bottom of the river and supporting them with wooden floats. Wires connected the two torpedoes, so that when a Union ship made contact, it would draw them toward the sides of its hull and at the same time pull friction primers that would detonate the explosives. Brown's creation was crude but effective; on 12 December, the Union ironclad gunboat *Cairo* fell victim to the twin torpedoes, settling to the bottom in twelve minutes to become the first warship to be sunk by an explosive underwater device.

The *Arkansas*' meteoric career had lasted 21 days, but her lone fight against an entire Union fleet on 15 July 1862 was sufficient to elevate the squat, rust-covered ironclad, her patchwork crew and her indomitable captain to the lofty realms of legend – in both nautical annals and among the revered Southern heroes of the 'Lost Cause'.

References

Gillespie, Michael L. 'Legendary Wake of Terror,' in *Military History Magazine Presents Great Battles*, November, 1988, pp. 4–9.

Martin, David. *The Vicksburg Campaign, April 1862–July 1863*, Combined Books, Inc., Conshohocken, PA, 1994, pp. 53–68

Scharf, J. Thomas. *History of the Confederate States Navy*, Fairfax Press, 1977.

Still, William N. Jr. *Iron Afloat: The Story of the Confederate Ironclads*, University of South Carolina Press, Columbia, SC, 1985, pp. 62–78.

CHAPTER 6
Swan of the East
SMS *Emden*, August – November 1914

On 1 November 1906, amid the massive battleship-building mania that would eventually lead Germany and Great Britain to war, the keel was laid at the Imperial Yard in Danzig for a light cruiser, tentatively named *Ersatz Pfeil*, that was intended to replace a small, obsolete cruiser named *Pfeil* (Arrow). By the time that the ship was launched on 26 May 1908, a subscription that had been taken up by the citizens of Emden towards her construction resulted in her being re-christened with the name of that city.

Trim and attractive for her time, *Emden* was otherwise singularly unimpressive among the mighty dreadnoughts and swift battle cruisers whose launchings dominated public attention. Nobody would have ever predicted that she, of all the warships in Germany, would attain legendary status as the protagonist of one of naval warfare's most swashbuckling sagas.

Built at a cost of 6.8 million gold Marks (£319,000), 387 feet long, 44 feet in beam and 17½ feet in draught, *Emden* was already behind the state of the cruiser's art. Powered by two standing triple-expansion engines of three cylinders each, drawing power from twelve coal-fed boilers for a maximum speed of 24 knots, she was the last piston-engined cruiser to be built in Germany – even her sister, *Dresden*, had turbines. *Emden*'s ten 4.1in high-velocity guns were already matched in range and surpassed in punch by the 6-inchers equipping Britain's newest generation of light cruisers, against which her armour, ranging from two to four inches, could not provide adequate protection. She did, however, also have two torpedo-tubes transversely mounted in the hull, which could launch a total of five 17.7in torpedoes broadside to a range of 11,000 feet.

After trials and reserve service, *Emden* entered active duty on 1 April 1910. Her first orders were to have her grey finish repainted in white for tropical service and, with flag-showing stops along the way, to replace the old cruiser *Niobe* at the northern Chinese port of Tsingtao which, since being seized in 1897, had been developed into the capital of Germany's empire in the Far East. *Emden* would never return to Germany.

Emden's first action came on 10 January 1911 when she joined the light cruiser *Nürnberg* in suppressing a native revolt at Ponape in the Caroline Islands. The two ships shelled a 1,000-foot fortified hill on the nearby island of Jokaj, then landed a force of sailors and native troops to storm the position, which they took in six hours. The rebellion on Ponape itself went on for another six weeks before the last of the rebels surrendered. On 1 March, *Emden* left the 'pacified' island to return to Tsingtao, where colonial patrols and courtesy visits resumed, broken up by semi-annual rotations of personnel. In March 1913, the German Cruiser Squadron came under the command of *Konteradmiral* (rear-admiral) Maximilian *Graf* von Spee and, on 29 May 1913, *Kapitänleutnant* (lieutenant-commander) Karl Friedrich Max von Müller took command of *Emden*.

Born in Hanover on 16 June 1873, Müller had originally trained to be an army officer as had his Prussian father, but in 1891 he talked his father into letting him transfer to the navy, where he made midshipman within two years. He served in numerous ships, from battleships in the North Sea to gunboats in German East and South-west Africa, where he contracted the recurring malaria from which he suffered for the rest of his life, and from which he would die on 11 March 1923. Müller's relatively slow progress up the ranks was largely the result of his self-effacing reserve; limiting the descriptions of his subsequent activities to the sparsest necessary details, his personality remains a mystery to this day, but his old-fashioned chivalry and innovative tactical genius were to be adequately spoken for by his deeds.

News of serious unrest in northern China brought *Emden* to Nanking on 12 August, joining comparable British, Japanese and American warships to protect Western interests against rebels reported to have been firing on steamers and gunboats along the Yangtse River. Steaming upstream of Wuhu, *Emden* came under fire from a rebel fort near Tongling, but 25 well-placed shells silenced the enemy guns. She then proceeded to Hangkow, exchanging small-arms fire with rebels along the way, and remained active during the next eight months of intermittent trouble.

Already the gunnery champion of the Cruiser Squadron, *Emden*'s gleaming white hull and graceful lines earned her the nickname of 'Swan of the East' among the local mariners. Her running of the Yangtse gauntlet earned her the reputation of being the most bold and dashing of the Western warships, while Müller was decorated for it with the Order of the Royal Crown, Third Class with Swords, and promoted to full *Fregattenkapitän* (commander) in March 1914. On 12 March, *Kapitänleutnant* Helmuth von Mücke from Zwikau, Saxony, was appointed his Executive Officer. As extroverted as his commander was modest, Mücke's job as disciplinarian over *Emden*'s 400-man crew was eased by his charm, humour and infinite resourcefulness. Equally ingenious was *Kapitänleutnant der*

Reserve Julius Lauterbach, a fat but muscular giant from Rostock who, against his family's wishes, had left military school aged 17 to pursue his love of the sea. After twenty years in the China Seas with the Hamburg–America Line, Lauterbach stood in boisterous, beer-swilling, worldly-wise contrast to his naval colleagues, but he had a seabag full of experience and local acquaintances that would come in handy in the year to come.

In mid-June, *Emden* lavishly hosted the visiting British heavy cruiser *Minotaur*, flagship of British Commander-in-Chief, China, Vice-Admiral Sir T. H. M. Jerram. On 20 June, Spee's squadron left Tsingtao on a south Pacific cruise, leaving only *Emden* and a few auxiliaries behind. On 29 June, the assassination of Habsburg heir Archduke Franz Ferdinand produced shock waves that could even be felt in the Far East. On 24 July, the old Austro-Hungarian cruiser *Kaiserin Elizabeth* arrived at Tsingtao, followed four days later by word that Austria–Hungary had declared war on Serbia.

On 31 July 1914, *Emden* left Tsingtao so as to be ready in case the war escalated. On 2 August, it was learned that war had been declared between Germany and Russia. The next day, France joined with Russia against Germany. On 4 August, near Tsushima Island, *Emden* encountered the 3,500-ton mail steamer *Ryaezan*, which led her on an hour-long 17-knot chase as the Russians sought sanctuary in neutral Japan and radioed Vladivostok for help. Jamming *Ryaezan*'s transmissions with her own radio, *Emden* caught up with the Russian and brought her to a halt with twelve shots across her bows. Appointed Prize Officer for now – and for the rest of *Emden*'s raiding career – Julius Lauterbach boarded the ship and, when her captain professed not to speak German, he laughingly reminded him that he had spoken it well enough when they had been drinking beer together at the club in Tsingtao a month earlier. *Ryaezan* carried 80 passengers but little cargo; nevertheless, her good turn of speed inspired Müller to keep her for later use as an auxiliary cruiser (with eight 4in guns installed from the gunboat *Kormoran*, she joined Spee's squadron as *Kormoran II* on 27 August, but achieved nothing before being interned at Guam in December).

On the way back to Tsingtao, *Emden* ran into five cruisers of the French squadron south-bound from Vladivostok, but to the Germans' relief and amusement the French sheered off, thinking *Emden* an outrider for Spee's squadron and fearing a trap. On that same day, however, a more serious naval adversary entered the picture: Britain had declared war on Germany. Japan, bound by a 1902 treaty of alliance with Britain, could be expected to cash in on it at German expense at any time. Tsingtao would be a death-trap for any German ship so, after a brief stay to replenish coal and stores, *Emden* left China for the last time to join up with Spee's squadron, which lay at Pagan Island, north of Guam in the Marianas.

As *Emden* entered Pagan harbour on 8 August and anchored along-side *Scharnhorst, Gneisenau* and *Nürnberg*, she was fervently cheered; her crew later learned that a wireless report had said that she had not only taken the *Ryaezan*, but that she had fought an engagement with the Russian light cruiser *Askold* in which both ships had been sunk – not the last voyage *Emden* would make through the rumour mills. On the 13th, Admiral Spee summoned his captains aboard *Scharnhorst* to discuss where to go from there. Spee wished to carry on the war in the East by maintaining a menacing 'fleet in being' which would divert and tie down elements of the Royal Navy. For this strategy, he judged the Indian Ocean logistically and tactically impractical, a British lake with no secure place to refuel. Instead, he decided to operate in the south-eastern Pacific, where the long coast of neutral but sympathetic Chile could provide hidden shelter and supply whenever necessary.

While agreeing that coaling considerations were important to Spee's squadron, Müller felt that the long voyage to that part of the ocean, and the paucity of worthy targets once there, would contribute little to the German war effort. He therefore proposed that *Emden* remain behind to fend for herself in the Indian Ocean, where she might cause disruption to the enemy while taking advantage of the flexibility of manoeuvre that a single warship might enjoy over a squadron. Spee considered the proposal overnight and then agreed, detaching *Emden* and the collier *Markomannia* on the morning of 14 August. The next day, Japan delivered an ultimatum to the Germans at Tsingtao: Germany was to remove or disarm all warships in the Pacific, and evacuate the port of Kiaochow by 9 September, acknowledgement and response to be made by 23 August. The Germans made no reply, but prepared for the siege to come. Japan was now in the war on the Allied side. Spee's squadron and *Emden* were now cut off from any friendly port of call, and would be hunted down by warships of the British Commonwealth, France, Russia and Japan.

Under the circumstances, Müller's idea of using *Emden* for lone privateering on the high seas seemed suicidal. With a range of 1,226 miles at 24 knots between coaling stops (3,790 miles at 12 knots), *Emden* had been built for scouting and fleet support in the North Sea, not for challenging the independent long-range patrolling of Britain's empire-guarding cruisers. Besides avoiding her enemies, her greatest challenge as a raider in the Indian Ocean would be in keeping herself fuelled and maintained.

Emden's greatest weapon, however, was neither her guns nor her torpedoes, but the minds of her captain and officers, who devised an ingenious strategy of self-help, making maximum use of whatever ships she captured, combined with carefully worked-out rendezvous points with *Markomannia* and prizes pressed into service as additional supply ships. Their excellent staff work and intelligence-gathering would also be instrumental in keeping *Emden* informed of the maritime routes to prey upon and the whereabouts of warships to avoid. A certain degree of deception was added to the formula by the fabrication of a dummy fourth funnel to make *Emden* appear British, like the light cruiser *Yarmouth*, known to be a regular patroller of Far Eastern waters.

Emden's cruise brought her no results at first, save for a near-confrontation in the East Indies on 27 August with the neutral Dutch battleship *Tromp*, until the two vessels' identities could be satisfactorily ascertained. When a victim finally did turn up on 7 September, it was the neutral Greek *Pontopouros* carrying some not-so-neutral English coal. Müller settled the tricky question of neutral rights by buying the Greek's charter. The prize and her useful cargo were then his – captured, bought and paid for.

On 10 September, *Emden* captured the 3,392-ton *Indus*, bound for Bombay to pick up cavalry horses. All that was aboard the ship were ballast and 150 cases of soap, but the latter were gratefully taken aboard, since in his haste to leave Tsingtao, Müller had neglected to stock properly in toilet soap for his crew, and with barely a fortnight's supply left, he had just recently been teased by First Officer Mücke about the necessity of giving first priority to the capture of a soap-ship. This minor incident was to inspire the following advertisement which turned up in *The Empire*, a Calcutta newspaper, on 25 September:

> 'There is no doubt that the German cruiser *Emden* had knowledge that the *Indus* was carrying 150 cases of North-West Soap Company's celebrated ELYSIUM Soap, and hence the pursuit. The men on the *Emden* and their clothes are now clean and sweet, thanks to ELYSIUM Soap. Try it!'

Commercial exploitation is the sincerest form of flattery, and one may imagine the delight and amusement aboard *Emden* when her crew came across this unique example aboard another of her victims about a month after its publication. If ever there were proof that *Emden* had achieved fame – and perhaps even a measure of popularity – among her enemies, here it was, in writing.

Emden's already-growing notoriety was all the more reason for Müller to continue to play a careful game, keeping an erratic course and sometimes exchanging friendly, though distant, greetings with passing merchant ships to keep the Allies guessing as to his whereabouts, before choosing to strike again. The day after taking *Indus*, *Emden* sank the *Lovat* and captured the *Kabinga* which, since she was carrying a neutral cargo, was pressed into service to accommodate *Emden*'s growing bag of prisoners. On 12 September *Emden* brought an end to the voyages of the collier *Killian* and the 7,600-ton steamer *Diplomat*. On the 14th Müller stopped the neutral Italian freighter *Loredano* and vainly appealed to her captain to take on some of his prisoners. After they parted company, Müller steered a southerly course until the Italian was out of sight, then changed direction to slightly west of north. Sure enough, *Loredano*'s captain could not wait to tell of his encounter with the Germans, and over the next few days no less than five ships, any one of which would have overwhelmed *Emden*, were being dispatched or alerted in hopes of trapping the Germans. They included *Yarmouth* – the light cruiser which *Emden* sought to impersonate with her false fourth stack – the armoured cruisers *Hampshire* and *Minotaur*, and the Japanese battle cruiser *Ibuki* and light cruiser *Chikuma*.

That night, Müller encountered the unladen steamer *Trabboch*, quickly took her and, after evacuating her crew, blew her up. He then released his latest captives on board *Kabinga*, after seeing that they signed the customary petition that they would never take up arms against Germany or her allies. *Kabinga*'s captain sent a letter to Müller thanking him for the way he, his family and crew had been treated during their detention, and before being sent on their way, the newly freed prisoners gave three lusty cheers to the *Emden*, her captain and crew. When they reached Calcutta, they spread word of their humane and chivalrous treatment, and both *Emden* and her skipper came to be known as the 'Gentlemen of War' throughout the Far East and back in Britain.

No sooner had *Kabinga* vanished into the night when Müller spotted another, east-bound merchantman which, he subsequently learned, had seen the great explosion of *Trabboch* and was trying to hasten away from the area. He gave chase, and with a shot across her bows forced her to heave-to for an exchange by megaphone:

'What ship?'

'*Clan Matheson*.'

'English?'

'No, British!', replied the irritated Captain William Harris, who was a Scotsman.

Soon afterwards, *Clan Matheson*'s nationality became a moot point; she was scuttled, and some of her crew were put to work farther south off the Andaman Islands, assisting in coaling up *Emden* from the *Pontopouros* – albeit for payment. Returning to the Singapore–Calcutta and Madras–Rangoon steamer lanes on 15 September *Emden* met only the neutral Norwegian steamer *Dovre*, whose master took aboard *Clan Mathe-*

son's crew and informed the Germans that he had seen two British auxiliary cruisers in the Malacca Strait and the French cruisers *Dupleix* and *Montcalm* in Penang. One of Müller's officers proposed the idea of raiding Penang, which he stored away in his mind for a later time.

For now, he chose to steam south until *Dovre* was out of sight, then swing westwards towards Madras, the chief port on India's south-eastern coast, with the intention of 'diminishing English prestige' by shelling the oil tanks there. While he did so, two Allied warships that had been in a position to stop him were elsewhere. Captain H. W. Grant's cruiser *Hampshire* was 300 miles to the east, steaming to investigate a false report of gunfire – more likely thunder misinterpreted by a nervous populace – near Akyab, on the north-east coast of Burma. Grant had left orders with his Japanese partner, *Chikuma*, that she guard the approaches to Madras against a possible visit by *Emden*, but *Chikuma*'s captain took his time coaling in Colombo before steaming to her appointed beat, certain that the Germans would not be so foolish as to strike so deep in British waters. That assumption threw away Japan's last chance to claim a naval victory of any sort during the First World War, and left Madras wide open for *Emden*'s attack on 22 September.

Although the war had been going on eight weeks, Müller found the city lit up like a carnival and, already aware of reports of German atrocities on the Western Front, took pains to angle his 25 salvos of 130 shells against the fuel tanks with a minimum of error. The result was that only five people were killed and twelve injured in the destruction of 346,000 gallons of fuel worth about £8,000. The damage was less than it might have been, but its psychological effect on the British was devastating. For days, trains were packed with people fleeing a possible return of the 'mystery ship'; the economy of the city was affected for weeks; the raid was the talk of the bazaars for months, and the word '*Emden*' took its place in the Madras dialect of the Tamil language to signify 'an enterprising and ingenious person'.

Having thus played her small part towards embarrassing the British in the eyes of their Indian subjects, *Emden* escaped none the worst for wear. Of nine shots fired at her by the elderly shore batteries, only three exploded close by her, and none hit.

An indirect consequence of *Emden*'s activities was that when Admiral Spee's Pacific Squadron was reported as having been sighted off British Samoa, there were no ships available to deal with it, all being either in or around the Indian Ocean hunting for *Emden*, or guarding convoys against her. On the same day that *Emden* bombarded Madras, Spee struck at Papeete in French Tahiti; the only opposition, the gunboat *Zélée*, was quickly overwhelmed by shells from *Scharnhorst*, *Gneisenau* and *Nürnberg*. Spee then steamed on, unopposed until 2 November when he won his greatest victory at Coronel, and 8 December when he met his end off the Falklands.

First Lord of the Admiralty Winston Churchill, who would later describe the German Pacific Squadron as '... a cut flower in a vase, fair to see and yet bound to die', was growing frustrated and angry about the continued invisibility of *Emden* everywhere save in the daily newspapers. In a letter to the Secretary of the Admiralty and First Sea Lord Prince Louis of Battenberg on 29 September, Churchill wrote: 'The escape of *Emden* from the Bay of Bengal is most unsatisfactory, and I do not understand on what principle the operations of the four cruisers *Hampshire*, *Yarmouth*, *Dupleix* and *Chikuma* have been concerted. From the chart, they appear to be working entirely disconnected and with total lack of direction.' On 1 October he reiterated the need for co-ordinated effort, and complained bitterly of the delays in transport schedules caused by *Emden*'s continued existence: 'I wish to point out to you most clearly that the irritation caused by an indefinite continuance of the *Emden*'s captures will do great damage to the Admiralty's reputation.'

No concerted effort, however, would have substituted for plain luck against Müller's principal weapon – space. Left entirely to his own devices, he could strike anywhere he chose in the Pacific, Indian or Antarctic Oceans. The science of radio directional ranging was in its infancy, and in any case *Emden* only used her wireless to listen in on others, as she had nobody to whom she herself could transmit. A chance sighting by any of her opponents would have been fatal to her, but *Emden* had so far succeeded in losing herself in the vastness of the sea.

She now set course southwards, ever deeper into enemy waters and into one of the busiest sea lanes in the East where, between 25 September and 19 October, she captured thirteen ships, whose stores kept her in business and whose newspapers, some dated to within a day of capture, kept Müller and Company ahead in their psychological impact on the region – causing growing panic and yet admiration among their enemies. *King Lud* and *Tymeric* fell victim to *Emden* on the 25th, and *Gryfevale* was captured the next day. The most fortunate prize of the cruise came on 27 September, the 4,350-ton collier *Buresk*, carrying 6,600 tons of first-class coal from South Wales to the British China Squadron in Singapore, as well as the steamers *Ribera* and *Foyle*. All prisoners were put aboard *Gryfevale* which was then sent off to freedom. After coaling from the almost depleted *Markomannia* off Miladunmadalulu Atoll in the Eastern Maldives, Müller dispatched her to restock from *Pontopouros*' hold at a future rendezvous point at Simaloer, then proceeded south in company with *Buresk*.

On 9 October, *Emden* stopped at the British-owned island of Diego Garcia, where her crew coaled-up once more, carried out some desultory hull-scraping and maintenance and took time to repair the engine of the motor-boat of the local coconut and copra plantation, whose people had not been visited from the outside world since late July, and did not even know there was a war on. They learned the truth when the auxiliary cruiser *Empress of Russia* arrived on 12 October, sent by Captain Grant to check in case *Emden* might have gone there, only to discover from the astonished residents that she had been and gone two days before. This latest addition to the *Emden* legend was headlined 'High Comedy on the High Seas' by at least one British newspaper.

More serious were the fates of *Clan Grant*, taken on 15 October and sunk the next day with a captured barge, and of *Ben Mohr*, sunk that night. *Emden*'s richest catch came on the 19th: the 7,562-ton *Troilus*, which went down with 10,000 tons of rubber, copper and tin easily exceeding £1 million in value, followed by the *Exford*, the *Chiltern* and the *St. Egbert*. At the end of that busy day *Emden*'s captives, including a woman who amiably recognised Prize Officer Lauterbach from having travelled aboard one of his peacetime commands, were released to safety aboard the freed *St. Egbert*. Müller then set course eastwards again. His next target would be the island port of Penang off the north-west coast of Malaya.

On the morning of 28 October, *Emden*, with her false smokestack raised to impersonate *Yarmouth* and – in a rare lapse of Müller's sense of chivalry – flying British colours, slipped into Penang Harbour and picked out among the many vessels there the 3,050-ton Russian light cruiser *Zhemchug*. Built in 1903, *Zhemchug* had participated in the Battle at Tsushima in May 1905, but had escaped that débâcle to be interned in neutral Manila. Now she had joined her former Japanese enemies in the hunt for *Emden*, arriving at Penang on 26 October to clean her boilers. Ignoring Admiral Jerram's advice that he take extra precautions, Captain Second Grade Baron Cherkassov had gone ashore that night to visit a lady friend, leaving his ship anchored up and down the tideway, her torpedoes disarmed, all but twelve shells stowed, and no extra men posted on watch.

At about 5.13 a.m. *Emden* struck her Union Jack, raised the Imperial German Naval Ensign, opened fire and, at 5.18 loosed her starboard torpedo. *Zhemchug* was unable to respond; half her shells had been left by the after gun, which was put out of action when a blown-away ship's boat fell on it, and the other six by the No. 2 starboard gun, which was pointing in the wrong direction. Her surprised crew dragged the ammunition to the forward gun and returned fire, but scored no hits; one shell passed over the German cruiser and struck a merchant ship in the harbour. After reversing course, *Emden* launched her port torpedo, which struck home below *Zhemchug*'s bridge and conning tower and blew her up, killing 91 of her men and wounding 108. Deciding not to press his luck, Müller then headed out of the dangerous confines of the harbour. In August, *Zhemchug's* Captain and First Officer were convicted of negligence by a naval court in Vladivostok, after which they were both sentenced to a 'house of correction' and stripped of their rank, their decorations and their status as members of the Russian nobility.

Of the French warships defending Penang, the third-class cruiser *D'Iberville* and destroyer *Fronde* were laid up with boiler trouble, but, although herself having problems with bearings, the destroyer *Pistolet* raised enough steam to set out in pursuit of the Germans at 20 knots. Meanwhile, *Emden*, mistaking an oncoming unarmed pilot boat for an armed ship, fired on her and left her in a sinking condition, fortunately without inflicting any casualties. Müller next encountered the tramp steamer *Glenturret* and stopped her only long enough to ask her captain to convey his apologies for shooting at the unarmed vessel and for not being able to rescue *Zhemchug's* crew. As *Emden* left harbour, she encountered another French destroyer, the 310-ton *Mousquet*, which fired one torpedo and engaged with one of her guns before being demolished in an unequal 10-minute fight. *Emden's* crew rescued one officer – whose leg would later have to be amputated – and 35 men, and cared for them as best they could while raising full speed to outrun the game little *Pistolet*, which they finally lost in a rain squall. Two days later *Emden* stopped the British steamer *Newburn*, to which the French prisoners were transferred, minus three who had died of wounds and were buried at sea with full naval honours.

While *Emden* lost herself in the open sea and laid low, the newspapers spread the word of her latest outrage against the Allies. In Germany, the Kaiser conferred on Müller the Iron Cross First and Second Classes and awarded the Iron Cross Second Class to fifty men to be picked from among his crew.

With enemy warships unlikely to be in the area for a while, Müller planned his next strike against Direction Island in the Cocos Islands, a major British communications cross-roads with a concentration of underwater cables and a large wireless tower. To preserve ammunition and lives, Müller decided to land a demolition team rather than use his guns to eliminate the facility.

At dawn on 9 November 1914, *Emden* approached Fort Refuge with her dummy stack up, but the British on Direction Island were not caught napping. Their suspicions were aroused by the absence of any flag flying from her mainmast, and they recognised her fourth stack as painted canvas. As *Emden* approached, the transmitter signalled: 'What ship? What ship?' *Emden* tried to jam them, but the British managed to get off two more transmissions in succession: 'Strange ship in entrance' and 'SOS, *Emden* here'.

At 6.30 a.m., Mücke led a landing-party of 48 men ashore, armed with four Maxim machine-guns, 29 rifles, 24 pistols and several boxes of ammunition and dynamite. The nine Englishmen who greeted them offered no resistance and the party split into three groups, one to herd the prisoners out of harm's way while another went to destroy the communications facilities and the third to the radio shack. Every piece of machinery was destroyed except for an ice-maker. The wireless tower, too strong to chop down, was dynamited, care being taken that it would fall away from the tennis courts. After a great expenditure of time and effort, the Germans found and severed three of the underwater cables.

While Mücke's landing-party was demolishing the communications facilities, an unidentified warship tried vainly to contact the station. From the strength of her signal, *Emden's* radio-operators judged her to be at least 200 miles away, and carried on with their overly thorough job of destruction. The ship was probably *Minotaur*, which was desperately relaying the news of *Emden's* presence in all directions. Among those who heard were three warships protecting an Australian convoy only 53 miles and two hours to the north of the Cocos: the modern Australian light cruisers *Melbourne* and *Sydney*, and the Japanese *Ibuki*. The convoy leader, Captain Mortimer Silver in *Melbourne*, deliberately failed to acknowledge receipt of the message, thereby leaving *Emden's* radio-operators unaware of his force's presence in their vicinity. Silver overrode the insistence of *Ibuki's* captain that his ship have the honour of dealing with the Germans, fearing that the battle-cruiser might not be able to outrun *Emden* should she decline to fight. While the Japanese officers wept in frustration, Silver dispatched Captain John Glossep in *Sydney*, whose 6in guns were more than equal to the task of taking on *Emden*, to investigate. At 7 o'clock *Sydney* peeled off from the convoy, making for Direction Island at twenty knots. At 9.15 Glossep sighted land – and smoke from a ship raising steam.

Mücke was getting worried about the time it was taking his party to finish their work, when a blast from *Emden's* whistle turned their attention to her. Running to the beach, they saw her putting to sea, and, looking eastward, saw the reason for her abandoning them: *Sydney*, coming on at full speed.

Müller knew he was undermanned, outgunned and outclassed, but he doubted that he could outrun the Australian, and was loath to abandon his men on the island. He saw no choice but to make a fight of it, and so *Emden* steamed full-tilt towards her oncoming nemesis.

At 9.40, *Emden* fired first and fired well, hitting *Sydney's* fire-control equipment on the third salvo and knocking it out. Glossep then wisely opened the range to use his larger guns to advantage while denying *Emden* the use of her torpedoes. The accuracy of the Australian gunners was poor at first, but quickly improved. Even firing independently in the absence of central fire control, *Sydney's* 6in guns were devastating, her 670 rounds doing more damage to *Emden* than the 1,500 4.1in shells fired by the latter were able to inflict – more often than not they bounced harmlessly off *Sydney's* 2-inch armour at 8,000 yards' distance. One German shell did set fire to *Sydney's* ammunition hoist, threatening a fatal magazine explosion, but one of the Australian crewmen braved the flames and extinguished the burning cordite. From then on, *Emden* was strictly on the receiving end. Soon fires were raging aboard her, their roar punctuated by occasional explosions of more shells striking home and the cries of the wounded and dying.

At 11.15 Müller, finding his ship to be a hopeless shambles and his last hope, the torpedo tubes, flooded and unusable, turned north-north-west for North Keeling Island and ran *Emden* on to the reef at 11.20. Since the Germans neglected to strike their colours, the cautious Glossep fired two more broadsides at them before the Germans noticed the reason for their continued punishment and ran up a white flag in place of the Imperial Naval ensign. A total of 128 officers and crewmen, a civilian cook, a barber and four Chinese laundry men were killed aboard *Emden*, while 65 were wounded. Müller was one of the 117 officers and men who were unharmed when they surrendered. *Sydney*, in contrast, had lost four men killed, four severely wounded and four slightly wounded from the sixteen hits she had taken in the unequal fight.

Sydney now set about mopping-up, starting with the recovery of *Buresk*. By the time Glossep caught up with her and ordered the prize crew's surrender, however, the Germans were scuttling their war prize, leaving the Australians with only a few lifeboats for their trouble. Allegedly cursing them for cheating him of the collier's recovery, Glossep dispatched one of *Buresk's* lifeboats to transport *Emden's* wounded ashore, then steamed south for Direction Island to collect Mücke's landing-party.

There, too, he was to be cheated of the full fruits of victory. Arriving at the island before nightfall, Glossep decided to wait until morning before landing, in anticipation of possible resistance from the small German force. He turned out to be right in believing that Mücke had no intention of surrendering, but when the Australians landed next morning they found that the Germans had commandeered the *Ayesha*, a 97-ton barquentine, and had sailed away twelve hours earlier.

The Allies had not been the only ones to be hoodwinked that day. The British on Direction Island had cordially and sincerely wished Mücke's departing group good luck on their hazardous enterprise. Then, after the Germans had vanished over the horizon, they set about uncovering a hidden emergency cache of spare equipment and parts and completely restored the island's communications facilities. For all its fatal thoroughness, *Emden*'s last raid had turned out to be the least productive.

Sydney returned to North Keeling where, in a gesture appropriate to naval warfare of a bygone age, Glossep had the following message delivered by longboat to Müller aboard his beached ship:

> HMAS *Sydney*, at sea
>
> The Captain, HIGMS *Emden*
> Sir,
> I have the honour to request that in the name of humanity you now surrender your ship to me. In order to show how much I appreciate your gallantry, I will recapitulate the position.
> (1.) You are ashore, three funnels and one mast down and most guns disabled.
> (2.) You cannot leave this island, and my ship is intact.
> In the event of your surrendering in which I venture to remind you is no disgrace but rather your misfortune I will endeavour to do all I can for your sick and wounded and take them to a hospital.
>
> I have the honour to be,
> Sir,
> Your obedient Servant,
> John Glossep
> Captain.'

Müller, after having made a last futile effort to destroy what was left of his disabled ship, accepted Glossep's terms and, after seeing his crew evacuated aboard *Sydney*, was the last to abandon *Emden* for eventual imprisonment for the duration of the war on the island of Malta. As *Sydney* steamed on for Colombo, Glossep radioed ahead to request that there be none of the traditional cheering to greet his triumphant ship as she entered harbour, in deference to his defeated foes, especially their wounded.

Although the respect that she and her crew elicited from their adversaries would be gained by many other German ships and commanders in future, no other warship could ever claim to have endeared herself to her enemies as had *Emden* in her genteel hundred-day rampage. Captain Müller had not only been a brilliant tactician, but a lone citadel of vanishing chivalry and daring, resourceful individualism in a war that was already sacrificing its innocence to the faceless slaughter of 20th-century technology. In a typical epitaph, *The Telegraph* in London spoke for many of its readers: 'It is almost in our hearts to regret that the *Emden* has been captured and destroyed ... There is not a survivor who does not speak well of this young German, the officers under him and the crew obedient to his orders. The war on the sea will lose some of its piquancy, its humour and its interest now that the *Emden* has gone.'

Almost in some hearts to regret, but not quite – certainly Churchill, Jerram and the British Admiralty shed few tears over the elimination of this small but irritating thorn in their side. They were pleased to let *Emden* take her rightful place in the history books, so long as she was now history.

Little did they know that the last chapters of the epic were yet to be written.

While Sydney was evacuating *Emden*, Mücke and his landing-party were sailing roughly north-westwards aboard the *Ayesha* – an inter-island trading ship built for seven passengers, now forced to accommodate 53. So seriously did the Allies still take anything and anyone associated with the *Emden* that a search for the fugitive windjammer was mounted with no less zeal than the hunt for the cruiser. On 17 December Admiral Jerram wrote to the Admiralty of *Ayesha*: 'She is a menace to trade until captured', and assured them that the French destroyers *Fronde* and *Pistolet* 'still remain in Penang for the defence of the harbour' – prompting the letter's bemused recipient to pencil in a sardonic query: 'Against what?' When he heard reports of *Ayesha*'s having stopped at Padang on 2 December, Jerram dispatched the armed merchant cruisers *Empress of Japan* and *Himalaya* to scour the south-east coast of Sumatra for her and for the fugitive collier *Exford*. The latter was indeed caught by *Empress of Japan* and her German prize crew taken into custody, but her commander, Julius Lauterbach, altered her compass to read falsely, causing her to run aground *en route* to Singapore.

Imprisoned in the Tanglin barracks in Singapore, *Emden*'s irascible ex-Prize Officer was visited by a half-French, half-Chinese lady friend from Shanghai, who brought him maps and arranged a boat to help him escape. The breakout itself was effected by fomenting a mutiny among the demoralised Indian prison guards, for which act the British subsequently placed a £1,000 reward on Lauterbach's head.

There followed an amazing odyssey in which Lauterbach, by means of disguises (an Arab merchant on one occasion), false passports (Swedish, Dutch and Belgian among others) and his merchant mariner's knowledge of the Far East, travelled from Singapore to Padang to Cebu to Manila in a matter of six weeks. During his eight-week stay in that neutral American port in the Philippines, he took time to mail nose-thumbing postcards to several British colonial acquaintances – including his former captor, the commanding officer at the Tanglin barracks. Lauterbach then caught a Japanese collier to Tientsin, thence to Shanghai to look up some friends – one of whom owed him $500 – and another lady friend who warned him of a British plot to kidnap him and extradite him from then-neutral China. Indeed, as he left the German Club, four men tried to seize him, but he broke free and, as a shot was fired after him, he escaped by jumping into the river.

Next, Lauterbach stole the real passport of US Navy Petty Officer W. Johnson, and took an American passenger ship to Nagasaki, only to learn that Japanese Intelligence had caught wind of the scheme and its agents were waiting to question a 'Mr. Johnson'. As luck would have it, another American stepped forward, introduced himself as Colonel Johnson of the US Army, and asked what the fuss was all about.

During a later stop in Yokohama, Lauterbach caught a private investigator searching his cabin 'for German officers'. After successfully establishing his American identity, Lauterbach befriended the Japanese detective and was shown around the city by him. There were several posters offering 250,000 yen for Lauterbach's capture, which the detective stated he, for one, would love to have earned. Later, he would receive a sarcastic postcard from his occidental guest, belatedly informing him of how close he had actually come to claiming that reward.

Lauterbach resumed his voyage to Honolulu and San Francisco, where he learned that his adventures were already in the newspapers. He took the train to New York, disguised as a Dane, and bribed his way aboard a Danish freighter in Hoboken, New Jersey, as a stoker. Off the Orkneys, the ship was detained by a British auxiliary cruiser as a suspected blockade-runner, but after five days of searching she was released and allowed to resume her course to Oslo, Norway. Lauterbach then made his way to the German naval attaché in Copenhagen and, on 10 October 1915, he arrived home at Warnemünde.

Meanwhile, on 14 December, Mücke had made contact with the German oiler *Choising* under Captain F. Minkwitz and, off the Palai Islands, transferred his crew and scuttled the leaking, worn-out *Ayesha*, while the crew gave three cheers and *Choising* dipped her flag to the sailing ship's memory. An overloaded firetrap capable of only eight knots, *Choising* nevertheless avoided discovery until she entered the Red Sea and disembarked *Emden*'s 53 fugitive crewmen at Hodeida – under the nose of the blockading French cruiser *Desaix*, which was anchored nearby. *Choising* then made her way to the port of Massawa in Italian-held Eritrea, where she still lay in May 1915, when Italy joined the Allies and interned her.

Mücke's sailors now found themselves having to adjust to the alien environment of the Arabian desert, and to the convoluted intrigues of their Turkish hosts, who for any number of reasons – inability to believe that Mücke's men were really Germans, or perhaps a desire to keep them as military advisers, by treachery if necessary – gave their guests false information regarding the best way to proceed. On 27 January 1915 – the

Kaiser's birthday – Mücke took the initiative and led his men north-east-wards, reaching Sanaa on 6 February. There, the military commander in the Yemen, Ahmed Tewfik Pasha, informed Constantinople, Germany and an astonished world of the latest whereabouts of the vanished *Emden* survivors.

From Sanaa, the Germans set out for Jiddah in two Arab *sambuqs*, sailing 300 miles along the Red Sea coast in four days and slipping past blockading Allied warships. One of the *sambuqs* struck a reef and sank. At Al Lith, one of the Germans died of typhus. Mucke led the rest overland on camels provided by the local sheikh.

On 31 March, the Germans were set upon at Ras al Aswad by Arab brigands, whose numbers quickly swelled from 70 to 300. Surrounded, the Germans formed a square of camels and held off their attackers for four days, losing three men before finally being rescued by a cavalry col-umn led by one Sherif Abdullah, second son of the Emir of Mecca. Although the Germans received a festive welcome in Jiddah, Mücke was convinced that his rescuers were, in fact, in league with the Bedouins and had ended the battle in the dunes only because the Germans, who still had four Maxim machine-guns, had defended themselves too well (40 Bedouins had been killed and 36 wounded in the fighting). Ignoring rec-ommendations by the local officials that he lead his men overland with their word of safe passage, Mücke made a secret deal with an anti-British Egyptian smuggler and, on April 8, his men slipped out of Jiddah aboard another *sambuq* and sailed 400 miles further up the coast in three weeks before reaching Al Wajh on 29 April.

With a Turkish escort, Mücke's party made a final 100-mile march eastwards over desert and mountains to the railhead at Al Ula, arriving on 7 May. Awaiting them – after a three-weeks' vigil – was Emil Ludwig, a reporter for the *Berliner Tagblatt*, whose greeting to *Kapitänleutnant* Mücke was in the best traditions of Stanley and Livingstone:

'A bath, or Rhine wine?'

'Rhine wine,' Mücke replied.

There followed a triumphant train ride to Constantinople where they arrived on 23 May. Prior to returning to their homes, the survivors of the German Pacific Cruiser Squadron lined up in two rows before Admiral Wilhelm Souchon, German naval commander in Turkey, the tat-tered naval ensign of *Emden* flying proudly from the pole of a boat-hook to which it had been attached with rusty nails. Mücke raised and lowered his sword in salute and said: 'Beg to report, landing-party from SMS *Emden* numbering five officers, seven petty officers and thirty-seven men, present and correct.'

So at last ended a remarkable voyage of 30,000 miles, in which a single obsolescent cruiser had done damage worth at least fifteen times the cost of building her – more than £5,000,000. She had sunk a cruiser, a destroyer and sixteen merchant ships, coaled eleven times from three captured colliers and had bombarded oil facilities in the heart of the British Empire while disrupting transport, raising the price of rice and insurance in the Indian Ocean region and drawing the attention of 78 warships from four navies. She had also left behind a legacy for the relatively young navy of which she had been part, and a set of tactics which would serve as the model for future campaigns by that same navy in two world wars.

An attempt was made by the British to refloat and restore the *Emden* for Far Eastern service, but she was too twisted and battered to be of use and, immediately after the war, she was scrapped for a fraction of her original cost – a bane on her enemies to the end. The Germans commissioned a replacement *Emden*, but that more modern light cruiser accomplished no more than did the rest of the German Navy by that time – driven from the high seas and idly swinging at their anchor chains in home waters. The first post-war German design for a major warship – another light cruiser – was also named *Emden*, and served mostly as a training vessel during the Second World War. Since then, two frigates of the Federal German *Bundesmarine* have perpetuated the proudest name in its history.

References

Hoyt, Edwin P. *The Last Cruise of the Emden*, London, André Deutsch, 1967.
Humble, Richard. *Hitler's High Seas Fleet*, Ballantine Books, New York, 1971.
Vat, D. van der. *Gentlemen of War*, William Morrow & Co., Inc., New York, 1984.
Zimmerman, Gene T. 'Direction Island, Swan Song of the *Emden*', in *Sea Classics*, vol. 5, No. 4, July 1972.

CHAPTER 7

A Submarine in Dire Straits
His Majesty's Submarine *B.11*,
13 December 1914

Although the exploits of lone submarines have received their share of acclaim, the accolades bestowed on them are usually tempered because of the stealth advantage of operating submerged. One of the more noteworthy exceptions to this generalisation was the British submarine *B.11*, whose unprecedented sortie through the Dardanelles and into the Turkish-controlled Sea of Marmara in the early months of the First World War was lent an unexpected element of melodrama. For one thing, she was old and primitive, even for her time. And she was operating in waters where both the ability to submerge and the benefits to be derived from it were severely limited. Whatever her deficiencies for tackling the unusual hazards that lay in her path, however, *B.11* possessed an essential asset – an outstanding commander and crew.

When Turkey declared war on Britain and France on 30 October 1914, all that was available to the two Allied navies in the eastern Mediterranean was a mixed force of mostly second-rate warships under a mediocre admiral. On 1 November, Vice-Admiral Sackville Hamilton Carden, commanding the British blockading force in the area, was ordered by the Admiralty to commence hostilities against Turkey, although a formal British declaration of war was not issued until 3 November. Commanding a force made up of the battle cruisers *Indomitable* and *Indefatigable*, French battleships *Vérité* and *Suffren*, two light cruisers, twelve destroyers and three submarines, Carden did not act until the latter date, with a desultory bombardment of the Turkish forts at Seddübidar and Kum Kale. Other than that, Carden's force was mainly concerned with watching for a breakout by the German battle cruiser *Goeben* and light cruiser *Breslau* from Turkish waters, as well as blockading Smyrna and the Bulgarian port of Dedeagach.

If Carden's force were less than impressive, it was none the less adequate to deal with the Ottoman fleet which had had no combat experience since 1877, and which consisted in the main of rusting, antiquated warships. The only serious threat the Turks possessed was the new addition to their fleet, the *Goeben* – renamed *Yavuz Sultan Selim*, but still manned by German officers and personnel under the command of Rear-Admiral Wilhelm Souchon. For the time being, the German battle cruiser, whose delivery into Ottoman hands had had so much to do with Turkey's entry into the war, was keeping a low profile between two hostile forces – the Anglo–French Mediterranean Fleet and the Russian Black Sea Fleet. Meanwhile, following Carden's bombardment of their forts in the lower Dardanelles, the Turks brought in reinforcements and made some long-overdue improvements to their defences. The consequence was a stalemate between the opposing surface forces.

Initially, Carden's submarine force consisted of the French submarines *Faraday*, *Leverrier*, *Coulomb* and *Circe*, and three Malta-based Royal Navy submarines, *B.9*, *B.10* and *B.11*, to which would later be added *B.6* and *B.7* out of Gibraltar. The submarine flotilla's senior officer, Lieutenant-Commander P. H. Pownall, established his headquarters in an old depot ship, the *Hindu Kush*, in the middle of Mudros harbour on the Aegean island of Lemnos. Assigned the task of supporting the surface ships in carrying out the Dardanelles blockade, the captains of the three British and four French submarines pressed for a more independent and aggressive role.

The matter of seeking out targets within the Dardanelles was, in fact, discussed between Pownall and his three senior officers, Norman Holbrook, Geoffrey Warburton and Samuel Gravener, behind the closed doors of *Hindu Kush*'s wardroom. One of the French boats had already penetrated above Sedd el Bahr and Holbrook's *B.11* had chased a Turkish torpedo-boat four miles into the straits beyond Kum Kale. A deep penetration into Turkish waters would be another prospect entirely, however.

For one thing, none of Pownall's submarines were top-of-the-line models. All three of the Vickers-built *B*-class boats, for example, dated back to 1906. With a surface displacement of 287 tons (313 tons submerged), a length of only 135 feet and a diameter of 13½ feet, the *B* class submarine was powered by a single-shaft, 600hp 16-cylinder Vickers petrol engine on the surface at a maximum speed of 13 knots, or at nine knots submerged by means of a 290hp electric motor. Her endurance was inadequate for any long-range raiding, even within the Sea of Marmara.

Venturing into the Dardanelles was dangerous for any ship, above or below the surface. The coastal guns of the fortresses on each side of the strait had been reinforced by mobile howitzer batteries and searchlights. Five lines of mines had been laid across the strait below Kephez Point, and another minefield lurked to the north across the Narrows. Although these mines had been laid against surface shipping, the propellers or diving planes of a submerged submarine could all too easily foul them.

In addition to the man-made obstacles, the Dardanelles presented their own share of natural hazards to an invading submarine. The Allies were well aware of the Strait's westward currents that varied in strength

from one to four knots. Less well-known at that time was the exact loca-
tion of a stratum of salt water which, in fact, lay 10 fathoms below the
fresh-water surface of the strait. In consequence, any Allied submarine
captain entering the strait was faced with an imponderable regarding the
nature and strength of the current at depth, for the difference in density
of fresh and salt water would affect the trim of his boat when dived.

Despite these daunting challenges and the limited area in which
they could operate, Pownall's captains all agreed that any demonstration
of strength in the Chanak area of the lower Dardanelles would be better
than nothing. They submitted a plan to Carden for an underwater raid
and he gave it tentative approval in early December.

The submarine commanders eagerly vied for the privilege of carrying out the sortie, but Pownall's choice was a foregone conclusion. The
French submarines had externally mounted torpedoes, which limited
their diving depth. Of the British boats, *B.11* had the most recently fitted
battery, which would give her the longest underwater endurance. Pownall also had plenty of faith in the abilities of 28-year-old Lieutenant-
Commander Norman Holbrook, who had been *B.11*'s commander since
30 December 1913.

The odds against passing the Strait were considerably lessened
when Pownall and Captain Coode, who commanded the destroyer
flotilla, devised a system whereby they believed a submarine could slip
through the moored mines. Under their direction, engineers from the
torpedo depot ship *Blenheim* improvised tubular steel guards which fitted
over *B.11*'s fore and aft hydroplanes. Since no dry dock was available, the
submarine's ballast tanks were alternately flooded to change her trim,
raising first her bow and then her stern high enough out of the water for
the hydroplane guards to be bolted into place. To provide vertical protection for the conning tower, compass binnacle and other outer projec-
tions on which a mine cable might also foul, stout steel jumping wires
were run fore and aft from the conning tower.

At 4.15 on the morning of 13 December, *B.11* cast off from the
Hindu Kush, which was then lying off Cape Helles, and made for the Dardanelles, some three miles away. Holbrook's mission was simply to penetrate as far up the Strait as possible, sinking any ships he encountered –
a *carte blanche* devoid of any specific action or target, leaving him with
considerable leeway.

Turkish searchlights swept the narrow waters as *B.11* approached
the entrance and Holbrook ordered his main engines shut down. He had
observed that the Turks switched off their searchlights just before dawn,
a habit that offered him a brief period in which he might slip through
undetected. Sure enough, at 5 o'clock the searchlights began to go out
one by one and Holbrook, using his electric motors so as to avoid attract-

ing a sharp-eared Turkish lookout's attention with the sound of his petrol engine's exhaust, brought *B.11* to within a mile of Cape Helles. After scanning the northern shore of the Gallipoli peninsula through his glasses, he ordered his executive officer, Lieutenant S. T. Winn, to 'take her down'. In the control room, Winn relayed the orders:

'Stand-by diving stations. Open vents. Flood Q ... flood main ballast. 'Planes hard a-dive!'

'Hatch shut and clipped,' Holbrook called as he came below and *B.11* silently slipped below the surface, then ordered: 'Steer zero-five-zero, Number One. Trim level at 20 feet. Maximum speed.'

Even at full power, the contrary current kept *B.11*'s submerged speed down to an extremely modest two knots, but Holbrook was satisfied with her progress as he scanned the area through the periscope. Then the hull began to vibrate at regular intervals. Figuring that something must have worked loose on the outside hull, Holbrook ordered Winn to take *B.11* back to the surface. Such an action risked discovery at an early stage of the mission, but Holbrook counted on the few remaining minutes of darkness to cloak his boat's presence from the eyes of the Turks.

Once on the surface, Holbrook and an engine room artificer (ERA) climbed out of the hatch and inspected the outer hull. It was a relief, at least, to find the cause of the trouble without too much delay – the entire forward port hydroplane guard was hanging loose, its securing bolts having sheered off. Holbrook ordered the stern tanks flooded in order to raise the bows higher, while the ERA and another crewman, secured to the submarine by safety lines, performed the difficult task of jettisoning the tubular steel guard. Just minutes before dawn, they finally worked it loose and let it drop over the side. Still not spotted by Turkish sentries, *B.11* submerged again and resumed her slow upstream progress while the crew ate breakfast in alternating shifts. Holbrook's breakfast was half of a lobster that had been graciously presented him by the French submarine captains before he left Mudros.

At 8.30, Holbrook would make out the mouth of the River Suandere over the port bow, a landmark that indicated that they were nearing the Kephez minefield. At 8.40 he ordered the submarine down to 80 feet and the crew braced themselves for the ordeal to come – hours of virtually blind navigation while the wires of the moored mines scraped along the side of the hull. More unsettling to the crew than direct contact with a mine was the danger of the now-unprotected forward port hydroplane snagging on one of their wires, forcing their vessel to the surface where it would be exposed to Turkish shore batteries.

After an hour, Holbrook ordered *B.11* back up to periscope depth so that he could get a new fix on their position. They had made better progress than he had expected, arriving just a little more than a mile away from Chanak on the Asian shore. After checking the shipping off Chanak, Holbrook turned his attention south-westward towards Sari Siglar Bay, a sheltered anchorage on the lee side of Kephez Point. Anchored there was what Holbrook described as 'a large old Turkish battleship' with twin funnels, a single mast and heavy guns in turrets fore and aft. He identified her as the *Messudieh*.

Built in the Thames in 1874, the ironclad battleship *Messudieh* had undergone a major reconstruction at Genoa, Italy in 1901, during which she was given water-tube boilers and engines of 11,000 horse power. In her modernised form, *Messudieh* was rated at 9,520 tons and carried two 9.2in guns, twelve 6-inchers and fourteen 3-inchers. Unknown to Holbrook, she had fallen victim to the neglect that had taken a general toll on the Ottoman fleet – the formidable-looking guns that projected from her main turrets were in fact wooden dummies. Her secondary armament was real enough, though, and it kept her useful as a coastal defence ship.

Lying at least a mile away, *Messudieh* was out of the range of *B.11*'s 18in torpedoes, besides which the angle of attack was too narrow to ensure a hit. 'We went down again,' Holbrook said later, 'but the tide got up and swept us into Sari Siglar Bay and now the ship was on our port bow.' *B.11* now lay a little more than 800 yards abaft the battleship's beam, leaving only a slight adjustment in course to bring the submarine's bows in line with the enemy ship's forward section.

'I altered course and it needed full speed to combat the current and get into position for a shot,' said Holbrook. 'I fired one torpedo and then had to reduce speed because the lights were getting low and obviously our batteries were failing. We then found ourselves aground stern first and I could see the ship down by the stern and smoke from the shore suggesting that fire was being directed at us.'

While black smoke mushroomed from the stricken *Messudieh*, her gunners spotted *B.11*'s periscope and brought all guns to bear against her. They were still churning up the water around the submarine with a furious barrage when *Messudieh* suddenly capsized, trapping many of her crew within her hull.

While *Messudieh*'s guns were no longer a threat, the Turkish shore batteries had now joined in, and there was no time for Holbrook and his men to savour their kill. 'By using full revs we got off but I couldn't see the way out of the bay,' said Holbrook in his account. 'I looked for the farthest bit of land through the periscope but the Coxwain said the spirit compass lenses had packed up and all he could see was black spots.'

Holbrook's luck seemed to have run out. In the *B*-class submarines, as in most others at that time, the steering compass was fixed outside the pressure hull to prevent its being unduly affected by the hull's residual magnetism, and an image of the compass card was reflected to the helmsman through a primitive – and, as it turned out, vulnerable – system of lenses and prisms. At that crucial moment, sea water leaking into the tube or excessive condensation had fogged up the lenses, causing the image of the card to be lost. Holbrook saw no choice but to rise to periscope depth, but when he did, he saw to his horror that the current had swept *B.11* deeper into Sari Siglar Bay. Cliffs seemed to tower on all sides, while an enemy torpedo-boat and other vessels were approaching from the shore at what seemed to be ramming speed.

Holbrook ordered a dive to 50 feet – the maximum expected depth in the area – but *B.11* had only descended 38 feet when she struck bottom. Holbrook ordered full speed ahead and his submarine clumsily extricated herself from the mudbank – only to slide into another. At the same time, Holbrook noticed that sunlight was streaming through the circular glass ports of the control room, indicating that the conning tower was awash. The Turkish shore batteries had also noticed this – they were firing again.

'I put the helm hard a-port,' Holbrook wrote in his official report, 'and went on to full speed, the submarine frequently touching bottom from 10.10 to 10.20, when we got into deeper water.' Despite the laconic description, those ten minutes must have seemed like as many hours to the crew, as the electric motors were pushed to their limits and the ammeter needles swung into the discharge segments of the dials. Still, Holbrook calmly took station in the conning tower, peering through the tiny glass ports as he conned his boat through extremely troubled waters, occasionally bumping along the bottom while shells exploded all around.

Finally, the boat reached deep water again and Holbrook took her down to periscope depth. *Messudieh* had disappeared and there was clear water to port. Holbrook kept *B.11*'s bows pointed towards the European shore for a few more yards until he was sure that they were in mid-channel, then altered course downstream.

By this time, *B.11*'s long underwater run at maximum power had drained her batteries to danger point and there were still sixteen miles between her and the open sea. Curbing his impatience, Holbrook lowered *B.11*'s speed to 1½ knots, letting the current enhance it.

With the compass out, it was not safe to go under the Kephez minefields, so Holbrook decided that *B.11* would have to thread her way through the five lines of mines at periscope depth. Few in the crew dared breathe until Holbrook saw the mouth of the Suandere, indicating that they were clear. But they were not yet out of danger. The shore batteries and fortress guns at the mouth of the Strait, now doubtless alerted, still lay ahead. *B.11* had to remain submerged for ten more miles, during which she was, in Holbrook's words, 'more or less swept out of the Straits' by the current.

93

Again, dinner was eaten in relays, while Holbrook finished the other half of his lobster and ordered rum to be issued to every member of his crew, to be drunk when – and if – they reached the successful conclusion of their ordeal.

Finally, at 2.10 p.m., *B.11* surfaced about two miles west of Cape Helles and made contact with the destroyers that were waiting to escort her back to Mitilini. After nine hours underwater, the air inside the little submersible had become so foul that a poisonous greenish-yellow cloud billowed out as the narrow circular hatchway was opened, and it took half an hour before sufficient oxygen had been restored inside for her petrol engines to start.

At Mudros, a group of Holbrook's flotilla colleagues presented him with a giant cardboard Iron Cross in a mock ceremony on the quarter-deck of the battle cruiser *Indefatigable*. The French commander-in-chief sent Carden a signal: 'Please accept my warm congratulations for the glorious deed of the submarine *B.11*.'

The Admiralty swiftly followed suit with a telegraph to Carden: 'Communicate to the officers and men of *B.11* their Lordships' high appreciation of the daring and skilfulness which have achieved this exploit.' Holbrook became the first British submariner to receive the Victoria Cross, his country's highest award for valour – and, for that matter, the first member of the Royal Navy to be so honoured during the war. His First Officer, Lieutenant Winn, was awarded the Distinguished Service Order and every member of her 13-man crew received either the Distinguished Service Cross or the Distinguished Service Medal, according to rank.

Back at Sari Siglar Bay, the crew entombed inside the sunken *Messudieh* endured a claustrophobic night, but on the following day holes were cut in her upturned keel and most of them were rescued. The Turks – and their navy in particular – were shocked and demoralised at the violation of their waters by such a puny opponent. The local German senior commander, *Vizeadmiral* Marten, was ungrudging in his admiration of Holbrook and his crew, calling their feat 'a mighty clever piece of work'.

It also proved to be a difficult piece of work to emulate. When *B.9* tried to repeat *B.11*'s feat on 14 December, she did not get far before the aroused Turks spotted her. Observation mines, detonated from shore, exploded all around her as she reversed course, but she was able to escape. Less fortunate was the French *Saphir* in her attempt; she was disabled when she struck bottom near Nagara Point, after which she surfaced and was destroyed by shore batteries.

The importance of Holbrook's success lay not so much in the sinking of an obsolete Turkish battleship as in its vivid demonstration of the capabilities of submarines when used in a strategic role. They had originally been developed for tactical use – and in the case of the *B*-class, primarily for coastal defence – but *B.11* had set a precedent for a much wider role.

Moreover, with the Western front in a state of stalemate, there was much discussion in London and Paris on the need to open a new campaign, with the Ottoman Empire a logical target. *B.11*'s exploit carried a good deal of weight in the London and Paris discussions, suggesting that a submarine campaign in the Dardanelles could sufficiently disrupt Turkish maritime communications as to make a decisive invasion of the Gallipoli Peninsula possible.

Urged on by his Chief of Staff, Roger Keyes – himself a former submarine commodore in charge of the Harwich flotillas at the beginning of the war – Carden sent the Admiralty an urgent request for a flotilla of the Royal Navy's latest *E*-class submarines, which were considerably larger than the *B*-class, with a much more powerful battery and an internal gyrocompass that would not flood. As it happened, the Mediterranean Fleet had an Australian *E*-class boat, Lieutenant-Commander H. D. G. Stoker's *AE-2*, and thanks to Holbrook's success Carden's request was granted with neither argument nor delay. Within weeks, four more *E*-class submarines were on the way to the eastern Mediterranean. Although the Gallipoli invasion, launched on 25 April 1915, would end in humiliating failure on 9 January 1916, the submarines would live up to expectations, causing considerable damage to the Turkish navy and winning three more VCs.

References

Gray, Edwyn. 'A Mighty Clever Piece of Work', in *Sea Classic International*, winter 1985, pp. 76–81.

Halsey, Francis Whiting. *The Literary Digest History of the World War*, vol. 8 *Turkey and the Balkans, August 1914-October 1918*, Funk & Wagnalls Co., New York and London, 1919, pp. 81–4.

Hough, Richard. *The Great War at Sea, 1914-1918*, Oxford University Press, Oxford and New York, 1983.

Kemp, Paul J. *British Submarines of World War I*, Arms & Armour Warships Fotofax, London, 1990.

Liddle, Peter H. *The Sailor's War 1914-18*, Blandford Press, Poole, Dorset, 1985, p. 62.

The Marshall Cavendish Illustrated Encyclopedia of World War I, 1986, vol. II, pp. 466–70.

CHAPTER 8

Holiday in Hostile Seas
Admiral Scheer, October 1940 – April 1941

Captain Edward Stephen Fogarty Fegen knew that he stood no chance against the warship he had challenged. When he first saw her coming head on, he had had no reason to believe her to be hostile ... then she turned to bring both her turrets into play, revealing the distinctive silhouette of a German pocket battleship, armed with six 11in and eight 5.9in guns. Against that daunting arsenal, Fegen's ship, the *Jervis Bay*, mounted eight 6-inchers. A thin-skinned armed merchant cruiser (AMC) converted from a 14,164-ton liner, *Jervis Bay* was escorting a large convoy of cargo vessels to Britain – all of them so much defenceless prey for the German raider unless they had time to disperse. Fegen had no illusions as to his chances of winning the fight he was about to start, but his duty to the convoy left him no choice but to try.

The German opened fire at 17,000 yards and her first salvo straddled *Jervis Bay*. Without hesitation, Fegen placed his ship between the raider and the convoy, and ordered the ships to scatter. The German captain watched in frustration as the ships made black smoke and made their best speed in all directions, but he knew that he must dispose of their valiant escort before he could give chase to any of them.

Salvo after salvo crashed into *Jervis Bay*. One shell demolished the charthouse, disabling the steering gear and killing or wounding every man on the bridge. Severely wounded in one arm, Fegen emerged from the debris and hurried aft through the flames and wreckage to the emergency steering position. Although *Jervis Bay*'s forward guns were out of commission and her after guns could not be brought to bear, Fegen steered his ship straight at the enemy, compelling the Germans to concentrate their 11in guns on his ship instead of the fleeing merchantmen. The pocket battleship did use her secondary guns to some effect, however, badly damaging the 8,073-ton tanker *San Demetrio* and the 3,082-ton cargo-liner *Rangitiki* before they vanished over the horizon.

Only when it was impossible to fight on did Fegen give the order to abandon ship. Her decks awash with blood, the burning *Jervis Bay* rolled on to her beam ends and sank. About 200 of her gallant crew were lost, including Fegen; 65 survivors were later rescued by a Swedish freighter.

GRENVILLE'S LONE *REVENGE*
Above: Sir Richard Grenville's gallant defence of the *Revenge*.

HAD BARFLEUR HAD NO MORROW...
Right: Le Comte de Tourville. The Count led the fine French fleet of 1692. (Musée de la Marine)

Above: In the heat of the Battle of Barfleur, Tourville directs the conflict from aboard *Le Soleil Royal* while fighting three English vessels at once. (Musée de la Marine)
Below: French vessels burning at La Hogue. (Musée de la Marine)

NELSON'S PATENT BOARDING DEVICE
Above: Admiral Jervis receiving
Calder's report of the Spanish
fleet. 'There are 27 ships of the
line, sir. Near double our own.'
'Enough! If there are 50, I shall
sail through them.' (Anne S. K.
Brown Military Collection)
Right: HMS *Culloden* at Cape St.
Vincent, 1797. (Anne S. K. Brown
Military Collection)

Above: Nelson received the the Spanish officer's swords on board *San Josef* (Anne S. K. Brown Military Collection)

THE ONE THAT GOT AWAY
Below: 'Old Iron Sides', the United States frigate *Constitution,* seen here in action with a British warship.

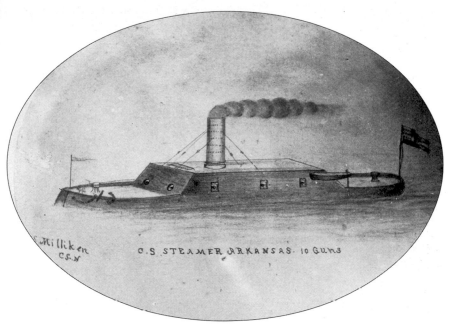

C.S. STEAMER ARKANSAS. 10 GUNS

TERROR FROM YAZOO
Above: CSS *Arkansas*.
Below: *Arkansas* running through the Federal Fleet on the Mississippi River, 1862.

SWAN OF THE EAST
Above: SMS *Emden* (Author).
Below: *Emden* on the rocks at North Keeling, November 1914, as seen from HMAS *Sydney*. (Author)

Above: The crippled *Emden*. (Author)
Below: The crew of *Emden* arrives at Constantinople. (Author)

A Submarine in Dire Straits
Above: The British Submarine *B.11*. (IWM)
Below: The crew of *B.11*, whose nine-hour dive defied belief.(IWM)

HOLIDAY IN HOSTILE SEAS
Above: *Nordmark* as seen in 1949 when she was the British *Bulawayo*. (IWM)

AN AGGRESSIVE DEFENCE
Right: Admiral Doorman, who was uncertain of his capability to deal with the enemy invasion force. (AMH)

Above: Admiral Doorman's flagship, *De Ruyter*. (AMH)

THE INGLORIOUS DEATH OF THE *HOKOKU MARU*
Above: The Japanese Armed Merchant Cruiser *Hokoku Maru* at Singapore in July 1942. (Author)
Below: *Aikoku Maru*, sister ship of the *Hokoku Maru*. (Author)

Above: HMIS *Bengal* returns to port after her success. (Author)

NIGHT OF THE LONG LANCE
Right: Rear Admiral Raizo Tanaka, commander of Japanese Destroyer Division 2. (USNHC)

Above: The crew of USS *Minneapolis* inspects her bow damage off Tassafaronga, 30 November 1942. (USNA)

FIGHTING RETREAT
Left: Vice Admiral Takeo Kurita, commander of Japan's First Striking Force. (USN)

Above: Ernest E. Evans, LCDR., USN, at the commissioning ceremony of USS *Johnston* at Seattle, 27 October 1943. He was *Johnston's* commanding officer until she was sunk on 25 October 1944. (USN)

Right: Rear Admiral Clifton Sprague who operated from the escort carrier *Fanshaw Bay* at Leyte Gulf. (USNA)

Opposite page, top: USS *Samuel B. Roberts* pictured just two weeks before being lost off Samar. (USNA)
Left: CVE *Kitkun Bay*, with Grumman FM-2 Wildcats departing, as CVE *Kalinin Bay* comes under attack in the distance. (USNA)
Above: *Yamato* takes two bomb hits off Samar on 25 October 1944. (USNA)

ALMOST TOTAL EXCLUSION.
Above: HMS *Brilliant,* one of the targets for *San Luis.*
Left: *Salta.* the sister vessel of *San Luis.* These Type 209 diesel-electric submarines were built in Germany.

The German raider was now unopposed in her pursuit of the merchant ships, but dusk was falling and she had little time in which to accomplish her gruesome task. Five ships, *Maidan* (7,908 tons) *Trewellard* (5,201 tons) *Kenbane Head* (5,225 tons) *Beaverford* (10,042 tons) and *Fresno City* (4,995 tons) were overtaken and sunk, and a sixth, *Andalusian*, was damaged. The slaughter would have been far greater, had *Jervis Bay* not bought the other ships time to escape. For his valorous sacrifice in the face of impossible odds, Captain Edward Fegen was awarded a posthumous Victoria Cross.

Britons are well-versed in the heroic saga of the *Jervis Bay*'s defence of her convoy against *Admiral Scheer*. But while *Jervis Bay*'s story came to a violent end at 8 o'clock on that evening of 5 November 1940, the voyage of her antagonist was just beginning. And, in its own way, the raiding cruise of the *Admiral Scheer* was no less remarkable and no less courageous, for she was about to carry out a lone raiding sortie that would extend over three oceans, in which the only other warships she was likely to encounter would be British.

Launched on 1 April 1933, *Admiral Scheer* was one of three unusual warships that the *Deutsches Kriegsmarine* tried to build within the 11in gun and 10,000-ton weight restrictions imposed by the 1919 Treaty of Versailles. Using diesel propulsion, welding, triple turrets and diminished armour, the first of the trio, *Deutschland*, only slightly exceeded the limit when she was launched in 1931. Her empty displacement was 11,700 tons, yet she packed six 11in guns and could steam at 26 knots. No match for a regular battleship, she could demolish an 8in-gunned heavy cruiser of her own weight class. Essentially, she was designed to outgun anything she could not outrun and outrun anything she could not outgun. The Germans called her a *Panzerschiff* (armoured ship), but the British referred to her and the two similar vessels that followed her as 'pocket battleships'.

By the time *Deutschland*'s slightly modified sisters, *Admiral Graf Spee* and *Admiral Scheer*, were launched, Adolf Hitler had become Chancellor of Germany and renounced the Treaty of Versailles. The *Panzerschiffe* were proceeded with, but the techniques that made them so weight-efficient were to be applied thereafter to larger, more powerful warships for a resurgent German *Uberwasserseestreitskräfte* (High Seas Fleet).

Admiral Scheer originally displaced 11,200 tons empty and 16,200 tons at full load. Her overall length was 616¾ feet, with a beam of 71¼ feet. Four MAN diesel engines powered each of her two propeller shafts, producing 56,800 horse power. Her thickest armour was 4 inches for the main waterline belt, bolstered by 1½ inches of internal armour. Main armament consisted of six 11in guns in two triple turrets; secondary armament eight 5.9-inchers. Anti-aircraft (*Flak*) protection was afforded by six 4.1in, eight 37mm and ten 20mm guns. There were also eight 21in torpedoes housed in quadruple tubes aft, and two aircraft that could be launched from a single catapult. Complement, 1,150 officers and men.

Commissioned at Wilhemshaven on 12 November 1934, *Admiral Scheer's* first mission began on 27 July 1936, when she arrived at Malaga to evacuate German refugees caught up in the Spanish Civil War. When *Scheer* steamed for Spain again on 1 October, her mission included observing and reporting Soviet vessels carrying weaponry to the Republicans in violation of the London Non-intervention Commission, while at the same time escorting and protecting 'special' steamers delivering German weapons to the Nationalist forces – equally in violation of the treaty. On 31 May 1937, *Scheer* bombarded Republican shore installations, barracks and batteries in the port of Almeria, in reprisal for an air attack on *Deutschland* in Ibiza Bay two days earlier (by two 3-engined aircraft in Nationalist markings) that killed 23 men and injured 78. By the end of June 1938, *Scheer* had completed a total of eight deployments to Spain.

The outbreak of the Second World War on 1 September 1939 found the *Kriegsmarine* still in the process of building up its strength, both in surface warships and submarines (*Unterseeboote* or U-boats). From the start, therefore, *Grossadmiral* Erich Raeder banished any thoughts of directly challenging the overwhelming might of the Royal Navy. Instead, he would harass the Allied maritime supply routes, ideally through a co-ordinated effort by his U-boats, warships and a supplementary fleet of armed and disguised auxiliary vessels. Raeder's strategy involved a dangerously contradictory combination of objectives. Essentially, his ships were expected to keep a high enough profile, through their occasional attacks on convoys or lone cargo ships, to disrupt Allied maritime traffic and stretch Allied naval resources over as wide an area of ocean as possible. At the same time, they had to keep a low enough profile not to be located and hunted down by a converging concentration of these same enemy warships.

The new war began with *Admiral Scheer* on the receiving end. On the evening of 4 September 1939, Bristol Blenheim IVs of 107 Squadron, Royal Air Force, attacked her in Wilhelmshaven. *Scheer* was struck by four bombs, but all were dropped at too low an altitude for their fuses to arm and they caused only minor damage. Four Blenheims were shot down by anti-aircraft fire, but *Scheer's Flak* also downed a defending German fighter, killing its pilot. A short time later, her nervous gunners also downed a passing Junkers Ju-52 which had failed to give the correct recognition signals.

While *Scheer* underwent an overhaul, her two sisters set out to play their part in Raeder's strategy. Operating in the North Atlantic, *Deutschland* only accounted for two ships before returning home. *Admiral Graf Spee* was more successful, sinking nine ships in a voyage that took her into the South Atlantic and the Indian Ocean. On 13 December 1939, however, she ran afoul of the British heavy cruiser *Exeter* and light cruiser *Ajax*, and the New Zealand light cruiser *Achilles* off the coast of Uruguay. In the ensuing Battle of the River Plate, *Exeter* and *Ajax* were badly damaged, but *Graf Spee* sustained enough damage of her own to put into the port of Montevideo. Over the next few tense days, the British moved the heavy cruiser *Cumberland* into the area, while convincing *Graf Spee's Kapitän zur See* Hans Langsdorff that even more heavy units had either arrived or were on the way. Finally, on 17 December, *Graf Spee* slipped her moorings, steamed down river and then exploded in flames as six of her own torpedo warheads went off. Three days after having ordered his ship scuttled, Langsdorff shot himself.

Although *Deutschland's* sortie had been a disappointment, the cruise of the *Graf Spee* had demonstrated the *Panzerschiffes'* potential as long-range commerce raiders. It had also shown the vulnerability of any German warship to being hunted down and destroyed if contact should be made with any of its British counterparts. *Graf Spee's* demise began a slow process in which the élan of the German surface raiders would be tempered – and later hobbled – by caution. The most immediate result, however, was an order from Hitler to re-christen *Deutschland* as *Lützow*, rather than risk the symbolic ramifications of the loss of a ship bearing the country's name.

Throughout the early months of the war, *Admiral Scheer* underwent a refit, followed by sea trials in the Baltic from August until October 1940. Then, on 14 October, Raeder obtained the permission of a reluctant Hitler to send *Scheer* into the Atlantic to strike at Britain's oceanic trade routes. Commanding her on this mission would be *Kapitän zur See* Theodor Krancke, a former commandant at the Naval College and a staff officer in Raeder's *Oberkommando der Kriegsmarine* during the Norwegian campaign of April–June 1940. The essential task of replenishment at sea would be performed at designated rendezvous in the Atlantic by the oiler *Nordmark*, which slipped out to sea on 19 October.

Scheer left Gdynia on 23 October and, after a brief visit to Brunsbüttel, arrived at Stavangar, Norway, on the 28th. Next day she steamed northwards into Arctic waters, striving to avoid detection by British reconnaissance planes. On the 30th, at a point midway between Jan Mayen Island and the north-eastern tip of Iceland, *Scheer* made a 350-degree alteration in course, heading south in the face of hurricane-force winds and heavy seas which swept two men overboard while they were trying to secure equipment on one of the 20mm guns. Given the sea conditions and the fact that the water temperature was -1 degree Centigrade, Krancke decided that stopping to rescue them was out of the question.

By 1 November, however, *Scheer* had made it through the Denmark Strait undetected and, despite the tragic loss of the two men, Krancke was satisfied with his progress. Moreover, the *Funkbeobachtungsdienst* or *B-Dienst* – the *Kriegsmarine*'s radio intelligence service, which had broken the British codes in 1936 and had been monitoring their radio traffic since the beginning of the war – had informed Krancke of a large British convoy, HX-84, that had left Halifax, Nova Scotia, on 27 October, and he carefully plotted its most likely route on his charts.

At 9.40 on the morning of 5 November, *Scheer* was in position to intercept the convoy and catapulted her Arado Ar-196 floatplane (T3+BH) to reconnoitre. When it returned some hours later, its pilot, *Oberleutnant zur See* Pietsch, was able to confirm the approach of eight ships and, even better, the absence of any normal warship escort.

Scheer's crew went to action stations as she turned toward her prey; but at 2.30 she encountered a lone steamship, which presented the disconcerting possibility of transmitting a distress call that would scatter the convoy and attract Royal Navy warships to the area. Unable to risk letting her go, Krancke closed in on the vessel, which turned out to be the 5,389-ton banana boat *Mopan*. Luckily for Krancke, *Mopan*'s crew complied with his order to stop and took to their lifeboats without sending a radio message. With no time to put a prize crew aboard, *Scheer* sank her first prize with a 4.1in shell below the waterline.

Even as *Mopan* went down, the 37-ship convoy appeared over the horizon. As Krancke sized-up his victims through his binoculars, a single-stack vessel that looked like a passenger liner left her position at the head of the convoy, raised speed in *Scheer*'s direction and signalled: 'What ship?'

Figuring the challenging vessel to be an armed merchant cruiser, Krancke withheld a reply, hoping to lure her within range of his main armament and finish her quickly, before the convoy could scatter. He was not to get his wish, thanks to the tenacious spoiling action put up by Captain Edward Fegen and the crew of the *Jervis Bay*. The five vessels that *Scheer* did manage to sink after dispatching *Jervis Bay*, combined with *Mopan*, gave her a total of 52,884 tons of shipping destroyed in six hours – a vivid illustration of what a battleship could do to a convoy, but far short of what might have been accomplished. Krancke would have been even more disappointed, had he known the fate of the *San Demetrio*, which had been set afire and abandoned by her crew. The next day, the tanker's crew drifted back to their still-floating ship, reboarded her, extinguished the flames and brought her home with the greater part of her cargo of oil intact.

The British reacted predictably to news of the attack on HX-84. Two other convoys that had already left Halifax for Liverpool were ordered to return to Canada. At the same time, the battleships *Nelson* and *Rodney* were deployed to block the Iceland–Faeroes passage, while the battle cruisers *Hood*, *Renown* and *Repulse*, together with the light cruisers

Dido, Naiad and *Phoebe,* patrolled the approaches to the Bay of Biscay. Additionally, the Admiralty decided that henceforth no large convoy would cross the Atlantic without at least one battleship among its escort – a significant policy decision that would have serious consequences for the Royal Navy in the Far East a year later, when it came up against the Japanese Combined Fleet.

Krancke, kept abreast of all these developments by *B-Dienst,* should have been gravely concerned about his prospects of returning home – if that is what he had planned to do. But he had no intention of curtailing his sortie yet. Instead, he steered *Scheer* in the direction that the British would have least expected him to take – southwards, deeper into the Atlantic.

En route to his rendezvous with the supply ship *Nordmark* at a position code-named *Zander,* on 12 November *Scheer* had an unexpected encounter with a German ship – the freighter *Eurofeld,* which had been caught in Tenerife when war broke out, and had been lying low there with chronic engine trouble. Her captain had, in fact, been told to venture out in hopes of finding *Scheer* so that the *Panzerschiff*'s chief engineer could investigate the problem. *Scheer*'s engineers made temporary repairs to *Eurofeld*'s leaky boilers. Four days later, *Nordmark* arrived and was given a musical greeting by *Scheer*'s band.

During the next four days, *Nordmark* supplied the spares necessary to effect permanent repairs to *Euromark* and pumped 1,327 tons of diesel oil into *Scheer.* After making arrangements for the next rendezvous, Krancke departed for the Equator, while *Eurofeld* set out to make contact with another German raider known to be operating in the Atlantic at that time – the auxiliary cruiser *Thor.*

On 24 November, *Scheer* encountered the 7,448-ton refrigeration ship *Port Hobart.* On this occasion Krancke let his victim transmit a raider distress signal. He wanted the British to send a warship or two to this remote position – he would be far away by the time they arrived. Before sinking the vessel, however, Krancke observed the Prize Law rules by having a motor-boat bring aboard her crew and passengers – which, somewhat to his chagrin, included seven women. Krancke had the men placed under guard but, gentleman pirate that he was, put cabins at the ladies' disposal.

A week later, *Scheer*'s Ar-196 sighted the 6,242-ton Harrison Line steamer *Tribesman* 900 miles off the coast of Gambia. As the armoured ship crept up for a night attack, the British vessel tried to make a distress call, but this time Krancke did not want his presence known and shot away her aerials. In the course of the chase that followed, *Tribesman*'s crew took to their boats. While most were captured, one boat, carrying the ship's master and chief engineer, vanished into the night. The rest of the crew was made up of eight European officers, who joined their compatriots on the forward mess deck, and 69 Lascar seamen who were confined under guard in another part of the ship.

After dispatching *Tribesman*, *Scheer* stole back into the central Atlantic, but a new problem arose – her engines were found to be in need of an overhaul. For the time being, Krancke's solution was to allow each engine to be stopped and attended to in alternating succession, while proceeding at a reduced speed of 22 knots.

Scheer had found no further prey by 14 December, when she met *Nordmark* to refuel and transfer her 150 prisoners. On 17 December, however, she caught the 8,652-ton refrigeration ship *Duquesa*. By now, Krancke had learned that Admiral Raeder had dispatched the heavy cruiser *Admiral Hipper* into the North Atlantic so, to draw some of the Royal Navy's attention away from her, he let the cargo vessel get off her QQQQ and RRRR distress calls before overhauling her. Although *Duquesa's* old coal-burning engines and low fuel supply made her a poor prospect to be sent back to Germany, her manifest revealed huge stocks of meat and eggs that were too tempting to waste – especially with Christmas just around the corner.

On 22 December *Scheer*, accompanied by the captive *Duquesa*, had another rendezvous with *Nordmark*, and the Germans transferred all the provisions they could into the latter's larders – 604 cases of eggs, 503 crates of tinned meat, 177 sides of frozen beef and mutton, and an unknown quantity of bacon. At the same time, Krancke thoughtfully moved his female prisoners to *Duquesa's* more commodious quarters. Hoping that the capture of an adequate supply of coal might yet allow him to steam *Duquesa* back to Germany, Krancke decided to keep her afloat for the time being. Then, after giving *Nordmark's* captain a new rendezvous co-ordinate code-named *Friedrich*, he took *Scheer* off in search of fresh prey.

Although *Scheer* had found slim pickings in December, she did better than *Admiral Hipper*, which had left Brunsbüttel on 30 November and slipped through the Denmark Strait on 6 December. Bad weather hampered *Hipper's* efforts and on Christmas Eve she was about to make for Brest when her radar picked up a large convoy – WS-5A, consisting of twenty transports carrying troops, tanks, guns and other equipment to the British Eighth Army in North Africa. *Hipper* shadowed the convoy throughout the night, but, as she prepared to attack the next day she found an unwelcome Christmas surprise waiting for her – the heavy cruiser *Berwick* and the light cruisers *Bonaventure* and *Dunedin*, accompanied by the old aircraft carrier *Furious*, which was ferrying aircraft to Africa. After a brief exchange of fire, during which slight damage was inflicted on *Berwick* and the transport *Empire Trooper*, *Hipper* broke off contact and fled to Brest, arriving on 27 December. The Royal Navy's commitment of major warships to convoy protection, made in the wake of *Scheer*'s destruction of *Jervis Bay*, had paid off, but *Hipper* was also handicapped by the inferior endurance and chronic unreliability of her 3-shaft turbine engines – as against *Scheer*'s diesels.

On the same day that *Hipper* reached Brest, the battle cruisers *Scharnhorst* and *Gneisenau*, with a destroyer escort, left Kiel in an endeavour to get through the Denmark Strait. Gale-force winds forced the destroyers to abandon the sortie on 29 December, and the weather further deteriorated. Titanic waves crashed over the bows of the battle cruisers, damaging their fire-control systems and fracturing several of *Gneisenau*'s deck beams. Conceding defeat to the elements, Admiral Günther Lütjens reversed course and returned to Kiel for repairs.

That left *Admiral Scheer* once more the only regular warship of the *Kriegsmarine* still at large on the high seas, and the Royal Navy was certainly not ignoring her. After receiving *Duquesa*'s signal, the British dispatched the cruisers *Neptune* and *Dorsetshire* from Freetown, formed a force off the island of St. Helena made up of the aircraft carrier *Hermes*, light cruiser *Dragon* and AMC *Pretoria Castle*, and diverted another unit bound for Freetown, Force K comprised of the carrier *Formidable* and the heavy cruiser *Norfolk*, to search for the German raider. Combined, these ships would have made short work of the pocket battleship, but they were too few and dispersed over too wide an area to find her – and, in any case, *Scheer* and *Duquesa* were moving away, farther south.

Scheer's crew celebrated *Weinachtsfest* with beef, beer, walnuts and cigarettes, all provided by the *Duquesa*, while their coloured paper Christmas decorations were topped by a fir tree lashed to the mainmast. Elsewhere, prisoners aboard the *Nordmark* made do with bread, jam and sausages, although on Christmas Eve *Nordmark*'s skipper did break out a bottle of champagne for the captive masters and officers quartered in the after part of the ship.

On Christmas morning, *Thor* and *Eurofeld* joined the trio. Although *Scheer* and *Thor*'s crewmen were allowed to visit one another's ships, *Scheer*'s crew were forbidden to take any photographs of the disguised merchantman. Meanwhile Krancke had a conference with *Thor*'s *Kapitän zur See* Otto Kähler. Although SKL (the *Seekriegsleitung*, or naval general staff) had favoured the idea of the two ships operating closely in the South Atlantic until the end of January 1941, Krancke and Kähler agreed that such an idea was not feasible, because *Scheer*'s distinctive silhouette would compromise *Thor*'s stealth advantage, while the slower *Thor* would cancel *Scheer*'s speed asset.

On 27 December, *Scheer* again rendezvoused with *Duquesa*, taking on 200,000 eggs and eight tons of frozen meat while her crew also took the occasion to repaint her in British-pattern camouflage. By the 29th, no less than five ships flying the German flag were meeting at a point code-named *Andalusien*, about 600 miles north of Tristan da Cunha. The guests were *Scheer*, *Nordmark*, *Eurofeld*, *Thor* and *Storstad*, a captured Norwegian tanker from which *Nordmark*'s tanks were replenished and *Scheer* took on another 656 tons of oil. Following a short, fruitless raiding patrol by *Scheer* and *Thor*, the *Panzerschiff* and the auxiliary cruiser rejoined *Nordmark* and *Eurofeld* on New Year's Eve, while *Scheer*'s Arado crew kept a vigilant eye overhead, lest British warships should unexpectedly turn up to crash the party.

It was an audacious way for the Germans to spend the holiday, receiving congratulations from Berlin on their success so far and flashing New Year's greetings at one another – 6,000 miles from home, in the middle of what was ostensibly regarded as a British lake. And they were not alone, for while no further regular warships had left German waters, three other auxiliary cruisers had broken out: *Pinguin*, *Kormoran* and *Atlantis*.

In addition to fuelling all these surface raiders from rendezvous point *Andalusien*, *Nordmark* was also tending to three Italian submarines operating in the South Atlantic. Her task as a supply ship was greatly eased by *Duquesa*'s still-generous food stores, while most of the prisoners were transferred to *Eurofeld* and dispatched to Occupied France, which she reached in March 1941. After *Storstad*'s fuel supply was used up, she too was sent to Europe with a fresh batch of prisoners.

On 2 January, *Scheer* again met *Storstad*. This Norwegian tanker, captured by *Pinguin*, her fuel tanks now empty, was sent back to Europe with another batch of prisoners. She reached the Gironde on 4 February, and was renamed *Passat* by the Germans. On 5 January, the last of *Scheer*'s engines had undergone their overhauls. The next day, after topping off her bunkers from *Nordmark* and taking on more provisions from *Duquesa*, the *Panzerschiff* resumed her hunting.

On 8 January 1941, *Scheer* struck north for the Cape Town–Freetown route off West Africa, hoping to catch the convoy that had eluded *Hipper*. She did not find it, but on the 17th she captured the 8,038-ton Norwegian tanker *Sandefjord*, which was carrying 11,000 tonnes of crude oil from Abadan to Anglo–Iranian Oil at Swansea. Putting a prize crew aboard, Krancke sent her off to Bordeaux.

On 20 January, *Scheer* encountered two ships, which posed a dilemma. Krancke's ingenious solution was to approach his first prospective victim, the 5,597-ton Dutch freighter *Barneveld*, bows-on, with one gun of *Scheer*'s distinctive three-gun turret depressed and two guns raised, visually impersonating an investigating Royal Navy cruiser until he was close enough to board and take her without firing a shot. The bluff paid double dividends. Observing these seemingly peaceful goings-on from their own ship, the British crew of the 5,103-ton *Stanpark* offered no resistance to the boarding-party that approached them by motorboat – and suddenly armed seamen in German uniform were clambering up the side and had seized the radio office before a distress signal could be transmitted. Three of *Scheer*'s torpedoes – only one of which struck home – hastened *Stanpark* to the bottom. *Barneveld* was carrying three Royal Naval officers bound for the Mediterranean, 48 Royal Marines and an Indian named Bazay, an anti-British supporter of the nationalist leader Mohandas Ghandi, who willingly provided the Germans with a five-page report on current conditions in England. Also aboard were five new Northrop Nomad light bombers that were to have been delivered to the South African Air Force at Port Elizabeth, as well as 86 army vehicles and 1,000 tons of ammunition and equipment. After noting down all the technical details they could glean from her cargo, the Germans used explosive charges to scuttle *Barneveld* the next day.

On 24 January, *Scheer* met *Nordmark* and *Duquesa* again, replacing her three torpedoes and picking up spares for her seaplane, at the same time depositing 250 prisoners aboard *Sandefjord*. *Thor* and *Eurofeld* also turned up. Plotting his next move, Krancke learned that SKL had originally intended *Scheer* to operate in the Antarctic Ocean, but had dropped the idea in favour of giving him a free hand. Krancke's choice was similar to that made by *Graf Spee*'s Captain Langsdorff back in 1939 – leave the South Atlantic, where his depredations might be drawing too much unwelcome attention from the Royal Navy, and try his luck beyond the Cape of Good Hope.

Departing on 28 January, *Scheer* arrived off the southern tip of Madagascar on 6 February and commenced a vain search for victims on the Durban–Perth route. On 14 February, Krancke made contact with the disguised German merchant cruiser *Atlantis*, accompanied by the supply ship *Tannenfels* and two captured vessels, the tanker *Ketty Brovig* and freighter *Speybank*, just north of Madagascar. *Atlantis'* *Kapitän zur See* Bernhard Rogge had been having a good run of luck in the area and, although bad weather hampered communications between the two raiders, Krancke learned from Rogge that operating at the northern end of the Mozambique Channel might be profitable. After refuelling from *Ketty Brovig*, the two raiders went their widely separate ways on 17 February.

Steaming westwards, *Scheer* marked her 123rd day at sea off the Seychelles Islands, 500 miles below the Equator and 2,000 miles beyond the northernmost point that *Graf Spee* had ventured in the Indian Ocean. On that same day, 20 February, *Scheer*'s floatplane finally spotted a ship heading south. Using the British signalling technique, *Scheer* was able to close on her latest victim, which proved to be the 6,994-ton *British Advocate*, carrying 4,970 tons of crude oil and 4,770 tons of petroleum. While a prize crew was being put aboard the tanker with orders to rendezvous with *Atlantis*, *Scheer*'s floatplane reported another sighting and the *Panzerschiff* set out after this fresh victim.

That night, *Scheer* caught up with the 2,546-ton Greek steamer *Grigorios C.*, whose master claimed he was carrying Red Cross supplies to New York. Her scheduled destination was, in fact, the Greek port of Piraeus and her cargo turned out to be British weapons, which were sent to the bottom with her next morning.

That evening, the Arado made another sighting and *Scheer* went to investigate, with two guns elevated to give the impression that she was a British cruiser. As she overtook her target, Krancke could make out the colours of the then-neutral USA painted on the ship's side, but he had his doubts. Turning broadside to the stranger, *Scheer*'s blinker signalled from her control tower: 'Stop at once. Do not force me to open fire. You are behaving very suspiciously.'

A hand-held Aldis lamp on the wing-bridge signalled the freighter's reply: 'So are you. You look like a German to me.' Moments later, *Scheer* opened fire. At the same time, the German wireless crew picked up the familiar RRRR call, and confirmation of their prey's true identity: 'Canadian Cruiser in 6° 36' S., 47°18' E., under attack by battle cruiser.' Immediately afterwards, the message was heard being repeated from shore-based wireless stations.

A burst of 37mm gunfire at *Canadian Cruiser*'s bridge persuaded her captain to surrender, but as an armed boarding-party climbed up the rope ladders, the Allied crew was offered some small amusement as their uninvited guests arrived with their white tropical uniforms smeared with the red and blue paint of the spurious American flag that had recently been painted on the hull side.

Canadian Cruiser's distress call could not have come at a more fortuitous time for the British – or at a worse time for the Germans. On that same day, Krancke received a message from *B-Dienst*, reporting that WS-5B, a 20-ship convoy escorted by the cruisers *Australia* and *Emerald*, had left Durban on 15 February and had arrived off Mombasa on the 21st. It was a tempting target, but, with *Scheer*'s presence in the Indian Ocean now known, also a dangerous one. Indeed, the Commonwealth cruisers *Canberra*, *Shropshire* and *Hawkins* were fanning out looking for the German raider, as was Force V, consisting of the aircraft carrier *Hermes* and the light cruisers *Glasgow*, *Emerald* and *Cape Town*. *Glasgow*, under Captain Harold Hickling, was lying only 400 miles west of *Scheer* when he responded to *Canadian Cruiser*'s distress call by altering course south-southeastwards in hopes of finding the enemy pocket battleship and directing more powerful units towards her. For the Germans, the ocean was shrinking and time was running out.

On 22 February, *Scheer* caught one more lone victim, the 2,542-ton Dutch steamer *Rantau Pandjang* carrying 3,000 tons of coal from Durban to Singapore and Sabang, which tried to escape in a rain squall but stopped when fired upon with 11in and 5.9in shells. There was no time to put a prize crew aboard, so Krancke sank her. Unknown to him, however, *Glasgow* was then only 140 miles away and *Rantau Pandjang*'s distress call came to Captain Hickling's attention. Just before noon, a Supermarine Walrus flying-boat launched from *Glasgow* sighted *Scheer*, whose crew in turn sighted the plane at 12.17. Krancke, mindful of Admiral Raeder's admonition to avoid any risks, abandoned any further notions of attacking convoy WS-5B and decided to leave the Indian Ocean. As a precaution, however, he turned *Scheer* eastwards, hoping to mislead the aircraft as to his course until it broke contact. At 12.48, the Walrus lost contact and returned to *Glasgow*.

Just before 2 p.m., *Glasgow*, now just 80 miles away, catapulted her Walrus skywards again, this time with orders to shadow the German raider while Hickling passed on all information of its whereabouts to the commander-in-chief of the East Indies station, Vice-Admiral Sir Ralph Leatham. At this juncture, however, the weather worsened, reducing visibility to three miles. Krancke, meanwhile, had reversed *Scheer*'s course as soon as the Walrus had completed its first over flight and was now steaming westwards. Some hours later, *Glasgow*'s fuel ran low, compelling Hickling to make for the island of Mauritius to replenish. In his memoirs, *Sailor at Sea*, Hickling later ascribed the frustrating outcome of his pursuit to '*Scheer* bad luck'.

Scheer, in contrast, seemed to be leading a charmed life. The heavy cruiser *Cornwall*, which had left Cape Town for the island of St. Helena on 2 March, crossed the German's path twice without either ship knowing it. On one occasion, *Cornwall* stopped a Vichy French transport, the *Ville de Majunga*, while the latter was carrying troops to Madagascar; had she not done so, her path and *Scheer*'s might have crossed again. As it was, after meeting *British Advocate* and Krancke's ordering her prize crew to proceed separately to western France, *Scheer* herself managed to slip through the closing British dragnet and into the South Atlantic on 3 March, without further incident.

On 8 March, *Scheer* met the supply ship *Ermland*, followed by the *Nordmark*. In addition to taking aboard provisions and transferring prisoners, *Scheer* put a film crew aboard *Nordmark* to take a newsreel of a simulated attack on a merchant ship for the benefit of the folks back home. On the 10th, the supply ship *Alsterufer* arrived to provide more 5.9in ammunition – although it turned out to be the wrong type – and spares for the *Panzerschiff*'s Ar-196.

Krancke now decided that it was time to quit while he was ahead, rather than risk a reprise of the *Graf Spee* fiasco. On 11 March, *Scheer* began her homeward run and crossed the Equator on the 15th. A day later, *Scheer* ran into the disguised raider *Kormoran* and the U-boat *U124*, the latter carrying a much-needed replacement *Seetakt* radar apparatus for the *Panzerschiff*'s worn-out unit. After exchanging information on the situation in the South Atlantic and Indian Oceans, the three German captains parted company and *Scheer* resumed her northward run. As she approached the Denmark Strait, the tops of her turrets were painted red as a recognition measure, to ensure that the *Luftwaffe* did not attack her once she neared German-controlled waters. On 25 March, Krancke was forced to wait for bad weather, without which his ship would be unable to elude the standing Royal Navy cruiser patrols that he knew were waiting for him. Finally, on the night of the 27th, he took advantage of a new moon to slip through, using his newly repaired radar to evade the light cruisers *Fiji* and *Nigeria*, patrolling the northern end of the passage.

Three days later, *Scheer* reached Bergen and anchored in Grimstadfiord for 24 hours while her crew smartened up their ship for the homecoming. On 1 April, Scheer entered Kiel for an inspection by Raeder himself, after which the Grand Admiral shook hands with each officer, mounted a flag-bedecked rostrum and gave a rousing welcome speech. Krancke had already been cited for the Knight's Cross on 21 February, and on his arrival he was also promoted to *Konteradmiral*. In addition, 40 of *Scheer*'s crew received the Iron Cross First Class and the rest the Iron Cross Second Class.

The jubilation was justified. In 161 days, *Admiral Scheer* had steamed 46,419 nautical miles through the Arctic, Atlantic and Indian Oceans, sinking or capturing sixteen merchant ships totalling 99,059 tons, as well as the AMC *Jervis Bay*. On top of that, in contrast to her unfortunate sister, *Graf Spee*, *Scheer* had returned to boast about her feats – and, at the same time, demonstrated what formidable raiders the diesel-engined *Panzerschiffe* could be.

In an ironic epilogue, on the night of 7/8 April, 49 Armstrong Whitworth Whitleys staged a bombing raid on the naval dockyard and industrial areas of Kiel, killing 88 people and injuring 184. *Scheer* was not damaged in that or five subsequent bombing raids on Kiel during the next six weeks, but it must have been sobering for her crew to observe that she had been in more danger at home than she had been during her lone foray in enemy-controlled waters.

Scheer's return marked the end of a triumphant few months for the *Kriegsmarine*. On 23 January, *Scharnhorst* and *Gneisenau* left Kiel again, and by the time they entered Brest on 22 March they had jointly accounted for 22 Allied merchant ships in the North and central Atlantic. Even the cruiser *Admiral Hipper*, which departed Brest on 1 February, had had some good hunting astride the Sierra Leone convoy route on 11 February when she ran into SLS-64, an unescorted 19-ship convoy, and sank seven ships totalling 32,806 tons before their distress calls and her own rapidly diminishing fuel stocks compelled her to return to Brest on 14

February. A minor setback was suffered on 8 May, when the disguised merchant raider *Pinguin* was intercepted and sunk in the Indian Ocean by the British heavy cruiser *Cornwall*.

But the climax of German surface ship operations was still to come. On 22 May *Bismarck*, which with her sister *Tirpitz* was the most powerful battleship in the *Kriegsmarine*, set out on her first operational sortie, accompanied by the heavy cruiser *Prinz Eugen*. The results would be far different from the previous few raids. On 24 May, *Bismarck* and *Prinz Eugen* ran foul of the British battleship *Prince of Wales* and battle cruiser *Hood* in the Denmark Strait, during which the latter was blown up and sunk with all but three of her crew. By 27 May, however, *Bismarck* had been hunted down and destroyed by an aroused Royal Navy. *Prinz Eugen*, which had left *Bismarck* to raid independently following the Battle of Denmark Strait, returned to Brest on 1 June without accomplishing anything.

Bismarck's spectacular five-day combat career, comprised as it was of a dramatic battleship duel, a suspenseful sea chase and a fiery, heroic finale with more *Sturm und Drang* than Richard Wagner's *Götterdämmerung*, was the stuff of which wartime legends were made, but it also marked a turning-point in the Atlantic War. More tellingly than *Graf Spee*, the loss of *Bismarck* brought German naval affairs to the attention of Hitler who, despite his admitted ignorance of naval matters, began to deprive Raeder of the relative free hand he had enjoyed up to that time. In consequence, the flexibility and scope of German surface ship operations would be severely restricted by an ill-defined policy from the *Führer* that placed an exaggerated emphasis on the avoidance of 'unnecessary risks'.

Admiral Scheer was not to take part in another significant operation against the Allies until *Unternehmen Rösselsprung*, an Arctic sortie against the Murmansk-bound Convoy PQ-17 on 2 July 1942 – and on that occasion, she and all other German surface ships involved were recalled before going to sea, leaving the job of slaughtering the dispersed convoy to aircraft and U-boats. Remembering *Scheer*'s earlier success and keen to repeat it, Admiral Raeder asked permission to send either *Scheer* or *Lützow* back into the Atlantic, but Hitler would not allow it until they had achieved at least one major success against the Russian-bound Allied convoys in Arctic waters, which he regarded as the *Kriegsmarine*'s 'Zone of Destiny'.

On 16 August, therefore, *Scheer* left Skjomenfiord to carry out *Unternehmen Wunderland*, an odd little operation which took her into waters far removed from her tropical hunting grounds of 1940–1. Her task was to seek out and attack convoys in the Kara Sea, despite a paucity of maps and information on the region itself, let alone of any ships steaming through it. Five Blohm und Voss Bv-138 flying-boats and two U-boats, *U251* and *U601*, were expected to provide supplementary intelligence for *Scheer*, but foggy conditions prevented them from doing so.

Although *Scheer* managed to penetrate the ice fields north of Uyedinyenya Island, her captain, *Kapitän zur See* Meendsen-Bohlken, adjudged the ice facing him at Wilkitzky Strait too forbidding to allow his ship passage into the Laptev Sea, and reversed course. As *Scheer* continued east, her floatplane (Arado Ar-196 T3+EK) reported seeing a 9-ship convoy escorted by one two-funnelled icebreaker. Over the next four days, the *Panzerschiff* searched the poorly charted waters south-west of the Wilkitzky Strait between Severney Zemlya and Cape Chelyuskin on Kharitona Laptev Land, venturing as far east as 96 degrees in her quest of the convoy. Finally, on 24 August, her floatplane crash-landed and was written-off as a total loss. Deprived of aerial reconnaissance, Meendsen-Bohlken abandoned his search and turned south-westwards for the Russian mainland. The Soviet convoy, actually escorted by two ships, *Krassin* and *Lenin*, passed by unmolested.

At dawn on 25 August, *Scheer* bombarded the Soviet polar settlement at Cape Zhelaniya, demolishing its meteorological station, warehouses and living quarters, and damaging the wireless house. She then moved on to exact similar destruction on the radio station at Novy Dikson. While on her way there, *Scheer* encountered the 1,384-ton Soviet icebreaker *Aleksandr Sibiryakov*, *en route* to erect a weather station at Cape Molotov on Severney Zemlya, and demanded updated information from her on ice conditions in the Kara Sea. Although German warships were anything but frequent visitors in the area, *Sibiryakov*'s *Kapitan* Karachava had a hunch about the strange ship's identity and, knowing there was a convoy in the vicinity, he demanded the intruder's name. A signal lamp flashed the answer from the warship's bridge: '*Shishiyama*'. The Soviet Union was not at war with Japan at that time, and to reinforce the illusion of neutrality, one of *Scheer*'s crewmen selected what looked like a red and white ensign and hastily ran it up the mast. When the flag unfurled, however, it revealed not the red rays of the rising sun, but the stars and stripes of the USA!

Karacheva was now convinced that he was confronted by a German warship – against which he knew he did not stand a ghost of a chance. Even so, *Sibiryakov* opened fire with her puny guns, hoping to distract the Germans and buy time for the convoy. It was *Jervis Bay* all over again, with a similar outcome – *Aleksandr Sibiryakov* was soon afire and sinking. *Scheer* picked up 22 of her crew before moving eastwards in search of the suspected convoy, but a discouraging barrier of ice and continuing poor visibility led once more to the abandonment of that enterprise.

Scheer next turned up off Novy Dikson at 1.05 on the morning of 27 August, and at 1.37 her 11in guns opened fire at three miles' range. Unlike Cape Zhelaniya, however, the settlement at Novy Dikson was armed and its garrison returned fire with 152mm shore batteries, as well as guns mounted on merchant ships in the harbour. In the course of the spirited exchange, *Scheer* expended 77 11in rounds and a total of 379 5.9in and 4.1in shells, claiming to have inflicted extensive damage to the wireless and port facilities, as well as sinking a 5,000-ton tanker and damaging other ships. In fact, the only Russian ships hit were the patrol vessel SKR-19 (*Dezhnev*) and the 433-ton steamer *Revolutsioner*, both of which were damaged but not sunk. *Scheer* herself took two direct hits and retired northwards, rounding the northern tip of Novaya Zemlya to re-enter the Arctic Ocean and resume her vain quest for Allied convoys. On 28 August, *Wunderland* was cancelled and by the 30th *Scheer* was back in Skjomenfiord. She had accomplished comparatively little for her effort, but from the crew's standpoint, the cruise through poorly charted enemy waters had constituted as exotic an adventure as *Scheer* had had earlier in the Indian Ocean – and it had buoyed their spirits no end just to have got out of port again.

Wunderland was to be *Scheer*'s last raiding cruise. On 10 September, she set out on a foray with *Hipper* and the light cruiser *Köln*, only to have it called off. During her passage from Narvik to Altenfiord, she was unsuccessfully attacked by a British submarine, HMS *Tigris*. In December 1942, she returned to Wilhelmshaven for another refit.

While this was under way, the *Kriegsmarine* underwent a major shake-up. Following the disappointing performance of German surface forces against a lightly defended British convoy in the Battle of the Barents Sea on New Year's Eve 1942, an enraged Hitler – conveniently forgetting the fact that the excessive caution shown by the German warships involved had been essentially a reflection of his own – ordered the entire High Seas Fleet scrapped. When Raeder tendered his resignation in protest, Hitler accepted it and appointed Karl Dönitz *Grossadmiral* in his place. Although Dönitz was pleased to be able to concentrate the *Kriegsmarine*'s efforts behind his U-boat campaign in the North Atlantic, he also managed to strike a compromise with Hitler that spared part of the German fleet from the scrap yards. *Scheer* was one of those retained, but for more than a year thereafter she served primarily as a training ship.

In the autumn of 1944, deteriorating German fortunes on the Eastern Front brought several of the High Seas Fleet's major units out of retirement. On 21 November 1944, *Scheer* joined *Lützow* in the Baltic to participate in *Unternehmen Hammer*, providing coastal fire support for German land forces on the Sõrvemaa Peninsula. Over the next two days, she exchanged fire with Soviet shore batteries. On the 23rd, air activity intensified; *Scheer*'s floatplane was shot down and she had to dodge bombs and torpedoes from Soviet aircraft. Later that night, the Germans evacuated the peninsula and both *Panzerschiffe* had returned to Goten-hafen by 25 November.

Throughout January and February 1945, *Scheer* and *Lützow* strove to stave off defeat along the Baltic coast, firing at enemy targets as far as 21 miles inland. In early March, *Scheer* had to be withdrawn because her 11in gun barrels, worn smooth by constant firing, needed to be relined. Leaving Gdynia, she returned to Kiel with 800 refugees and 200 wounded soldiers aboard. Even during this passage, on three occasions she passed close enough to shore to fire her worn-out guns at Soviet artillery units that were harassing refugee columns fleeing westwards.

On arrival at Kiel, *Scheer*'s crew learned that Admiral Otto Schniewind was going to inspect the ship. Scouring the bomb-scarred dockyard, *Scheer*'s captain was unable to find enough regulation grey paint to cover her superstructure, but did find several hundred drums of violet-blue paint in an old storage shed and put the crew to work apply-ing this over their war-weary ship. Schniewind's comments following his inspection have gone unrecorded.

On the night of 9/10 April 1945, Kiel underwent a massed bomb-ing attack by 591 Avro Lancasters. *Scheer*, berthed in the old inner basin of the dockyard, was missed in the first twenty minutes of the attack, but then a stick of bombs fell close alongside. Their blast tore away plating on the side of her hull and she capsized in minutes. Most of her crew were ashore in bomb-proof shelters, but 32 of those who had remained aboard to maintain essential machinery and man her anti-aircraft guns lost their lives.

Following the German surrender on 8 May 1945, the last of Nazi Germany's warships were either distributed among the victorious Allies or, in the case of those that had been sunk in harbour, scrapped. *Admiral Scheer* was the unique exception. Like a soldier fallen in battle, she was buried under the rubble of the ruined berth where she had made her final, hopeless stand. Buried in the annals of naval history, too, is her dar-ing lone raid into the Atlantic and Indian Oceans, which despite its suc-cess was eclipsed in posterity's eyes by the more dramatic sorties of *Admiral Graf Spee* and *Bismarck*. But then, unlike those ships, *Scheer* came back to die at home.

References

Gray, Edwyn. *Hitler's Battleships*, Naval Institute Press, Annapolis, MD, 1992.
Humble, Richard. *Hitler's High Sea Fleet*, Ballantine Books, Inc., New York, NY, 1971.
Turner, L. F. C., Gordon-Cumming, H. R., and Betzler, J. E. *War in the Southern Oceans*, Oxford University Press, Cape Town, South Africa, 1961.
Whitley, M. J. *German Capital Ships of World War II*, Arms & Armour Press, London, 1989.

CHAPTER 9

An Aggressive Defence
Badoeng Strait, 19–20 February 1942

During the first six months following their surprise attack on the American fleet at Pearl Harbor, Hawaii on 7 December 1941, the armed forces of Imperial Japan enjoyed an almost uninterrupted string of victories and conquests across the western Pacific Ocean and in East Asia. Great Britain and the USA were astonished as their overseas possessions were swiftly overrun – and complacent beliefs as to the inferiority of the Yellow Race nurtured for almost a century were shattered.

While news from the Far East became more depressing daily for the stunned British and American public, new propaganda was churned out to soften the blow. Efficient and effective though the raid on Pearl Harbor had been, the Americans were told – with considerable justification – that it had still been a 'sneak attack', and that retribution would soon come, once a resurrected US Navy met the enemy on more equal terms. Subsequent Japanese victories were attributed to sheer weight of numbers, by Asiatic hordes who would have neither the skill nor the courage to stand up to the Allies once the latter had mobilised forces that would match or exceed the enemy's in numbers.

The truth was that the Japanese were highly skilled, well equipped and motivated by a warrior code of victory or death – the code of *Bushido* – that essentially took valour for granted. To be sure, the courage and resourcefulness with which many of their Allied opponents resisted their advance could easily have stood up on their own merits, with or without the propagandists' embellishments. But there were several occasions, even during their heady days of success, when a freakish twist of fate turned the tables on the Japanese so that they were the ones who were outnumbered and outclassed. It may even be argued, in fact, that one of the most remarkable demonstrations of courage by Japanese naval personnel occurred during the early days of victory, rather than during the later, desperate hours of impending defeat.

On 15 January 1942, as the Japanese turned their attention towards the oil-rich Dutch East Indies, the American Asiatic Fleet, the Royal Navy and Royal Australian Navy combined their available ships with those of the Royal Netherlands Navy under what became known as ABDA (American, British, Dutch, Australian) Command. Intrinsically, the force appeared capable of putting up a good fight, but it lacked co-ordinated air support and was further handicapped by the inability of many of its English-speaking officers to speak Dutch or read Dutch charts.

Significantly, ABDA Command's first success involved the warships of a single country. Led by Commander Paul Talbot, four old US Navy four-stack destroyers – *John D. Ford*, which flew Talbot's pennant, *Pope*, *Parrott* and *John Paul Jones* – intercepted a Japanese invasion fleet in Balikpapan Bay, Borneo, on 21 January, and succeeded in sinking four cargo ships, as well as the 750-ton patrol craft *PC-37*. The Americans, who escaped without loss to themselves, could claim a tactical victory in this, their first surface engagement since 1898. But the stinging damage they inflicted was not enough to save Balikpapan and its oil fields from being overrun by the Japanese.

The next ABDA sortie involved a more powerful bi-national force, commanded by Dutch Rear-Admiral Karel W. F. M. Doorman and comprised of the American heavy cruiser *Houston* and light cruiser *Marblehead*, the Dutch light cruiser *Tromp*, and four Dutch and four American destroyers. Sallying forth to attack Japanese shipping in the Macassar Strait on 4 February, the Allied warships came under air attack off Kangean Island by Mitsubishi G3M bombers of the 11th Air Fleet, newly established at Kendari airfield on Celebes. *Houston* had her after turret knocked out by a bomb hit, while *Marblehead* was so badly mauled as to be forced to limp back to the USA. Doorman cancelled any further offensive action for the time being. *Marblehead*'s voyage half-way round the world in her damaged state was one of the war's great epics of seamanship and resourcefulness. She finally made it to the Brooklyn Navy Yard in New York on 4 May.

By 16 February, Singapore had fallen, the Palembang oil fields on Sumatra had been overrun and the islands of Ambon, Borneo and Celebes were under Japanese control. Their next target would be the island of Bali. The Japanese landing force consisted of units of the Sixteenth Army, based at Macassar Town after having overrun that Celebes seaport on 9 February. On the night of 18 February the troops were loaded aboard the transports *Sagami Maru* and *Sasago Maru*, and left Macassar at 1 a.m. Escorting them was a small naval task force under Rear-Admiral Kuji Kubo in the light cruiser *Nagara*, accompanied by Destroyer Division (Desron) 8 under Captain Toshio Abe, consisting of *Oshio, Asashio, Hatsushimo, Arashio, Wakaba, Nenohi* and *Michishio*.

The invasion force was attacked by a few Allied aircraft during the day, but arrived off Bali at 1 a.m. on 19 February and put its troops ashore without incident. Sometime after 7 a.m. the ships were subjected to further air attacks, during which *Sasago Maru* was slightly damaged and

Sagami Maru had a propeller shaft disabled. These minor hindrances apart, the Bali landing was a complete success and Kubo's warships escorted the *Sagami Maru* out of the area before any further attacks could be made on her. *Sasago Maru* lingered behind, with *Oshio* and *Asashio* in attendance.

Back at Tjilatjap, ABDA's Admiral Doorman still had a powerful enough fleet at his disposal to annihilate Kubo's force, if only he had been aware of the fact. As it was, he doubted whether he had the capability to deal with the enemy invasion force, but nevertheless he reversed to attack it off the beachhead and do as much damage as he could.

Doorman's plan called for a three-phase onslaught. First, the main ABDA fleet out of Tjilatjap, spearheaded by his flagship, *De Ruyter*, and the light cruiser *Java*, would strike at the enemy landing force. The second wave would come from Surabaya and would be led by Commander J. B. de Meester in *Tromp*, accompanied by American Destroyer Division 58, comprised of the four-stack destroyers *Stewart, Parrott, John D. Edwards* and *Pillsbury*. The third phase would be a mopping-up operation by five Dutch torpedo-boats. Good as it looked in conception, Doorman's strategy had the inherent weakness of dividing his forces into separate echelons that were expected to mount successive raids against an enemy who would be alerted by the first wave.

The operation got off to an ominous start on 18 February when one of Doorman's destroyers, *Kortenaer*, ran aground in the narrow harbour mouth of Tjilatjap. His destroyer screen reduced to *Piet Hein* leading the older American ships *John D. Ford* and *Pope*, Doorman carried on with what he had, arriving off the south-east coast of Bali at 9 p.m. on 19 February. An hour later, *De Ruyter* led the column northwards into Badoeng Strait between Bali and Nusa Besar. There the Allies had the disappointment of encountering what remained of the enemy invasion fleet: a single transport, escorted by two destroyers. The rest had already moved on.

There was nothing to do save destroy the targets that presented themselves. But even disposing of these would prove easier said than done. In threatening even one straggling Japanese transport, Doorman stirred up a two-ship hornet's nest.

Asashio (whose name, in accordance with the Japanese navy policy of christening first-class destroyers after poetic meteorological descriptions, translates as 'Morning Current') was the progenitor of three classes of destroyer that would collectively play a vital role in the Japanese naval effort. Built after Japan renounced the 1922 Washington Treaty with its warship tonnage restrictions, the 1,961-ton *Asashio* combined the best elements of previous designs, especially the highly innovative *Fubuki* class which had been introduced in 1927.

Like *Fubuki*, *Asashio* had a main armament of six 5in guns, arranged in twin turrets, one forward and two superimposed aft. Also in common with previous classes was the use of the Type 93 torpedo, one of the most formidable nautical weapons of its time. Perfected by Rear-Admiral Kaneji Kishimoto and Captain Toshihide at the Kure Technical Institute in 1933, the Type 93 used an enriched-oxygen propulsion system that endowed it with a wakeless track, a speed of up to 49 knots and an effective range of up to eighteen nautical miles. Almost 30 feet long, 24 inches in diameter and packing a 1,100-pound warhead, the Type 93 would eventually be known and feared in Allied naval circles as the 'Long Lance'. While the *Fubuki*s carried nine such torpedoes in three triple mountings, *Asashio* and her sisters carried eight in two quadruple mounts. Unlike their counterparts in other navies, the Japanese destroyers also had the significant advantage of being able to reload their torpedo tubes while under way or in action.

Built to outfight ships much larger than themselves, Japanese destroyers were less effective in anti-aircraft defence, although their 5in guns did have dual-purpose capability. A more serious deficiency lay in their anti-submarine capability, which was far behind the state of the art of the time – and for which the Japanese would later pay dearly as Allied submarines began to prey on their merchant fleet.

Below decks, *Asashio* introduced 2-shaft geared turbines that produced 50,000 SHP and a speed of 35 knots. Initial design flaws in the new turbines caused breakdowns, but these teething troubles were rectified by 1941. During early sea trials, *Asashio*'s steering characteristics were also found to be unsatisfactory, but a differently shaped stern and new rudders on subsequent vessels improved their turning circle.

Normally carrying a crew of 200, *Asashio* was to be joined by nine sisters. Further refinements produced the similar *Kagero* class, of which eighteen were built, and the more streamlined *Yugumo* class, of which a further twenty were built.

On the morning of February 20, *Asashio*, commanded by Commander Goro Yoshii, forged six miles ahead of *Sasago Maru*, while one of her improved sisters, the *Oshio* ('Big Current'), steamed along in closer attendance. Skippered by Commander Kiyoshi Yoshikawa, *Oshio* also flew the pennant of Captain Abe, leader of Desron 8.

The Dutch light cruiser *Java* was the first to spot the Japanese and opened fire at 10.25, to which the two Japanese destroyers responded with searchlights, starshell and gunfire that struck *Java* on the stern but failed to cause any significant damage. At the same time, *Piet Hein* zigzagged and launched a torpedo at a vague target she perceived in the gloom. The Dutch destroyer then lay a smoke-screen, obscuring herself from the perplexed officers in *Ford* and *Pope*. Plunging through the smoke at 28 knots, the Americans relocated their leader and took station 1,000 yards astern. At about 10.50, *Ford* spotted *Sasago Maru*, accompanied by a ship which her skipper thought to be a light cruiser; actually, it was the destroyer *Oshio* which had inadvertently 'crossed the T' of the Dutch cruisers and had opened fire on *Java*. Despite their point-blank proximity, the two ships' high speed and the poor visibility caused their salvos to miss. *Sasago Maru*, on the other hand, was struck by Dutch gunfire, as well as by at least one of a spread of torpedoes fired at 11.37 by *Ford* and *Pope*.

Asashio, meanwhile, had turned south towards the Allied column and loosed a torpedo at a destroyer. Soon afterwards, at 11.40, this deadly 'Long Lance' stabbed *Piet Hein*, which burst into flames and stopped, dead in the water and sinking. Doubling back in a tight circle, *Asashio* then encountered *Ford* and *Pope*.

In accordance with Doorman's plan, *De Ruyter* and *Java* had moved on northwards out of the Strait, but the American four-pipers, outgunned and now being pursued by both Japanese destroyers, were unable to follow them so switched to a contingency plan. After a brisk exchange of torpedoes and gunfire, *Ford* laid smoke, after which she and *Pope* retired southwards. Taking charge from aboard *Ford*, Commander E. N. Parker led his two-ship division towards Nusa Besar in the hope of being less visible and protecting the port side of his ships, which were short of torpedoes. Running parallel with the Americans, *Asashio* and *Oshio* traded shots with them for six minutes. As the Americans crossed *Oshio*'s bows, *Pope* launched five torpedoes at her, covered from Japanese return fire by a well-timed screen of heavy smoke laid by *Ford*.

Pope's torpedoes failed to hit the charging *Oshio*, but at that point *Asashio* emerged from the smoke and was mistaken by her sister for another enemy ship. The two Japanese were still shooting at one another as the two Americans emerged from the Strait and turned westwards for Tjilatjap.

After a few minutes, the pugnacious pair identified each other and ceased fire – neither had scored a hit, so they would be able to look back on the incident as comic rather than tragic. By now, the Strait was clear of Allied ships and Captain Abe ordered *Asashio* to take the lead as she and *Oshio* headed north to rejoin *Sasago Maru* – which, though further damaged by shell and torpedo hits, was still afloat.

Meanwhile, *Tromp* had rendezvoused with the American four-pipers of Commander T. H. Binford's Desdiv 58 off the southern coast of Java. On linking up, Binford put his four ships under de Meester's command and the second-wave attack group arrived at Bali on schedule at midnight. De Meester's plan was to have the American destroyers, led by Binford in *Stewart*, enter Badoeng Strait first and attack with their torpedoes. *Tromp* would then finish off any disabled Japanese vessels with her six 5.9in guns.

Hoping to get a better idea of the enemy's strength and deployment, and the extent of damage inflicted by the first strike, Binford tried to radio *Ford* or *Pope*, but was unable to make contact. To add to Binford's problems, an offshore mist cloaked the Bali shoreline as the Americans entered the Strait. As they neared the suspected beachhead at Sanur Roads, Binford and *Stewart*'s skipper, Lieutenant-Commander Harold Page Smith, saw green flares on the horizon, but had no idea of what message they were conveying, or even whether they emanated from friend or foe. Binford decided – correctly – that the twinkling lights must be enemy and, on his order, *Stewart* and *Parrott* each launched six torpedoes in their direction, to which *Pillsbury* added another three. All missed, having served only to alert the Japanese to the fact that their night's work was not yet over.

Swinging around to starboard, *Asashio* and *Oshio* burst out of the mist as full of fight as they had been a few hours earlier, although this time their zeal was subdued somewhat by the earlier incident in which they had traded shots with each other. Wishing to make sure of the identity of the new intruders, one of the Japanese ships flashed a challenge with a small signal searchlight. *Stewart* replied by illuminating the enemy vessel with her own searchlight, firing torpedoes at 1.36 and opening up with her 4in guns at 1.43. Her first two salvos fell short, the third overshot the rapidly advancing targets, but the following nine seemed to produce hits.

Rushing up to join the fray, *Edwards* tried to launch four torpedoes at the Japanese, but only two would leave their tubes, and those missed their targets. *Asashio* and *Oshio*, for their part, were giving better than they were getting. Their accurate gunfire straddled all four of Binford's ships. At 1.46, a shell struck *Stewart* a glancing blow and sprayed fragments across her deck, killing Seaman Second Class Eugene Stanley and wounding her executive officer, Lieutenant Clare B. Smiley. Another salvo splashed the bridge and forecastle.

This was enough for the Americans. Binford ordered his column to retire north-eastwards up the Strait, while Lieutenant-Commander Smith ordered 'Cease fire!' and 'Out searchlight!', then turned *Stewart* hard to starboard. The old four-piper had been hit astern, rupturing steam lines and flooding her steering-engine room, but for the time being she was able to take evasive action at 28 knots. *Stewart*'s turn was so abrupt, in fact, that in the course of trying to follow it *Parrott* and *Pillsbury* almost collided, the latter ship consequently falling out of formation.

While Desdiv 58 fled up the Strait, the small Dutch light cruiser *Tromp* arrived on the scene and the two Japanese warships, probably misidentifying her as another destroyer, turned their attention to her for an easy kill. As they reversed course and took up a parallel course with de Meester's ship, however, *Tromp* slammed a 5.9in salvo into *Oshio*'s bridge. Seven Japanese were killed, but these included neither Captain Abe nor Commander Yoshikawa. Taking aim on the bright blue glow of *Tromp*'s searchlight, *Oshio* scored several damaging hits on her larger antagonist. *Asashio* was also sniping away at the Dutch cruiser until she, too, took a hit that caused negligible damage but killed four of her crew and wounded eleven. Their first casualties of the night seemed to take some of the fight out of the Japanese duo and they broke off, or simply lost contact with *Tromp* – though not before they had landed a total of ten hits on her. Eight of *Tromp*'s crew were killed, and two more of her thirty wounded would die shortly after the action.

As the ABDA group made its way north through Lumbok Strait, it ran into new trouble. At 10.22, Admiral Kubo had learned of the attack off the Bali beachhead and turned *Nagara* round to join his embattled ships, followed by *Wakaba*, *Hatsushimo* and *Nenohi*. He was too far away to get back in time, but he did have a couple of ships that might – *Arashio* ('New Current') under Commander Hideo Kuboki, and *Michishio* ('Route Current') with Commander Masami Ogura at the helm, which were escorting the slow-moving *Sagami Maru* back to Macassar. Kubo therefore radioed the two destroyers to leave the transport and head south for Badoeng Strait at maximum speed. They arrived at the Strait's northern entrance at 2.19 a.m., just in time to meet de Meester's group practically head-on.

Closing to point-blank range, *Stewart* and *Edwards* exchanged vicious salvos of shells, torpedoes and oaths with *Arashio* and *Michishio*. *Pillsbury*, coming up on the port quarter, landed a full salvo of 4in shells squarely on *Michishio*. The stricken Japanese destroyer swerved to starboard – and squarely into the trajectory of a shell from *Edwards* which her skipper, Commander H. E. Eccles, followed with his eye as it arched through the night sky and landed with a bright explosion on *Michishio*'s starboard superstructure. *Michishio* was staggering along from this double punch when Tromp arrived and gave her a passing broadside of 5.9in shells. As *Tromp* and her American consorts continued their retirement into Lumbok Strait, they left *Michishio* dead in the water with 96 of her crew dead, dying or injured.

Kubo's column was still too far away to prevent their getting away, but the Allies were not out of danger yet. Steaming along at 28 knots, *Parrott*'s steering controls suddenly jammed and she veered off to the left – and towards a deadly group of offshore rocks. Lieutenant J. N. Hughes ordered full astern, preventing a complete disaster; although *Parrott* ran aground on the shoal at 2.20, she was able to work herself free and her crew was able get her under way again.

If *Parrott*'s crew had reason to ponder on the fickle, arbitrary nature of Dame Fortune, so would a handful of *Piet Hein*'s crewmen. Earlier in the action, *John D. Ford* had jettisoned a motor-whaleboat, which was subsequently found by 33 of *Piet Hein*'s survivors. Shortly afterwards, they came upon another welcome piece of flotsam – a gasoline tank which had been dropped from *Parrott*. Using this to fuel their boat's motor, they were eventually able to make their way to Java.

By 3 o'clock all Allied ships were clear of Bali. And what of the third phase, involving the five Dutch torpedo-boats? Curiously, they claimed to have steamed right through the Strait without encountering a thing.

On the morning of 21 February, *Oshio* was found to be capable of doing no more than 10 knots, so at 10 a.m. Abe transferred his flag to *Asashio* and *Oshio* was escorted by *Wakaba* to the nearest base for repairs. *Michishio*, more seriously damaged and leaking badly, had to be taken in tow by *Arashio*.

In addition to the sunken *Piet Hein*, the Allies lost the use of two other ships as a result of the encounter off Bali. After some minor repairs had been carried out at Surabaya, light cruiser *Tromp* left for Sydney, Australia, for more extensive repairs on 23 February. By the time she arrived there on 4 March, the remaining elements of the ABDA fleet had been wiped out in the battles of the Java Sea and Sunda Strait, and the fate of the Dutch East Indies was sealed. The only Dutch cruiser to survive the campaign, *Tromp* continued to serve in the Indian and Pacific Oceans, and would eventually be the first Dutch warship to return to the East Indies.

A more bizarre fate befell the destroyer *Stewart*. Although her Chief Machinist's Mate, Paul R. Seiffert, managed to keep her going long enough to lead her division back to Surabaya, she had to be dry-docked. Poorly placed keel blocks and shoring gave way and she rolled over in twelve feet of water, bending her port propeller shaft and causing further damage to her hull. *Stewart*'s crew was evacuated aboard other destroyers and, while an attempt to blow her up was not successful, Lieutenant F. E. Clark, in charge of the demolition detail, dismissed the flooded wreck as being 'of no value to the enemy'.

At first, the Japanese seemed to agree, leaving her *in situ* for about a year after occupying Surabaya. Then, wishing to use the dry dock, they refloated the old ship and frugally set about repairing her. In February 1943 *Stewart*, her silhouette slightly altered by her two forward smoke-stacks having been trunked together, and redesignated as Patrol Boat 102, entered Imperial Japanese service. On 24 August 1944, she and the Japanese-built *Kaikoban II*-class Type D escort No. 22 were escorting the merchantman *Niyo Maru* to Cavite in the Philippines when three torpedoes from an American submarine narrowly missed No. 22. The *Kaikoban* made two depth-charge attacks and managed to sink her assailant, the

American submarine *Harder*, which had previously accounted for no less than four destroyers and two escorts.

For her own part, Patrol Boat No. 102 somehow managed to survive the war, including an attack in April 1945 by US Army Air Force bombers at Mopko, Korea, and she was found at that port after Japan surrendered. Since the name of the lost *Stewart* had been passed on to a destroyer escort (DE-238), the US Navy re-christened the vessel *RAMP-224* (for 'Recovered Allied Military Personnel') and towed her home to San Francisco, California. The *Stewart's* strange saga came to an end on 24 May 1946, when she was towed out to sea again and used as target practice for naval bombers until finally sunk.

Ironically, none of the four Japanese protagonists of Badoeng Strait was destined to last as long as the resurrected *Stewart*. *Sasago Maru*, which had been the Allies' principal target, finally met her end on 14 October 1942, bombed by American aircraft based on Guadalcanal and fatally struck by a torpedo launched from a Consolidated PBY-5A flying-boat piloted by Major Jack R. Cram. Shortly after assisting in the evacuation of Japanese troops from Guadalcanal on 5 February 1943, *Oshio* was fatally ambushed by the American submarine *Albacore*, 70 miles north-west of Manus Island, on 20 February. Both *Asashio* and *Arashio* were skip-bombed and sunk by US Army Air Force aircraft in the Battle of the Bismarck Sea on 4 March 1943. *Michishio* met her end during the Battle of Leyte Gulf in the early hours of 25 October 1944, blown up in Surigao Strait by torpedoes from the American destroyers *McDermut* and *Hutchins*.

Given the Allies' faulty battle plan and poor co-ordination, it is easy to dismiss the Battle of Badoeng Strait as a textbook case of how not to attack an invasion fleet. As defeats went, its magnitude would soon be eclipsed by the more significant Japanese victories in the Java Sea and Sunda Strait. Nevertheless, the officers and crewmen of the four Japanese destroyers involved, particularly those of *Oshio* and *Asashio*, deserve their due credit for saving the transport they were assigned to protect, and in the process repelling two successive formations of enemy ships, each of which had them outnumbered and collectively outgunned. Had *Oshio* and *Asashio* been Allied destroyers, their captains and squadron commander might well have been considered for Victoria Crosses or Medals of Honor. But the Japanese did not give out medals for the sort of aggressive defence that their destroyer crews put up in Badoeng Strait; for them, such valour was not exceptional, but expected.

References
Gray, Edwyn. *The Devil's Device: Robert Whitehead and the History of the Torpedo*, Naval Institute Press, Annapolis, MD, 1991, pp. 216–18.
Hanks, Robert J. 'Ghost Ship of the Pacific Fleet', in *American History Illustrated*, October 1988, pp. 18–48.

Morison, Samuel Eliot. *History of United States Naval Operations in World War II, Volume III, The Rising Sun in the Pacific*, Little, Brown and Co., Boston, Mass, 1988, pp. 321–30.

Roscoe, Theodore S. *Tin Cans*, Ballantine Books.

Watts, A. J. *Japanese Warships of World War II*, Ian Allen, London, 1966, pp. 139–41.

CHAPTER 10

The Ship that Avenged Herself
SS *Stephen Hopkins*, 27 September 1942

A gloomy Sunday morning greeted the crew of the 7,181-ton American Liberty Ship *Stephen Hopkins* on 27 September 1942. Rain squalls, high winds and poor visibility were cause enough for misery, even without the rare but real possibility of stumbling across a venturesome enemy submarine as the cargo vessel made her way from Cape Town, South Africa, to Paramaribo, Dutch Guiana. She was in the southern Atlantic Ocean, east of Brazil – far from the crucial North Atlantic sea lanes between the USA and Great Britain, which were then the object of a desperate struggle between the U-boats of Adolf Hitler's *Deutsches Kriegsmarine* and the Allied merchant fleets and their naval escorts. Even so, it was German naval policy to maintain as world-wide a presence as possible, even if it were merely a token presence. Whether one encountered a North Atlantic wolf pack or a lone sub taking a relative 'breather' from the main action for easier pickings, all it took was one torpedo in the right place to bring the voyage to a tragic and violent end. If anything, though, the dirty weather was to *Stephen Hopkins'* advantage, having more adverse an effect on the visibility, speed and sea-keeping qualities of a surfaced submarine than it had on her own.

At 8.52 a.m., *Stephen Hopkins* was approaching a rain squall when suddenly the ghostly silhouette of another merchantman took shape in the rain, followed by yet another. As the strangers emerged from the squall, Third Mate Walter Nyberg, standing watch on *Stephen Hopkins'* bridge, ordered the helmsman to turn the rudder hard left to prevent a collision. As *Stephen Hopkins'* master, Paul Buck came up to look over the two ships, they hoisted the Swastika-bedecked ensigns of the *Kriegsmarine. Stephen Hopkins* turned away and took flight, to which action the leading German ship reacted by opening fire with 37mm cannon – followed six minutes later by the 5.9in guns of a light cruiser – while taking off in pursuit at half again the American's best speed. Earlier, Captain Buck had remarked to his men that he would fight if he ever encountered a German surface raider; now, as the enemy vessels rapidly closed on his ship, he would have his chance, for misfortune had brought him across

123

the paths of the armed merchant cruiser *Stier* and her supply ship, the blockade-runner *Tannenfels*.

Stier, also known as '*Schiff 23*' in German naval circles and '*Raider J*' to her British enemies, had originally been the 4,418-ton merchant ship *Cairo*, built at the Krupp-Germaniawerft at Kiel. With a length of 408.5 feet, a beam of 56.6 feet and a draft of 21.4 feet, *Cairo* was operated by the Atlas–Levant Line before the war. In April 1941, the ship was placed under the military command of *Kapitänleutnant* Horst Gerlach, who proceeded to arm her with six 5.9in, two 37mm and four 20mm guns, as well as two 21in torpedo tubes. The ship also carried two Arado Ar-231 reconnaissance aircraft.

Schiff 23 was formally commissioned on 11 November, Gerlach christening her *Stier* (bull), in reference to Taurus, the astrological sign of his wife, Hildegard. Although Gerlach doubted whether he would have occasion to capture many ships, he was confident that *Stier* would serve her strategic purpose as a distraction to Allied warships. One of his officers, *Fregattenleutnant* Ludolf Petersen, did not share his optimism. A veteran who had served as prize officer aboard the *Panzerschiffe Lützow* and *Admiral Scheer*, as well as the raider *Pinguin*, Petersen felt that *Stier*'s maximum speed of 14.5 knots was too slow, her crew was too inexperienced, and the mounting of all her armament above decks severely limited their ability to disguise her – all of which were factors to take into consideration if the ship was to play a useful role in the 'second wave' of disguised raiders that the *Kriegsmarine* was about unleash in 1942.

The earlier surface raiding campaign of 1940–1 had been remarkably well co-ordinated and brilliantly successful for the number of ships and the world-wide scope involved. Although the number of Allied cargo vessels sunk or captured was in no way comparable to their losses to U-boats, the disguised raiders had accounted for far more than had the regular surface warships of the *Kriegsmarine*, and had been far more successful than the latter in accomplishing their other objective: to maintain a long-standing menace at sea that compelled the Royal Navy to stretch its resources thin over the world's oceans. In the process, the daring and resourceful tactics of these lone privateers had put the names of *Orion, Widder, Komet, Pinguin, Thor, Kormoran* and *Atlantis* in the newspapers and in the history books. All this had been achieved at very low cost in proportion to the damage inflicted. In addition to the devastation they wrought on unarmed and weakly armed merchantmen, *Thor* sank the British armed merchant cruiser *Voltaire* and damaged two others, while *Kormoran*, when cornered and sunk on 19 November 1940, had managed to take her adversary with her – the Australian light cruiser *Sydney*, blown up with all hands.

By the middle of 1941, all the raiders had returned to their home ports except *Kormoran, Pinguin* and *Atlantis*, which had been caught and sunk by Allied cruisers. Then followed a succession of events that forced a re-appraisal of raider tactics. On 27 May 1941, the five-day cruise of the mightiest warship in the German navy, the battleship *Bismarck*, came to a dramatic end as British battleships, cruisers and destroyers overtook her and pounded her to a watery grave. Even as the consequences of this disaster were being appraised, Hitler launched his invasion of the Soviet Union on 22 June. As the Western nations began sending goods and *matériel* to their new Russian allies via Murmansk, Hitler ordered his High Seas Fleet north to concentrate against the Arctic convoys. In February 1942, the major warships remaining in France – the battle cruisers *Scharnhorst* and *Gneisenau* and heavy cruiser *Prinz Eugen* – succeeded in dashing up the English Channel to complete the concentration of Nazi sea power in the Arctic. Their successful passage was a profound embarrassment to the British, but it also gathered the German surface warships in a much smaller area in which the Allies could concentrate their own forces to safeguard the convoys, keep the Germans under surveillance, hunt them down and destroy them.

By early 1942, German hopes of re-opening the commerce-raiding campaign had to contend with the loss of one of their key routes for slipping past the Royal Navy; the Denmark Strait, between Iceland and Greenland, was now heavily patrolled following *Bismarck*'s foray through it. The entry of the USA into the war on 8 December 1941 added the ships of its powerful fleet to the Allied cause. On the other hand, Japan now offered the option of sanctuary in her ports to any German raider that should break out into the open sea. If things got too hot to slip home through the Allied gauntlet to Kiel or Brest, they could carry on, for the duration of the war if need be, from Singapore or Yokohama.

In any case, with the Battle of the Atlantic reaching a new peak, it was hoped that the presence of new raiders in the southern oceans might again distract Allied warships from their more vital tasks. The challenge would be in getting them out to sea; in all cases, they would be sailing the route of the 'Channel Dash' in reverse, via the Bay of Biscay ports before making for open waters.

The first of the 'second wave' was *Thor*, leaving Bordeaux on 14 January, followed by *Michel* out of Kiel on 9 March. It was the second voyage for both ships, and both made their breakouts smoothly. *Stier*, on her first foray, was to be less fortunate.

The British were becoming more vigilant in the Channel, and during *Michel*'s breakout in the week of 13–20 March, the Germans had thought it prudent to provide her with a torpedo-boat escort. *Stier* received an even bigger one as she left Rotterdam on 12 May 1942: six *Raumboote* (motor minesweepers) and six larger vessels from the 2nd and four from the 8th Minesweeper Flotillas preceded her in three V-formations, while *Seeadler, Iltis, Kondor* and *Falke* of the 5th Torpedo Boat Flotilla closely boxed her within a diamond formation.

This time, the Germans might have overdone it. A convoy of that size was impossible to disguise and, despite orders to limit *Stier's* speed to seven knots in order to reinforce the impression that she was an ordinary merchant vessel, a single such ship afforded so many consorts could only have led the British to conclude that she was a special target worth taking equally special pains to dispose of.

As the convoy passed within sight of Dover, the British 13.5in coastal batteries spotted it and opened fire. They failed to score any hits, but they did alert all motor torpedo-boats in the area, and at 4.04 on the morning of 13 May the lookouts in *Iltis* sighted a torpedo track to port. *Iltis' Kapitänleutnant* Jacobsen ordered both engines full astern, but it was too late. Struck just abaft her forward funnel by a torpedo launched by *MTB-221, Iltis* broke in two. As she sank off *Stier's* starboard side, taking Jacobsen and 33 others with her, a confused battle erupted between German guns and British torpedoes in the night, during which *Stier's* inexperienced forward gunners fired into the sinking wreckage of their own escort. Five minutes after *Iltis* was hit, *Seeadler*, at the forward point of the protective diamond, took an amidships torpedo hit from the inshore side – courtesy of *MTB-219* – and rolled over to port, throwing her captain off the bridge and into the sea. From his watery vantage point, the German skipper saw his ship go the way of *Iltis* – broken in two and quickly vanishing with 84 of his crewmen. Eventually the running fight ended as the British disengaged, having lost *MTB-220* to German return fire and having failed to do any damage to *Stier*. They had, however, sunk *Iltis* and *Seeadler*.

On 20 May, as *Stier* left the port of Royan in the Gironde and headed south-west into the Atlantic, Gerlach – who was promoted to *Korvettenkapitän* on 1 June – and his crew hoped that they might see to it that the sacrifice of their escorts had not been in vain. That could only be done by sinking as much enemy mercantile tonnage as possible, while simultaneously distracting and evading as many Allied warships as possible, for as long as possible.

Their first opportunity came on 4 June, when *Stier* encountered the 4,986-ton British freighter *Gemstone* in the Atlantic Narrows 175 miles east of Brazil's St. Paul Rocks. *Gemstone* was carrying a load of iron ore from Cape Town to Baltimore, which ended up on the bottom of the Atlantic while her master, E. J. Griffiths, and her crew became unwilling guests of the Reich. That night, three aircraft flew over *Stier*, but Gerlach ordered her hove-to in order to subdue her bow wave and wake, and was rewarded by going unnoticed.

Stier ran into a feistier victim on 6 June, in the form of the 10,170-ton Panamanian-flag tanker *Stanvac Calcutta*, whose captain, Gustaf O.

Karlsson, ordered full speed while his 3in bow and 4in after guns fired between 20 and 30 shells at the raider, scoring two hits and wounding two of *Stier*'s crew. The tanker was taken only after *Stier* had expended 148 rounds and a torpedo, killing Karlsson, helmsman Nelson Oskander, and twelve others of her crew. Fortunately for the Germans, their first salvo destroyed *Stanvac Calcutta*'s wireless and killed the radio officer before he could get off a distress signal.

After an unsuccessful attempt to correct *Stanvac Calcutta*'s list by shifting ballast, her chief officer, Aage H. Knudsen, ordered 'Abandon Ship!' Of the 37 oil-soaked crewmen picked up by the Germans, one died of his wounds aboard *Stier* and another died later, in Japanese captivity.

These promising first successes were to be *Stier*'s last for more than two months. If the raider managed to lose herself to her enemies in the vastness of the southern Atlantic, so too were the rare lone merchantmen lost to her. On 10 and 15 June, she met and refuelled from one of the blockade-running cargo ships delegated to sustain her at sea, the *Charlotte Schliemann*, also transferring 68 prisoners from the *Gemstone* and *Stanvac Calcutta* aboard the supply ship.

Early in July, Gerlach tried using his aircraft to locate a victim but found the Ar-231, a tiny machine designed for stowage aboard U-boats, and of which only six had been built, to be too under powered and fragile to be of practical use. In the course of several attempts to take-off, its pilot, Sergeant Karl Heinz Decker, found that he was only able to get airborne after removing the radio and draining one-quarter of the fuel from the tank. On landing, the starboard float strut broke, capsizing the aircraft. The Ar-231 was repaired and, on 5 July, Decker made another desultory flight, only to break the port undercarriage strut on landing and nosing over again. Having no better luck with the second attempt, Gerlach gave up, noting in his log that the Ar-231 was 'totally unsuited for the Atlantic even under the most favourable circumstances'.

After a long, fruitless patrol, *Stier* transferred the last of her prisoners aboard *Charlotte Schliemann* on 27 July, and next day rendezvoused with the raider *Michel* north of Napoleon Bonaparte's last place of exile, the island of St. Helena. The two raiders approached each other warily, with mutual distrust until their identities were positively established. Gerlach and *Michel*'s Kapitän Helmuth von Rückteschell attempted to conduct a joint raiding operation, but *Stier* was out of sight and out of communication with *Michel* at 8.15 a.m. on 9 August when she sighted the 7,072-ton British merchantman *Dalhousie* 250 miles east of Trinidad. Giving chase, *Stier* caught up with her quarry at 12.20 and fired a warning salvo. *Dalhousie*'s first reaction was an attempt at flight while radioing her situation and firing with her 5in gun. After a 28-minute pursuit, however, *Stier* signalled *Dalhousie*'s 37-man crew to 'Leave your ship!' and they finally complied. By the time *Michel* arrived, *Dalhousie* was sinking by the stern, keel up. Their presence compromised by *Dalhousie*'s wireless transmission, at Rückteschell's urging the two German raiders went their separate ways.

At this juncture, Captain Gerlach wanted to round the Horn and try his luck in the Indian Ocean, but the SKL (*Seekriegsleitung*, the Operational Staff of Naval Headquarters) ordered him to remain in the Atlantic, astride the Cape Town–River Plate route, and investigate Gough Island for its suitability as a possible raider base. After completing that assignment, on 27 August Gerlach again rendezvoused with *Charlotte Schliemann* and transferred his latest bag of prisoners aboard her. It was an unfortunate move for the prisoners, for *Charlotte Schliemann* was *en route* to the East Indies, where they would eventually be left in the less than compassionate care of the Japanese.

On 4 September *Stier* sighted the French ship *Pasteur*, but this potential victim managed to show a clean enough set of heels to escape. Another vessel was picked up on radar on 19 September, only to be lost after a 24-hour pursuit. Following another rendezvous with *Michel* on 24 September, *Stier* met the blockade-runner *Tannenfels* 650 miles north-northwest of Tristan da Cunha on the 25th. The two steamed together until the morning of 27 September when, at 24° 44′ S, 27° 5′ W, they were greeted by the welcome sight of an American freighter emerging from a squall – a vessel that Gerlach promptly ordered taken.

Stier's quarry, the *Stephen Hopkins*, had been launched at Kaiser's yard in Richmond, California on 14 April 1942, and was among the first twenty of an eventual 2,750 Liberty Ships to be mass-produced in the USA. Delivered to the Maritime Administration on 11 May and subsequently managed by the Luckenbach Steamship Company, *Stephen Hopkins*' first port of call was in New Zealand, followed by stops in Australia and Africa. She was on the return leg of this maiden voyage, steaming in ballast from Cape Town to Paramaribo to load bauxite, when she ran into *Stier*. Capable of no more than 11 knots, she was rapidly overtaken by the German raider.

Captain Buck's announced intention of making a fight of it seemed equally hopeless. Against *Stier*'s formidable firepower, *Stephen Hopkins* mounted one gun on the stern, of First World War vintage, firing a 4in, 33-pound projectile, plus two 37mm guns forward and six machine-guns. Despite the gross imbalance in armament, however, as the confident Germans closed to 1,000 yards' range, Buck ordered his ship cleared for action, while his Radio Officer, Hudson Hewey, tried to get off an 'RRRR' raider alert (which was jammed by *Stier*).

Gunner's Mate Paul B. Porter, just in from the 4–8 a.m. watch, had had breakfast and gone to sleep when he was aroused by a sensation like a sledgehammer hitting the deck. Peering out of the porthole of the starboard midships cabin, he saw two ships, one of which was blazing away at his ship. Grabbing a peacoat, sweater and helmet, he dashed off to his station at the aft .50-calibre mount, passing a crewman whose buttocks had been shot off. Removing the canvas cover of his machine-gun, he found that excessive exposure to moisture had rendered it inoperative, so he rushed off to assist the 4in gun crew.

Ordinary Seaman Roger H. Piercy also saw the two ships, and 'knew they were no friends of ours' when the first shells hit, wounding the Chief Mate, Richard Moczkowski, with schrapnel. Piercy ran to the 4in gun and found it being commanded by the youngest member of the ship's company, Cadet Midshipman Edwin J. O'Hara, from the US Merchant Marine Academy at King's Point, New York. During the voyage, O'Hara had become friends with the commander of *Stephen Hopkins'* foutreen-man naval armed guard, Ensign Kenneth M. Willett, US Naval Reserves, and had been practising at the gun with him during his time off from duty in the engine room. Ensign Willett was felled by a shell fragment while making his way to the 4-inch, but Piercy saw him arrive, his entrails hanging out from a stomach wound, to take charge of the gun.

Porter's decision to assist at the 4in gun was a good one, for its crew was being cut down one by one, to be replaced in turn by volunteers like himself. Glancing forward, Porter saw one of the 37mm guns vanish in an explosion, taking with it a friend of Porter's who back in Cape Town had warned him of the possibility of encountering a raider and who had remarked: 'I just feel that something is going to happen. I'm not going to make it.'

This time, however, *Stier* was not having things completely her own way. As luck would have it, *Hopkins'* first shot jammed the raider's helm and her second cut a water feed pipe in *Stier's* engine room, leaving her unable to move or bring her torpedo-tubes to bear. None the less, *Stier* managed to bring the American to a halt with her 5.9in guns and, augmenting their fire with that of the 37mm weapons, wrought devastation upon her. *Tannenfels* joined in the mêlée, raking *Hopkins'* deck with machine-gun fire.

Willett's gun crew defended their ship as best they could with a steady, accurate fire, assisted by their own 37mm guns under the direction of Second Mate Joseph Layman. All scored repeated hits on *Stier*, including several below the water line. One shell set the fuel bunker on fire, others hit the officers' quarters, both hospitals and the bridge. The seventh of fifteen 4in shells to hit *Stier* penetrated the crew's quarters near No. 2 hold and struck the diesel generator, setting fire to the wooden lockers and mattresses in an adjoining compartment.

As flames spread aboard *Stier*, another of *Stephen Hopkins'* shells knocked out the raider's electrical power, paralysing the ammunition hoists. Further shell hits severed the fire mains, rendering the fire hoses useless and compelling the Germans to form bucket chains to fight the blaze. The main engine stopped, leaving *Stier* adrift. *Fregattenleutnant* Petersen found his best friend, ship's doctor Meyer-Hamme, mortally wounded; his last words were: 'It is easy to die, greet our friends.' Two other members of *Stier's* crew were killed, five severely wounded and 28 suffered less serious wounds amid the carnage.

At length, however, the overwhelming fire of the Germans took its toll, cutting down Layman and his 37mm gunners and killing or wounding the last of *Stephen Hopkins'* 4in gun crew except for the indomitable Ensign Willett. Even as he tried to man the gun alone, the magazine blew up, and he too fell. With *Stephen Hopkins'* main defence silenced and the engine room ablaze, Captain Buck reluctantly ordered the ship to be abandoned. His order was barely audible over the shriek of steam from ruptured pipes.

As the crew carried out that melancholy order, they again heard the harsh bark of their 4in gun, now being manned by Cadet O'Hara. As he came up from the burning engine room and saw Willett being carried away, O'Hara rushed to the gun tub. Finding five unexpended shells, he loaded and fired them at the closing Germans and managed to score hits on both *Stier* and *Tannenfels*. After that, he joined his comrades over the side.

Chief Engineer Rudolf A. Rutz and 2nd Assistant Engineer George S. Cronk were engaged in carrying wounded and burned men from the engine room and from their quarters. Rutz ordered Cronk to see to the boat decks, where he found only one lifeboat intact and helped lower it. As this was being done, Cronk saw Captain Buck throw *Stephen Hopkins'* code book overboard and then walk to the other side of the bridge. Cronk went after him, but when he reached that side of the bridge, he could not find Buck and was himself cut off from his comrades by spreading flames fanned by the incendiary shells that continued to pelt the ship. Cronk therefore jumped overboard and swam for twenty minutes before finding the lifeboat. He then managed to pick nine other men out of the sea and off improvised life-rafts. At least one crewman was less fortunate, being mangled by *Stephen Hopkins'* still-revolving propeller as he tried to swim clear. Soon afterwards, the survivors vanished into the same rainstorm whence their attackers had come. At 10 o'clock the unequal engagement ended as *Stephen Hopkins* went down in flames.

For the 23 seamen aboard *Stephen Hopkins'* lifeboat No. 1, the ordeal was far from over. Two died of gangrene early on. The rest had to live on a ration of pemmican and some malted milk tablets. Captain

Buck, Chief Moczkowski, Second Mate Layman, Radio Officer Hewey, Ensign Willett, Cadet O'Hara and Chief Engineer Rutz had not been saved, which left 2nd Assistant Engineer Cronk the senior officer aboard the boat. Ironically, arguably the man most instrumental in getting the crew through the hard days ahead was German-born August Reese, nearly 60 years of age and an old salt with previous experience in Cape Horn sailing ships.

By mid-October, the death toll in lifeboat No. 1 had risen to five. Food had given out and one survivor remarked that he could eat a skunk. At this point, a tern alighted on the boat and was promptly seized by one of the crewmen, who remarked, 'Well, here is the meal we wanted.' 'But not a man among us had nerve enough to hurt the bird,' Piercy recalled. 'The poor thing had been fighting for its life and needed just as much help as we did.' Instead of killing the tern, Stephen Hopkins' survivors left it alone to recuperate and, when it finally flew off, Piercy noted that everyone 'felt better for it'.

On 25 October, the lifeboat's log noted: 'Saw butterfly and two moths.' Then, on the 27th: 'Hurrah, sighted land at 4 a.m.' Thirty-one days after Stephen Hopkins had gone down, the fifteen men who remained of her crew of 57 stumbled ashore at the remote Brazilian fishing village of Barro de Stapanoana. Cronk had lost more than 40 pounds, but he and Reese had kept the last of their comrades going through the 1,800-mile ordeal. A Navy lieutenant sent to meet them commented that they 'were never for one moment beaten. After thirty days of being battered together in a cramped lifeboat, they were still lavishing praise on one another, helping one another.'

Not until after the war did the survivors learn the full story of what they had accomplished. Even while Stephen Hopkins was slipping beneath the waves, Stier herself was in serious trouble. Struck by fifteen of the 35 shells fired at her by the Americans, she was on fire and in a sinking condition. Captain Gerlach tried to radio Michel for help, but failed to make contact. The damaged Tannenfels tried to bring her fire hoses into play against Stier's flames, but the rough seas foiled the attempt. After a final consultation with his officers, a miserable Gerlach assembled his men. After leading them in four shouts of Sieg Heil – one for the Führer, one for the Vaterland, one for their ship and one for their late adversary – Gerlach ordered Aussteigen! (Abandon Ship!). At 11.57, a scuttling charge went off, followed by a second two minutes later. As Stier went down by the stern, Gerlach managed to exhort a round of Deutschland Über Alles from his demoralised crew.

Tannenfels conducted a search for survivors of the American ship, but was unable to locate them in the storm. Her holds crowded with prisoners as well as Stier's survivors, the blockade-runner managed to make her way to Bordeaux. Subsequently, Gerlach wrote his final combat report, declaring that 'It was immediately clear that this was not an ordinary merchantman,' and maintaining that his voyage had probably been cut short by 'an auxiliary patrol vessel or even an armed merchant cruiser' with one 6in and six 4in guns. Even when the true identity of his last victim became known, he refused to believe that she had not been secretly fitted with more heavy armament than was officially reported. Petersen, however, gave credit where it was due: 'We could not but feel that we had gone down at the hands of a gallant foe ... that Liberty Ship had ended a very successful raiding voyage. We could have sunk many more ships.' On second thoughts, however, he added: 'She may have sunk us, but she saved most of our lives. We would not have lasted much longer out there those days and there would not always have been a *Tannenfels* around to pick us up.'

Petersen's philosophical appraisal was not that far off the mark. *Stier* was, in fact, the last German commerce raider to leave German waters for the open sea. *Thor*, berthing in Yokohama after sinking ten ships totalling 56,037 tons, was burned out when her nearby supply ship, the *Uckermark*, blew up. On 14 October 1942 *Komet*, escorted by the torpedo-boats *T-4*, *T-10*, *T-14* and *T-19* of the 3rd Flotilla, was attempting a breakout when she was ambushed off Cap de la Hague and sunk by a torpedo from the British motor torpedo-boat *MTB-236*. In another break-out attempt, the raider *Togo* was hit by a bomb during an attack by Westland Whirlwind fighter-bombers on 10 February 1943 and forced to put into Boulogne. She was bombed again while at Dunkirk, limped back to Kiel on 2 March and never tried to run the Channel again. That left only *Michel* at large to sink seventeen ships totalling 121,994 tons in the South Atlantic, Indian and Pacific Oceans. On 18 October 1943, three days from Yokohama, to which she was returning after a raiding sortie, *Michel* herself was torpedoed and sunk by the US Navy submarine *Tarpon*. With her loss, Germany's world-wide surface raiding campaign ended.

Ensign Kenneth M. Willett was posthumously awarded the Navy Cross, while Captain Paul Buck and Cadet Midshipman Edwin J. O'Hara were posthumously awarded the Merchant Marine Distinguished Service Medal. The Americans named a destroyer escort for Willett, and Liberty Ships in honour of Buck and Chief Mate Moczkowski. Buildings at the US Merchant Marine Academy at King's Point were named after Willett and O'Hara, and that school remains the only civilian institution in the United States that is allowed to fly a battle flag, in recognition of O'Hara and of its other cadets who served, fought and died in action for their country. Both *Stanvac Calcutta*, which had chosen death over surrender to *Stier*, and *Stephen Hopkins*, which brought the raider's career to an ignominious end, were listed among the US Maritime Administration's 'Gallant Ships' – two of only eleven American merchant ships so honoured.

References

Humble, Richard. *Hitler's High Seas Fleet*, Ballantine Books, Inc., New York, NY, 1971.

Muggenthaler, August Karl. *German Raiders of World War II*, Prentice-Hall, Inc., Englewood Cliffs, NJ, 1977.

Stanford, Peter. 'How an Ugly Duckling Fought Back and Sank Her Assailant', in *Sea History*, No. 35, spring 1985.

Turner, L. F. C., Gordon-Cumming, H. R., and Betzler, J. E. *War in the Southern Oceans*, Oxford University Press, Cape Town, South Africa, 1961.

Whitley, M. J. *Destroyer!*, Naval Institute Press, Annapolis, MD, 1983.

CHAPTER 11

The Inglorious Death of the *Hokoku Maru*
Cocos Islands, 11 November 1942

Although commerce raiding by disguised armed merchant ships during the Second World War is associated closely with the Germans, who were the most successful at it, they were not alone in such activity. Another combatant nation that tried its hand at surface raiding was Japan, although her effort was token and half-hearted at best in comparison with the finely co-ordinated campaign pursued by Germany in 1940–1. The brief career of the armed merchant cruiser *Hokoku Maru* typifies Japan's anti-maritime strategy, although her end was exceptionally dramatic.

The Japanese themselves were no doubt conscious of the incongruity of the world's third greatest naval power resorting to playing pirate with disguised merchantmen. Such furtive raiders made cost-effective sense to Germany's small fleet by forcing the Royal Navy to disperse its overwhelming numbers around the globe in an effort to protect its merchant shipping and hunt down their attackers. Japan, however, perceived no such need as she confidently entered the war. Her naval planners sought decisive battle, hoping to crush the Far Eastern fleets of the Western powers as quickly as possible, before they could bring their industrial capacity into full play; they had little interest in a shadowy side-show war in the trade lanes. Indeed, to do so would have been tacit acknowledgement of the possibility of a protracted war of attrition – a war that even the most optimistic of Japan's war leaders suspected she would lose.

None the less, the Japanese did convert no fewer than fourteen merchant ships to commerce raiders, although they seem to have been intended less as a menace to the commerce of their British enemies so much as counters in bargaining with their German allies. Japan was suspicious of any Western presence in the Far East, including that of her erstwhile ally, whose Far Eastern colonies and concessions she had seized during the 1914–18 War (as an ally of Great Britain!). By 1941 the Japanese, like everyone else in the world, had heard of the far-ranging exploits of Germany's sea raiders, whose depredations – in both world wars – had reached into the Indian Ocean. Japan felt it necessary to maintain a presence of her own there, against the day that she and Germany should find themselves negotiating the boundaries of their respective empires.

The issue of operational areas in the Indian Ocean was in fact the subject of discussion as early as 17 December 1941 between Vice-Admiral Nomura, the Japanese Naval Attaché in Berlin, and Admiral Fricke, Chief of Staff, *Oberkommando der Marine* (OKM). The Japanese proposed a line set at 70° E to delineate the operational limits for the two navies, whereas the Germans sought a diagonal line running roughly from Aden to Australia. Eventually the Japanese proposal was agreed upon, subject to change as situations might require.

By May 1942, some of the realities about maintaining their presence in the Indian Ocean were sinking in among the Japanese admiralty. Although British sea power – and colonial power in general – in the Far East had been irreparably humbled by the Japanese Combined Fleet's foray into the Bay of Bengal in April 1942, it had not been eliminated. Perhaps it might have been, had there not been a new and growing threat for Japan to contend with farther to the east: the battered but rapidly recovering US Navy. From May 1942 on, it was clear that the Japanese fleet would have to concentrate on eliminating the Americans, especially their aircraft carriers, in the Pacific, leaving the Indian Ocean with a lower priority. Under those circumstances, the sort of nuisance tactics employed by the Germans became more attractive.

Like the Germans, the Japanese combined the use of raiders and submarines in their anti-shipping campaign, but their effort was planned – typically – in the manner of a fleet operation, lacking the depth, the wide-ranging scope, the contingency plans and the flexibility that made the German raiding campaigns so much more long-lived and successful. A key to German success that was completely lacking in the Japanese strategy, was the dispersal of British sea power by means of attacks on a variety of widespread targets. For all intents and purposes, the Japanese submarines and the two not very well-disguised raiders that entered the Indian Ocean in May 1942 might as well have been the carrier task forces that had struck there in March and April.

Armament of the Japanese armed merchant cruisers varied from ship to ship, the size of their guns ranging from 4.7in to 5.9in. Some carried one or two seaplanes and three – *Bangkok Maru, Kinjosan Maru* and *Saigon Maru* – also carried mines. The 10,439-ton *Hokoku Maru* and her identical sister and usual consort *Aikoku Maru* had both been built in 1939 at the Tama Shipyard. With a length of 492 feet, a beam of 66⅓ feet and a draught of 40¾ feet, they were converted at the start of the war with an armament of eight 140mm (5.5in) guns, four 25mm cannon and four 13mm heavy machine-guns in twin mountings and two 21in torpedo tubes. Two Aichi E13A1 floatplanes were carried for scouting purposes, one of which was stowed in reserve.

No attempt was made to conceal the guns of the Japanese auxiliary cruisers, as had the German raiders; other than using the vastness of the ocean itself, stealth had not really entered into the Japanese formula. Shortly after their conversions, both ships were additionally modified to accommodate ammunition, gasoline, bombs and about 80 torpedoes for the submarines with which they were expected to operate in the Indian Ocean.

Aikoku Maru and *Hokoku Maru* commenced operations in May 1942 in support of the 8th Submarine Flotilla, 1st Division under Rear-Admiral Ishizaki. The flotilla was comprised of submarines *I-10* (flagship), *I-16*, *I-18*, *I-20* and *I-30*, which between them also carried three midget submarines and two Yokosuka E14Y1 floatplanes. The intention was that the I-boats would be most actively committed around the Indian Ocean, the raiders taking up a roughly central position to provide logistic support and strike at targets of opportunity. *I-30* reconnoitred Aden on 7 May, and Djibouti the next day. The first success, however, was scored by the surface raiders on 9 May when they encountered and captured the 7,987-ton Dutch tanker *Genota* 480 miles south-southeast of Diego Suarez.

I-30 was in evidence again off Dar-es-Salaam on 19 May, and on 29 May *I-10*'s aircraft was spotted over Diego Suarez. The next day, *I-16* and *I-20* launched their midget submarines – *I-18* failed to get hers off – and at least one of these penetrated the harbour at Diego Suarez to torpedo the British battleship *Ramillies*, flooding a compartment. The corvettes *Thyme* and *Genista* dropped depth-charges against the intruder; then the other midget struck, hitting the tanker British *Loyalty*, which settled to the bottom. It was arguably the greatest success achieved by Japan's midget subs, but after the raid one of them was found aground on the outer reef and its two crewmen were caught and killed by British Commandos on 2 June. The other midget was never recovered, and perhaps had fallen victim to the corvettes.

Another success came on 5 June for *Aikoku Maru* and *Hokoku Maru* when they sank the cargo ship *Elysia*, but three other vessels were sunk that same day by the I-boats in the Mozambique Channel. The submarines had accounted for another nine vessels by 13 June, on which date *I-30* was dispatched to France. She would make Lorient on 2 August, but while returning with valuable cargo, she fell victim to a British mine off Singapore on 13 October.

Meanwhile, the other submarines were continuing their rampage off the coast of Mozambique, accounting for another nine ships – including the neutral Swedish vessel *Eknaren* – between 26 June and 8 July. These successes demonstrated how effective the Japanese submarines could be against enemy commerce when used for that purpose, but it also displayed on several occasions how poor their marksmanship was whenever they surfaced to finish their victims off with their deck guns. One of their more fortunate intended victims was the 6,889-ton British merchantman *Dallington Court*, which was shelled by I-boats in the northern approaches to the Mozambique Channel on 1 July, and managed to escape not only their gunfire but also their torpedoes.

It was left for the two raiders to conclude the successful campaign on 12 July, when they caught the 7,113-ton *Huakari* bound from Fremantle to Colombo and sank her 780 miles south-east of Diego Suarez for their third victim. They and their undersea partners then retired to Penang. The results should have been encouraging: between them the Japanese had crippled a British battleship and sunk nineteen British merchantmen totalling 120,000 tons, as well as six vessels of other nationalities, for the loss of two midget submarines and the four men of their crews. Yet the Japanese never conducted another commerce-raiding campaign of comparable scope.

From August to October 1942, *I-27* and *I-29* penetrated the Arabian Sea and sank five ships. Then, on 24 October, the Japanese announced to the *Seekriegsleitung* (Operational Staff) of the OKM that they planned to send three raiders into the Indian Ocean, and asked that the German raider *Michel* be withdrawn; recently arrived, she had added two merchant victims to the eight for which she had already accounted in the South Atlantic. The Germans complied and *Aikoku Maru* and *Hokoku Maru* were sent out again, apparently carrying their supplementary stock of fuel and torpedoes to keep open the option of supporting another submarine offensive.

So it was that on 11 November 1942, the 6,341-ton Royal Dutch/Shell tanker *Ondina* and the escort ship HMIS *Bengal* were 500 miles south-west of Cocos Island, about half-way *en route* from Fremantle, Australia, to Diego Garcia, when *Bengal*'s captain, Lieutenant-Commander W. J. Wilson, reported: 'About 1145 an unknown vessel was sighted steaming straight for us ... a second vessel was seen over the horizon.' As the two interlopers closed on the Allied ships they opened fire. Had *Ondina* been alone, she probably would have surrendered. But her Indian Navy escort was duty-bound to defend her, and despite the overwhelming, if inaccurate, firepower he faced, Lieutenant-Commander Wilson chose to make a fight of it.

Bengal was an Australian-built 650-ton *Bathurst*-class 'minesweeping sloop', whose role was to defend her consort from submarines, not surface warships. Her single 12pdr and three 20mm cannon – one Bofors and two Oerlikons – were no match for the armament of either one of her two antagonists. The Japanese seemed to be aware of this, for when Wilson ordered *Ondina* away and turned to oppose them, *Aikoku Maru* left *Hokoku Maru* to dispose of *Bengal*, while she herself swung around the engaged escort and went after the tanker. As the raider rapidly overhauled her, the *Ondina*'s crew gamely fought back with their single 4in gun.

Suddenly, the one-sided engagement took an unexpected turn. Wilson reported that *Bengal*'s sixth shot caused 'a terrific explosion ... flames leaping high in the air'. The fuel and *matériel* aboard *Hokoku Maru* destined for future rendezvous with I-boats had proved her undoing. Even so, the Japanese raider's crew fought on with vengeful fury, as did *Aikoku Maru*'s, each gun crew bringing their weapon to bear at whichever Allied vessel presented itself.

Bengal was holed by near misses and took a direct hit from *Aikoku Maru*, but kept firing at both raiders until her ammunition was nearly exhausted. *Ondina* took the worst of it as *Aikoku Maru* put at least one shell and two torpedoes into her, killing her Master and setting her on fire. The Dutch fought their gun until they ran out of ammunition, then abandoned ship.

At about the same time, *Bengal* was squaring off with *Hokoku Maru* again when Wilson reported '... another terrific explosion ... flames leapt hundreds of feet in the air, and when the smoke cleared away nothing could be seen'. Hoist by her own petard – *Hokoku Maru* had blown up.

This took the starch out of *Aikoku Maru*, which turned away to avoid sharing her sister's fate, and to search for and rescue any survivors – after her machine-gunners had fired parting shots at *Ondina*'s lifeboats. The raider's departure and the damage to their boats prompted the tankermen to reboard their ship and try to save her. This they eventually managed to do, putting out *Ondina*'s fires and making their way back to Fremantle. *Bengal*, which had miraculously emerged from the mêlée without a single casualty, proceeded to Colombo, Ceylon.

The little-known action fought so gallantly by *Bengal* and *Ondina* effectively brought Japan's fling with armed merchant cruisers to an end. During the next year *Aikoku Maru* and most of her cousins were re-rated as transports. The six that were not found themselves on the receiving end of Allied bombs, mines or torpedoes without accomplishing anything like the first successes of *Aikoku Maru* and *Hokoku Maru* ... modest those these had been. A final sortie into the Indian Ocean was made by two regular Japanese warships, the heavy cruisers *Chikuma* and *Tone*, which sank the 7,840-ton motor vessel *Behar* 720 miles south-west of Cocos Island on 9 March 1944 and brutally murdered most of her crew – for which atrocity Vice-Admiral Naomasa Sakonju and *Tone*'s Captain H. Mayazumi would be brought to justice after the war. By the time of that raid, all commerce raiding by the Japanese – on or below the sea – had already faded into insignificance against the crippling losses inflicted on their merchantmen and warships alike by the established master highwaymen of the Far Eastern oceans: Allied submarines.

References

Turner, L. F. C., Gordon-Cumming, H. R., and Betzler, J. E. *War in the Southern Oceans*, Oxford University Press, Cape Town, South Africa, 1961.

Watts, Anthony J. *Japanese Warships of World War II*, Doubleday & Co., Inc., Garden City, NY, 1967, pp. 317–18.

Additional information courtesy of the Imperial War Museum, London.

CHAPTER 12

Night of the Long Lance
Tassafaronga, 30 November 1942

November 1942 was the month in which Allied forces went on to the offensive all over the world. At El Alamein, German and Italian forces under Field Marshal Erwin Rommel were defeated and put to flight, with British General Bernard Law Montgomery's Eighth Army in hot pursuit. In Russia, the Germans abandoned all hope of taking the city of Stalingrad, and it became the survival of the German Sixth Army that was in doubt as the jaws of a massive Soviet trap began to close around it.

On the other side of the world, a series of fierce naval battles around the island of Guadalcanal reached its climax, leaving the American forces with almost complete control of the air and of the waters surrounding the island. In consequence, Japanese army forces on Guadalcanal were isolated from reinforcements and supplies, while units of the US Army's Americal Division could be shipped in to relieve the long-suffering Marines who had first landed, taken vital Henderson airfield and held it for three desperate, critical months. By the end of November 1942, it was no longer a question of whether Guadalcanal could be completely secured by the Americans, but a simple matter of when.

The Japanese navy recognised the inevitability of Guadalcanal's loss and was all in favour of evacuating the island. The Japanese army high command, however, rejected this proposal and repeated its standing demand for more troops and supplies.

Since August 1942, the task of bringing in reinforcements had been carried out primarily by the Japanese Destroyer Division 2 (Desdiv 2), commanded by Rear-Admiral Raizo Tanaka, which escorted transport ships down the passage known to the Americans as 'the Slot' because it lay between two roughly parallel island chains. The punctuality and seemingly unerring precision with which his ships made their nocturnal runs to 'Cactus', as the US forces code-named Guadalcanal, earned Tanaka's convoys the nickname of 'Cactus Express' by the Americans, a sobriquet that was later changed to 'Tokyo Express'. Tanaka himself earned a grudging degree of respect from his American adversaries – a

140

rare honour for a Japanese in those rancorous days – and acquired a nickname of his own: 'Tenacious Tanaka'. After losing seven out of eleven transports during the decisive naval battles between 13 and 15 November – some of which he had ordered run aground in order to get their cargoes ashore – Tanaka was called upon to use his own destroyers as fast transports, the use of slow-moving freighters being dispensed with entirely.

While visiting the Japanese naval base at Truk, Tanaka's chief of staff, Commander Yasumi Toyama, summed up Desdiv 2's new role during a conversation with his friend, Captain Tameichi Hara:

'We are more a freighter convoy than a fighting squadron these days. The damn Yankees have dubbed us the "Tokyo Express". We transport cargo to the cursed island, and our orders are to flee rather than fight. What a stupid thing! It is doubtful whether we could fight, anyway. Our decks are stacked so high with supplies for Guadalcanal that our ammunition supply must be cut in half. Our cargo is loaded in drums which are roped together. We approach near the island, throw them overboard and run away. The idea is that the strings of barrels will float until our troops on the island can tow them ashore. It is a strenuous and unsatisfying routine.'

Captain Hara's own destroyer, the *Amatsukaze*, had recently emerged from the confused night engagement of 13 November, where she had used her powerful 24in Type 93 torpedoes to sink the American destroyer *Barton* and cripple the light cruiser *Juneau*, which was later finished off by the submarine *I-26*. In that same engagement, *Amatsukaze* herself had come under fire from the American light cruiser *Helena*, and had to limp out of the fight on manual steering, with 43 of her crew dead. Hara had a respectable fighting record, and Commander Toyama asked him to recount his impressions on American and Japanese strengths, weaknesses and mistakes – including his own – that Hara had observed during the battle. Hara did so in an objective, professional manner, including what he regarded as the most important lesson he had learned in the recent night battles:

'Whatever our mission, we must always be ready for battle. I think it is wrong ever to consider fighting as merely secondary. Caution is necessary to be sure, but excessive caution is crippling. Please tell Admiral Tanaka not to repeat our mistakes.'

Soon after, Toyama flew back to Rabaul, Tanaka would have a fresh occasion to test the lessons that both he and Hara had learned the hard way. The situation was becoming desperate for the Japanese troops on Guadalcanal, from whom appeals for food and medicine were coming daily. On 27 November, Tanaka proposed to lead eight destroyers to the island, each loaded with at least 100 sealed metal drums containing food, medical supplies and just enough air to stay afloat. At about 200 to 300 metres from the shore off Tassafaronga, the drums would be rolled overboard, after which the soldiers would· swim out or use small boats to retrieve the precious cargo.

That evening, the Japanese relief force left Rabaul and steamed southwards for the Shortland Islands. Tanaka's flagship, the new destroyer *Naganami*, took the van position in his convoy, followed by the destroyers *Makinami*, *Oyashio*, *Kuroshio*, *Kagero*, *Kawakaze* and *Suzukaze*. About 3,000 metres ahead and slightly to port of the column, the destroyer *Takanami* served as a scout.

At 10.45 on the night of 29 November, Tanaka's force left the Shortlands for the final leg of its run. In an attempt to throw Allied observers off as to their intentions, the Japanese feinted east towards Roncador Reef and Ramos Island. Then, on the morning of November 30, the column again turned south for Guadalcanal.

The precautions proved futile. At 8 a.m., an Allied patrol plane spotted the Japanese convoy. Tanaka's doubts as to the secrecy of his mission were confirmed when he passed a Japanese observation post on Guadalcanal, which signalled that a dozen Allied destroyers had been observed off Lunga Point. True to his nickname, however, Tenacious Tanaka had no intention of turning back.

At 3 p.m., Tanaka issued a directive to his squadron: 'It is probable that we will encounter an enemy force tonight. Although our primary mission is to land supplies, everyone is to be ready for combat. If an engagement occurs, take the initiative and destroy the enemy.'

Meanwhile, coming to meet the Japanese was US Navy Task Force 67, a mixed unit of cruisers and destroyers commanded by Rear Admiral Carleton H. Wright. As other American admirals had done in past engagements, he advanced in an extended single-file formation, with the destroyers *Fletcher*, *Perkins*, *Maury* and *Drayton* in the van, followed by five cruisers, *Minneapolis*, *New Orleans*, *Pensacola*, *Honolulu* and *Northampton*. Two more destroyers, *Lamson* and *Lardner*, brought up the rear.

Fletcher, the lead destroyer in Wright's van, was the first of a new class, equipped with the latest SG radar, which was capable of producing an image on the screen. She was already a veteran, having been the only American ship to emerge completely undamaged from the wild night battle off Guadalcanal on 13 November. On that occasion, her radar had been wasted by her having been placed at the very rear of the American formation – a grievous error which Wright was clearly not about to repeat.

As Tanaka's column approached its drop-off point, everything was adding up to a crushing defeat for the Japanese and a glorious victory for the Americans. Although Tanaka knew that Allied units were in the area, he did not know where, nor did he know that there were powerful American cruisers as well as destroyers waiting to pulverise his 'tin cans'.

Forewarned and forearmed by Allied Intelligence, Wright 'crossed the T' of Tanaka's oncoming column. Tanaka did not realise that Wright was astride his path, nor did he suspect anything at 11.16 p.m., when *Fletcher*'s radar detected the Japanese destroyers, broad off the port bow, steaming slowly along the shoreline as they neared the rendezvous where they were to drop their cargo.

The time was ripe for slaughter, and *Fletcher*'s skipper, Commander William M. Cole, got on the talk between ships (TBS) system to Admiral Wright, fixing the enemy at a distance of 7,000 yards and requesting permission to launch his torpedoes.

At this point, things started to go awry for the Americans.

Uncertain as to whether the range was short enough for an effective engagement, Wright thought it over for a few minutes and asked Cole if he thought so. Cole replied in the affirmative, and at 11.20 Wright finally ordered the destroyers to loose their 'fish'. Cole eagerly complied with two salvos that sent a total of ten torpedoes spreading out from *Fletcher* toward the Japanese.

But Wright's four minutes of vacillation had changed the entire situation, for even at reduced speed the Japanese had not waited for his firing order. Tanaka's destroyers had passed *Fletcher*'s beam and moved away off the starboard quarter, opening up the range while the American destroyer men hastily re-adjusted their fire-controls. As a result, instead of a broadside shot with a favourable track-angle, *Fletcher* had to make do with a difficult shot up the sterns of the departing enemy vessels.

Behind *Fletcher*, *Perkins* fired eight torpedoes after Tanaka's destroyers. *Maury*, equipped with SC, an older, less effective model of radar, was unable to make out the enemy ships against the Guadalcanal coastline and refrained from wasting her 'fish'. Although similarly equipped, *Drayton* hazarded a shot with two of her torpedoes at an estimated range of 7,000 yards.

Meanwhile, with his column only 5,000 yards from the cargo-dropping point, Tanaka was busily studying his charts on the bridge of his flagship when *Naganami*'s lookouts reported seeing two torpedo wakes pass by the ship. Then a message came in from *Takanami*, his scout ship: 'Enemy ships bearing 100 degrees. Identified as three destroyers.'

Before Tanaka could react, *Takanami*, on her captain's own initiative, launched eight torpedoes at the Americans and then opened fire with her guns. A minute later, Tanaka ordered: 'Belay supply schedule! All ships, prepare to fight!'

Takanami paid the ultimate price for her brave but, as it turned out, rash decision to open fire. Deluged by 8- and 6in shells from all five

American cruisers, she was quickly set ablaze and stopped dead in the water.

But *Takanami's* sacrifice had not been in vain – Tanaka and his destroyermen saw to that. Shielding his flagship, and hence her radar signature, behind the burning scout ship, he brought *Naganami* around in a 180-degree turn, followed with remarkable precision by the other six destroyers, and placed his column on a parallel course with that of the Americans. Raising full speed, he led his ships closer to the cruisers, fixed the cruiser *Minneapolis* in *Naganami's* searchlight, opened fire with her 5in guns and then loosed a spread of eight torpedoes. His six consorts promptly followed suit.

Two of *Naganami's* torpedoes slammed into *Minneapolis*, shattering her bow and exploding her No. 2 boiler room. Flames leapt up forward of the cruiser's bridge, but moments later her bow collapsed just forward of No. 1 turret, scooping up a cascade of sea water which smothered the blaze. *Minneapolis'* forward guns fired three more times, then the electric power to the turret gave out. Moreover, with water filling her hull forward, her momentum was much reduced and she began to list slightly.

As *Minneapolis* slewed to a halt, *New Orleans* narrowly avoided a collision with her. Then another torpedo, launched by *Makinami*, hit *New Orleans* in the port bow, exploding two forward magazines and blowing off 120 feet of her forward section, right back to her No. 2 turret. The broken bow section slithered down her port side, gouging holes in the hull. As it passed by *New Orleans'* stern, some of the sailors farther aft believed that *Minneapolis* had just been sunk, and that their ship had run over her. All the men in *New Orleans'* forward section went down with it, while those aboard what remained of the ship laboured desperately to keep her afloat.

Pensacola, turning hard a-port to avoid a collision with the two cruisers in front of her, took a torpedo from *Kawakaze* that struck her port side directly below the mainmast, ignited her fuel tanks and transformed her into a floating torch.

Next in line was the light cruiser *Honolulu*, which reacted to *Pensacola's* sudden left-hand turn with a sharp turn in the opposite direction. Her swerve to starboard not only avoided a collision, but carried her clear of the glare of the burning heavy cruisers. *Honolulu* then zigzagged away to the north-west, untouched by torpedoes or gunfire.

Northampton, at the end of the line, was unaware of what was going on until she got closer to her now-burning colleagues. She was about to follow *Honolulu* to the north-west when her lookout spotted some Japanese destroyers dashing off to the west. *Northampton's* skipper decided to give chase and turned west, firing a blind, ineffective salvo with her 8in guns. Then, she herself was suddenly hit in the port side by two of eight torpedoes launched by *Kagero* and *Oyashio*. A monstrous explosion rocked the big cruiser, then flames swept over her.

While Tanaka's squadron swung north-west at full speed, *Honolulu*, which was running a parallel course with them, found two more destroyers coming up from the other side and fired on them until they turned and fled. Her captain and crew later learned to their regret that the ships they had been shooting at had been their own rearguard – *Lamson* and *Larner*.

As *Naganami* retired with her torpedo tubes empty and some shell splinters in her rear stack, Tanaka tried to contact *Takanami*, but got only silence. Not long afterwards, *Oyashio* and *Kuroshio* found *Takanami*'s burned-out hulk lying motionless off Cape Esperance. *Oyashio* was lowering her lifeboats and *Kuroshio* was about to come alongside when ominous silhouettes, identified as two cruisers and three destroyers, were sighted looming out of the darkness. The two Japanese ships withdrew, leaving *Takanami*'s 211 crewmen to their own devices. Remarkably, *Takanami* had lowered a cutter full of army troops during the action, and after she finally sank, a number of her crew also managed to swim ashore.

Tanaka put fifty miles between his ships and Guadalcanal before slowing to take stock of his losses. Aside from the loss of *Takanami* and the splinter damage to *Naganami*, there had been no other damage inflicted on his ships and no losses to their crews. Still grieving over the loss of *Takanami*, Tanaka considered the idea of returning to Tassafaronga to rescue any survivors and take on the Americans if they tried to interfere. Taking inventory of his available resources, he learned that a total of 44 torpedoes had been fired. Of his seven destroyers, four had expended all their torpedoes, one had fired half its supply and two – *Kuroshio* and *Suzukaze* – had not fired at all because they had been at a bad angle during their firing runs. Tanaka finally concluded that his ships were no longer fit to engage the enemy and ordered them to return to Rabaul.

Tanaka's prudence may have made a vital difference to three badly damaged American cruisers, which might have been scuttled, had he made a return appearance. His retirement left their hard-pressed crews free to concentrate on saving their ships, during which the sailors aboard *Minneapolis* and *New Orleans* demonstrated that a lot had been learned about damage control since the loss of their sisters, *Astoria*, *Quincy* and *Vincennes*, off Savo Island on 9 August 1942. After a masterful display of courage and ingenuity on the part of her crew, *Minneapolis* was able to raise three knots. *New Orleans*' crew, too, managed to keep her afloat during a painfully slow passage to Tulagi.

Pensacola's crew had even more problems to overcome. While one engine room was completely flooded and power was lost in three of her four turrets, it was fire, fed by ruptured oil tanks, that threatened her survival as it raged over her rear quarter and set off secondary explosions in her ammunition supply. Working throughout the following morning, *Pensacola*'s crew finally managed to put out the last of the fires at about noon, by which time her total casualties amounted to 125 dead and 68 wounded.

Northampton, too, was in serious trouble. Water was pouring in through the two torpedo gashes in the port quarter of her hull and the area around her mainmast was ablaze, cutting the forward and aft damage control parties off from one another. The influx of water could not be stemmed and after three hours she was settling by the stern while her crew began to abandon ship.

Much later, in a 1983 reunion, *Northampton*'s veterans would express long-harboured resentment toward *Honolulu*'s crew for not stopping to pick them up, but the undamaged light cruiser was carrying out specific orders to seek out the enemy and continue the fight rather than engage in rescue work. Still under fire – some of it from American ships – *Honolulu*'s commander ordered two destroyers to rescue survivors from the other cruisers. In consequence, it was to be the destroyer *Fletcher* that would be honoured by *Northampton*'s survivors for her timely arrival and the alacrity with which she fished them out of Guadalcanal's notoriously shark-infested waters. Remarkably, only 58 of *Northampton*'s sailors died – less than half the casualties suffered by *Pensacola* – while 773 were rescued.

At Tulagi, *New Orleans* had her lost bows covered over by jury-rigged patches made of coconut logs. Later, in Australia, a temporary metal bow section was fitted for the long trip back to Bremerton, Washington, where her bows were completely reconstructed. A few days after *Minneapolis'* arrival at Tulagi, the temporary repair work of crewmen and Seabees on her was almost rendered in vain when a gas explosion nearly sank her, but by 12 December she was on her way to Espiritu Santo for the temporary metal bows. From there, she steamed to Pearl Harbor and San Francisco for the installation of new bows. *Pensacola*, too, went to Espiritu Santo for more substantial repairs before setting out for Pearl Harbor, where she would undergo permanent repairs. *Minneapolis* rejoined the US fleet in August 1943, joined by *New Orleans* in October, but *Pensacola* did not return to service until November of that year.

With only one heavy cruiser permanently lost, the Battle of Tassafaronga would hardly rate among the most grievous defeats in US naval history, but it may well be the most humiliating. Task Force 67 had all the advantages that night: overwhelming firepower, advance intelligence, superior night detection equipment, a well-laid trap and the element of surprise. Yet, in an action lasting fifteen minutes, a surprised enemy had turned the tables on the Americans and given them a sound thrashing – all because of a four-minute delay, poor communications and the fatally unanimous decision by all the cruisers' commanders to concentrate their fire on the same enemy ship.

Even at the time, however, the Americans also placed credit for the débâcle where it was due – on the quick-thinking professionalism of the Japanese destroyermen and the outstanding leadership of their commander. Naval historian and Second World War veteran Rear Admiral Samuel Eliot Morison wrote: 'It is always some consolation to reflect that the enemy who defeats you is really good, and Rear-Admiral Tanaka was better than that – he was superb ... In many actions of the war, mistakes on the American side were cancelled by those of the enemy; but despite the brief confusion of his destroyers, Tanaka made no mistakes at Tassafaronga.'

It might have surprised the Americans to have known of how unenthusiastically Tanaka's superiors took the news of the night action. Although Tanaka's initial claim to have sunk a battleship and two cruisers and damaged four other cruisers was a considerable exaggeration, the truth was impressive enough. Even that, however, made less of an impression on his commanders than did his decision to retire to Rabaul without having unloaded the vitally needed supplies at Guadalcanal. In so doing, he failed to accomplish his mission which, in the technical sense, rendered Tassafaronga a strategic defeat for the Japanese.

Tanaka himself, discussing the battle at his little farm fifteen years after the war with his colleague, Tameichi Hara, was more critical of himself than his American opponents had been:

'I have heard that the US naval experts praised my command in that action. I am not deserving of such honours. It was the superb proficiency and devotion of the men who served me that produced the tactical victory for us.

'In this I am not rejecting glory in order to escape criticism. I accept the principal criticism levelled by fellow officers. It was an error on my part not to deliver the supplies according to schedule. I should have returned to do so. The delivery mission was abandoned simply because we did not have accurate information about the strength of the enemy force ... I saw no percentage in having our seven destroyers, low on ammunition and decks loaded with cargo drums, fight another running battle against eight US destroyers. Had I but known that only one cruiser and four destroyers remained in fighting trim! ...

'We were able to defeat Admiral Wright's ships in this action only because of *Takanami*. She absorbed all the punishment of the enemy in the opening moments of the battle, and she shielded the rest of us. Yet we left the scene without doing anything for her or her valiant crew.'

On 3 December, Tanaka had the opportunity to redeem himself. Commanding a force of four cruisers and eleven destroyers, he came prepared for trouble, but no surface force awaited him that night – the Americans were still licking their wounds after the beating they had taken on the last night of November. Some American aircraft attacked Tanaka's convoy, but only succeeded in causing light damage to a destroyer. A total of 1,500 drums of supplies were successfully dropped off Guadalcanal.

On 7 December, Tanaka led eleven destroyers down the Slot, but this time the Americans were waiting for him. During the day, aircraft from Henderson Field attacked. A near miss blew in the side of the destroyer *Nowaki*, flooding her engine room and boiler room and killing seventeen of her crew. *Tachikaze*'s bows were blown off and she too was forced to retire. That night, eight PT (patrol torpedo) boats harassed Tanaka's force, *PT-59* getting into a close-range gun duel with *Oyashio* that resulted in the destroyer scoring ten small-calibre hits on the torpedo-boat and taking ten casualties herself from *PT-59*'s machine-gun fire. Tanaka finally decided to call off the operation and returned to base.

On the night of 11 December, Tanaka tried again with a convoy of nine destroyers. An American air attack was brushed off, but as the Japanese reached Blackett Strait, they were again ambushed by PT boats. *PT-44* scored two torpedo hits on Tanaka's flagship, the destroyer *Teruzuki*, setting her aflame and slightly wounding Tanaka himself. He transferred his flag and, despite valiant efforts at damage control, *Teruzuki*'s fires reached her depth-charge stowage, the resultant explosions forcing her crew to abandon her. The rest of Tanaka's 'Express' arrived on schedule and dropped 1,200 supply drums, but he later learned to his chagrin that only 220 of them were recovered by Guadalcanal's garrison.

While in hospital at Rabaul, Tanaka dictated a memorandum to the naval high command, recommending that Guadalcanal be evacuated. The response was an order re-assigning him to Singapore. After leading one more transport run on 15 December, he was formally relieved of command by Rear-Admiral Tomiji Koyonagi.

For a time, the Japanese effort to support its hopeless campaign on Guadalcanal continued, using submarines as well as destroyers, but no more than a trickle of supplies got through, while the Japanese position on the island became completely untenable. Finally, in the first week of February 1943, Japan's high command bowed to the inevitable. With stunning efficiency, Koyonagi supervised three destroyer runs that evacuated the last of the 11,000 Japanese troops from Guadalcanal on 8 February 1943. The next day, troops of the Americal Division swept the western side of the island and discovered to their surprise that there were no Japanese left. Their commander, Major General Alexander M. Patch, radioed a message to Admiral William F. Halsey: 'Total and complete defeat of Japanese forces on Guadalcanal effected today ... Tokyo Express no longer has terminus on Guadalcanal.'

Rear-Admiral Raizo Tanaka was never placed in command of another destroyer division for the rest of the war – a misuse of his talents by the Japanese high command for which the US Navy, in retrospect, could feel profoundly grateful. Retiring quietly to a small farm after the war, Tanaka died in 1959, honoured as much by the Americans who once fought him as he was by the destroyer captains who had served under him.

References

Coombe, Jack D. *Derailing the Tokyo Express*, Stackpole Books, Harrisburg, PA, 1991,

Ewing, Steve. *American Cruisers of World War II: A Pictorial Encyclopedia*, Pictorial Histories Publishing Company, Missoula, MT, 1984.

Hara, Tameichi, Saito, Fred, and Pineau, Roger. *Japanese Destroyer Captain*, Ballantine Books, New York, NY, 1972.

Morison, Samuel Eliot. *The Two-Ocean War, The Definitive Short History of the United States Navy in World War II*, Ballantine Books, New York, NY, 1972.

Roscoe, Theodore. *Tin Cans, the True Story of the Fighting Destroyers of World War II*, Bantam Books, New York, NY, 1968.

CHAPTER 13
Fighting Retreat
Samar, 25 October 1944

Even with a historian son to prompt his memory, former US Navy Photographer's Mate 3rd Class Paul D. Guttman's recollections of the action were sketchy – most of the memories blocked out by subconscious choice. As a combat cameraman for CINCPAC (Commander-in-Chief, Pacific) he vaguely recalled being aboard the escort carrier *Fanshaw Bay*, making a brief stop there while being transported from the US Navy oiler *Cache* to the aircraft carrier *Hornet*, operating with Admiral William F. Halsey's Third Fleet. Only one memory stands out in stark relief: 'I saw those shells travelling through the air.'

What he was witness to was one of the most improbable scenarios in the annals of naval warfare – and one of the most desperately heroic actions in US naval history.

It was the morning of 25 October 1944. Five days earlier, the first of 103,000 troops of Lieutenant General Walter Krueger's Sixth Army had splashed ashore on the island of Leyte and secured the local capital of Tacloban, thus beginning the fulfilment of General Douglas MacArthur's vow to return to the Philippines, from which he had been ignominiously driven by the Japanese two and a half years earlier. Supporting the troops was Vice Admiral Thomas C. Kincaid's Seventh Fleet, a mixed bag of veteran American and Australian warships that included an air element of escort carriers, Task Group 77.4, under the command of Rear Admiral Thomas L. Sprague. Also providing protection for the landing was Halsey's Third Fleet, a fast attack force made up of the newest and most potent fleet carriers and surface warships in the US Navy.

The Imperial Japanese Navy had tried to oppose the landing, but thus far it had been mauled in every attempt, in the Sibuyan Sea and at Surigao Strait. And then, everything went terribly wrong for the Americans as a large Japanese battle fleet appeared, seemingly out of nowhere, off the island of Samar. Suddenly, the American beachhead was in serious jeopardy. And the only thing standing between the Japanese and their objective was a small escort carrier unit which was fighting for its own survival.

Since the Battle of the Philippine Sea on 19–20 June 1944, during which the carrier air component of the Japanese Combined Fleet was dec-

150

imated in what the Americans came to call 'The Great Marianas Turkey Shoot', the Imperial Navy lacked the ability to engage the US Navy on equal terms, even though it still boasted some of the most powerful surface warships in the world. To a good many Japanese admirals, it seemed as though they would be utterly powerless to contribute any further to the empire's defence – a prospect they regarded as intolerable.

The American invasion of Leyte cast a faint ray of light over that gloomy picture. The Philippines offered hundreds of islands among which the Japanese ships could hide from American aircraft and radar. There, then, their fleet might yet strike a resounding blow against the enemy. The chances of success remained slim, but it was the last remaining opportunity of any sort, and the Japanese admiralty, under Admiral Soemu Toyoda, seized upon it for all it was worth by formulating Operation 'Sho-1' ('Victory').

Similar to earlier operations devised by Toyoda's late predecessor, Admiral Isoroku Yamamoto, 'Sho-1' was a complex scheme that depended largely on the use of a decoy force to lure a sizeable portion of the American fleet away from the target area. The decoy was a small task force built around four aircraft carriers (*Zuikaku*, *Zuiho*, *Chitose* and *Chiyoda*) and two old battleships (*Ise* and *Hyuga*), commanded by Vice-Admiral Jisaburo Ozawa and given the misleading designation of 'Main Body'. Ozawa's sacrificial mission was to stand off the northern Philippines until he attracted a large element of Halsey's Third Fleet, then retire northward, leading the Americans on while staving off destruction of his own fleet for as long as possible.

While Halsey's fleet was so occupied, three other Japanese strike forces would move on Leyte Gulf from two directions. Vice-Admirals Shoji Nishimura and Kiyohide Shima were to combine their two units and attack the beachhead from the south, via Surigao Strait. At the same time, the most powerful Japanese element, called the First Striking Force, was to come down from the north through San Bernardino Strait, destroying any Allied warships that barred its path before annihilating the American beachhead under a deluge of shells.

Commanded by Vice-Admiral Takeo Kurita in the heavy cruiser *Atago*, the First Striking Force's main punch was provided by the battleships *Yamato*, *Musashi*, *Nagato*, *Kongo* and *Haruna*, and heavy cruisers *Atago*, *Takao*, *Chokai*, *Maya*, *Myoko*, *Haguro*, *Kumano*, *Suzuya*, *Chikuma* and *Tone*. They were escorted by two destroyer squadrons. Desron 2, commanded by Rear-Admiral Mikio Hayakawa, consisted of the light cruiser *Noshiro* and the destroyers *Shimakaze*, *Hayashimo*, *Akishimo*, *Kishinami*, *Okinami*, *Naganami*, *Akishimo*, *Hamanami* and *Fujinami*. Desron 10, under Rear-Admiral Susumu Kimura, was composed of the light cruiser *Yahagi* and the destroyers *Nowaki*, *Kiyoshimo*, *Urakaze*, *Yukikaze*, *Hamakaze* and *Isokaze*.

'*Sho-1*' did not get off to a promising start. Just after midnight on the morning of 23 October, Kurita's force was rounding the north-western tip of Borneo when it was sighted and waylaid by two American submarines, *Darter* and *Dace*. *Darter*'s torpedoes sank *Atago* and so damaged her sister, *Takao*, that she had to withdraw for repairs, while *Dace* sank *Maya*. In the course of trying to escape vengeful Japanese destroyers, *Darter* ran aground and became a total loss, but her entire crew evacuated safely.

After being fished from the sea, a shaken Kurita resumed command aboard the giant battleship *Yamato* and pressed on. About 24 hours later, however, he was spotted in Philippine waters by night-flying American reconnaissance aircraft. On the morning of 24 October, 150 aircraft from Vice-Admiral Shigeru Fukudome's Luzon-based Second Air Fleet tried to take some pressure off Kurita by attacking Rear Admiral Frederick C. Sherman's Task Group 38.3. They managed to sink the light carrier *Princeton* and caused heavy damage to the light cruiser *Birmingham*, but they were slaughtered in the process, Commander David McCampbell from the carrier *Essex* personally accounting for nine aircraft while leading Grumman F6F Hellcat fighters of his Air Group 9 against the attackers.

At the same time, Rear Admiral Gerald F. Bogan's Task Group 38.2 launched its air element against Kurita's force in the Sibuyan Sea. Brushing aside a puny air screen from Fukudome's depleted Second Air Fleet, Bogan's air groups – later joined by those of Sherman's task group – concentrated on *Yamato*'s sister, the 72,609-ton super battleship *Musashi*, finally sinking her after scoring nineteen torpedo and seventeen bomb hits on her. The heavy cruiser *Myoko* was also damaged by a torpedo hit and had to retire.

Elsewhere, aircraft of Rear Admiral Ralph E. Davison's Task Group 38.4 were attacking Nishimura's Force C in the Sulu Sea, inflicting minor damage to the battleship *Fuso* and the destroyer *Shigure*, but failing to deflect Nishimura from his determined course towards Surigao Strait.

Having seen one of the two largest battleships in the world overwhelmed, Kurita was less determined than Nishimura; he turned westwards to regroup beyond the range of the American carrier aircraft. Admiral Halsey learned of Kurita's retirement and, at about 4 p.m., he also received a report from a Curtiss SB2C Helldiver crew that they had spotted Ozawa's carrier force to the north, off Cape Engano. Convinced that the beating Kurita had taken in the Sibuyan Sea had eliminated him as a threat, and unaware that Ozawa's impotent carriers posed far less of a danger to the Leyte operation, Halsey gathered all three of his available carrier task groups and combined them with an escort of four battleships, five light cruisers and fourteen destroyers under Vice Admiral Willis A. Lee, dubbing the resultant composite unit Task Force 34. Halsey then headed north, leaving the northern approach to Leyte Gulf wide open. In drawing the most powerful units of the Third Fleet away from San Bernardino Strait, Ozawa's contribution to 'Sho-1' was succeeding beyond all expectations.

Unaware of this development, at 6.15 p.m. Kurita was still trying to decide what to do next when he received a message from Admiral Toyoda in Japan that made up his mind for him: 'With confidence in heavenly guidance the combined force will attack.' In essence, it was a chiding reminder that retirement was not an option, and Kurita dutifully turned his force eastwards again.

On the night of 24 October, the Leyte beachhead was being guarded only by its direct naval support component, the Seventh Fleet, the most powerful units being drawn south to meet Nishimura and Shima's forces at Surigao Strait. The result was an almost perfect ambush, with Allied battleships, cruisers and destroyers killing Nishimura and sinking the battleships *Yamashiro* and *Fuso*, the heavy cruiser *Mogami* and the destroyers *Asagumo*, *Michishio* and *Yamagumo*, while a motor torpedo-boat, *PT-137*, scored a crippling torpedo hit on the light cruiser *Abukuma*. The Americans paid for this overwhelming success with the loss of *PT-493* and damage to the destroyer *Albert W. Grant*.

The southern threat to the Leyte beachhead had been eliminated, but at the cost of drawing most of the Seventh Fleet away from the northern approaches. Meanwhile, as the 65 ships of Halsey's Task Force 34 steamed north at 16 knots to engage Ozawa's 17-ship decoy force, Kurita's First Striking Force made its way through San Bernardino Strait, guided by shore lights set up by Japanese army troops. As fortune would decree, a Consolidated PBY 'Black Cat' flying-boat, sent by Kincaid on a routine mission to reconnoitre the northern approaches to Leyte Gulf, passed over San Bernardino Strait just before Kurita arrived.

So it was that the Japanese First Striking Force managed to steam 150 miles in seven hours, completely undetected. Unknown to Kurita, the only obstacle that now lay between him and his objective were the escort carriers (CVEs), of the Seventh Fleet's air component, Rear Admiral Thomas L. Sprague's Task Group 77.4.

Even without Halsey's fast carriers, Task Group 77.4 was a formidable deterrent in itself, being comprised of sixteen escort carriers, 21 destroyers and destroyer escorts (DEs), and 444 aircraft – more than double the number of aircraft that the Japanese had in the Philippines. Although the CVEs were smaller, slower and more vulnerable than fleet carriers, their aircraft carried the same loads of bombs, torpedoes and bullets as those serving their larger cousins – and could deal out just as much punishment to enemy ships.

Working in Kurita's favour, however, was the fact that Sprague's group was divided into three task units, referred to on the radio as

'Taffies'. On the morning of 25 October, Task Unit 77.4.1, or Taffy 1, was lying off Mindanao under Tom Sprague's personal command and committing its aircraft to the pursuit of what remained of Nishimura and Shima's decimated forces following the Battle of Surigao Strait. Taffy 2, under Rear Admiral Felix B. Stump, was lying off the entrance to Leyte Gulf, while Taffy 3, commanded by Rear Admiral Clifton A. F. Sprague (no relation to Thomas Sprague), lay fifty miles north, off the southern coast of Samar Island – and right in the path of Kurita's First Striking Force.

Clifton 'Ziggy' Sprague's flagship was the escort carrier *Fanshaw Bay*, conned by Captain D. P. Johnson. In company with *Fanshaw Bay* were the escort carriers *St. Lo*, *White Plains* and *Kalinin Bay*, together with two others of Rear Admiral Ralph A. Ofstie's Carrier Division 26, *Kitkun Bay* and *Gambier Bay*. Their combined air element was made up of 97 FM-2s (General Motors-built versions of the Grumman F4F Wildcat), 71 TBM-1Cs (General Motors-built Grumman TBF-1C Avengers) and one TBF-1C. The screening force for the carriers, Destroyer Division 95 led by Commander William D. Thomas, consisted of the destroyers *Hoel* (Thomas's flagship), *Heermann* and *Johnston*, and the destroyer escorts *Dennis*, *John C. Butler*, *Raymond* and *Samuel B. Roberts*.

For Taffy 3, the morning of October 25 began at 5.30 with the dispatch of a combat air patrol (CAP) of twelve fighters over Leyte Gulf, followed at 6.07 by an anti-submarine patrol by four TBMs, escorted by two FM-2s. Just before sunrise, between 6.14 and 6.27, the crews secured from general quarters and settled down to breakfast before resuming what looked like a routine day's operations.

The routine ended at 6.44, when a lookout at *Yamato*'s masthead sighted several American carriers. A minute later, Ensign William Brooks, piloting one of *Kalinin Bay*'s sub-hunting TBMs, saw ships coming from the north and flew towards them to investigate, to be greeted with a ragged volley of anti-aircraft fire. At 6.46, *Fanshaw Bay* made an 'unidentified radar contact', and a man on her radar watch heard what he thought were 'Japs gabbling' on the inter-fighter direction net. At 6.47, TBM pilot Ensign Hans L. Jensen from Taffy 2's *Kadashan Bay* reported seeing four Japanese battleships, eight cruisers and a number of destroyers twenty miles from Taffy 3. He made a glide-bombing approach on one cruiser and reported that he was being fired at. Reckoning it more likely that Jensen was attacking ships of the Third Fleet, Sprague replied with an urgent cry of: 'Check identification!' But Jensen's radar operator, Radioman D. G. Lehman, confirmed what Sprague's own lookouts were now seeing: the distinctive pagoda masts of Japanese warships. Any last doubts evaporated at 6.58, when the Japanese opened fire, raising coloured shell splashes just astern of Taffy 3's ships.

Aboard *Yamato*, Kurita was just as surprised as Sprague. Typically for both sides throughout the war, he over-estimated the size of the ships he observed to the south-east. In Japanese eyes, the escort carriers seemed to be *Independence*-class light carriers, or even large fleet carriers. Destroyers became cruisers, even battleships, while DEs became destroyers. Kurita thought that he had run into a component of Halsey's Third Fleet.

The captains of the Japanese ships were elated at the prospect of using their guns. Only Kurita was uneasy. On first sighting the Americans, he ordered his four columns of ships to regroup in a circular anti-aircraft formation, but before this directive was carried out, he cancelled it by signalling: 'General Attack!' Kurita apparently felt that, given the threat of the aircraft carriers, his only hope lay in his ships closing to gunnery range with them as quickly as possible, and that there was no time to organise a line of battle. In consequence, however, he was committing his ships piecemeal, leaving each to its own initiative but depriving his fleet of the combined might that would have made it most effective. Even so, two loose columns of cruisers were soon closing in on the Americans from the port quarter, while the battleships were dead astern. 'A perfect set-up to polish off this unit,' remarked Captain D. J. Sullivan of the CVE *White Plains*. 'We could only go in the direction the Japs wanted to go themselves, to Leyte Gulf.'

Sprague, meanwhile, tried to make the most of his resources. Turning his carriers due east so that they could launch into the wind, he ordered their speed up to 16 knots, then to flank speed of 17½ knots. Every operational aircraft was to be launched and all ships were to make smoke.

At 6.30, Admiral Kincaid was holding a leisurely breakfast conference aboard his flagship, the amphibious command ship *Wasatch*, lying in San Pedro Bay, between Leyte and Samar, when he learned that Halsey had gone north with his entire fast carrier force, leaving the northern approaches to Leyte Gulf unprotected and vulnerable. Half an hour later, at 7.02 a.m., Kincaid received even more alarming news: Taffy 3 was under attack.

Kincaid responded to Clifton Sprague's plea for assistance by calling his units north. Thomas Sprague requested and got immediate permission from Kincaid to launch all his available aircraft against the Japanese. Sprague's own Taffy 1 lay 130 miles south by east from Taffy 3, but Felix Stump's Taffy 2 was much closer. Within ten minutes of the Japanese opening fire, every operational aircraft in Task Group 77.4 was either flying to Taffy 3's aid or on the flight decks, being readied for take-off. Meanwhile, officers in *Fanshaw Bay* took some grim amusement in the way Stump's voice rose in excitement as he tried to assure Clifton Sprague over the TBS (talk between ships) system: 'Don't be alarmed,

Ziggy – remember, we're in back of you – don't get excited – don't do anything rash!'

'Ziggy' Sprague was, in fact, doing nothing rash – most of his actions that morning were about the best that could be made under the circumstances. Even so, at 6.59, shells began falling near his flagship even as she got eleven torpedo-bombers and the last of her fighters off the deck. Three 14in shells, loaded with dyes to mark their fall for Japanese observers, straddled *White Plains*, throwing up yellow and purple geysers of water. 'They're shooting at us in Technicolor!' cried one of *White Plains'* seamen. While Kurita's ships were independently sniping at targets of opportunity, a similar problem was being faced by Commander Robert L. Fowler, leader of the air group on Ofstie's flagship *Kitkun Bay*. Staying aloft throughout the battle for a total of eight hours, he tried to co-ordinate air strikes against the Japanese, but found it virtually impossible to do so – the majority of air attacks were being carried out in twos and threes.

At 7.06, Taffy 3 passed into the temporary sanctuary of a rain squall and Sprague decided, now that his aircraft were launched, to change course to south-southwest, hoping to meet help from the rest of the Seventh Fleet as he made for Leyte Gulf. At 7.15, Taffy 3 emerged from the squall and, one minute later, Sprague ordered his three destroyers, *Hoel*, *Heermann* and *Johnston*, to conduct a torpedo attack on the enemy ships.

Johnston was closest to the Japanese when they attacked, and she had already engaged them before Sprague issued his order. Just two days short of a year old, *Johnston* was nicknamed 'GQ Johnny' because she had been at General Quarters so often in her short operational life, during which she assisted fellow destroyers *Franks* and *Haggard* in the destruction of a Japanese submarine, *I-176*, off Cape Alexander, Buka, on 16 May 1944. Now, on sighting Kurita's force, *Johnston's* Cherokee Indian skipper, Commander Ernest E. Evans, called all hands to general quarters once more and ordered them to 'prepare to attack major portion of Japanese Fleet'.

Dashing at a Japanese heavy cruiser column amid the splashes of several cruisers' guns, *Johnston* concentrated on the leading ship, *Kumano*, and fired about 200 5in shells at her. When Evans got Sprague's order to commence a torpedo attack, he was already in the best position to comply. Raising her speed to 25 knots, *Johnston* closed to 10,000 yards of *Kumano* and fired off all ten of her 'tin fish', then turned and retired under smoke. *Johnston's* senior surviving officer later claimed to have observed two or three explosions. Kurita reported only one, but it blew the bows off *Kumano*, flagship of Cruiser Division 7. Vice-Admiral Kazutaka Shiraishi transferred his flag to *Suzuya*, but she was already so badly damaged by aerial bombs that both ships had to drop out of the fight.

Moments after scoring her torpedo hit, *Johnston* paid for her audacity. Her senior surviving officer later wrote: 'At this time, about 0730, this ship got it. Three 14in shells from a battleship, followed thirty seconds later by three 6in shells from a light cruiser, hit us. It was like a puppy being smacked by a truck. These hits knocked out the after boiler room and engine room, lost all power to the steering engine, all power to the after three 5in guns and rendered the gyro compass useless.'

Sliced from the mast by an enemy shell, *Johnston*'s SC radar crashed down to the bridge, killing three officers. Evans' clothes above the waist were blown off, and two fingers of his left hand. Her speed reduced to 17 knots, *Johnston* was afforded a much-needed 10-minute reprieve by a rain squall, while steering was shifted to manual aft, damage was assessed and brought under control, and enough power was restored to allow partial fire control for two of her guns.

Aboard *Hoel*, Commander Leon S. Kintberger set course for the battleship *Kongo*, 7½ miles north-east of where *Johnston* had engaged *Kumano*. At 14,000 yards' range, the antagonists opened fire on each other. At 7.25, *Kongo* scored a hit on *Hoel*'s bridge that knocked out all voice radio communication. At 9,000 yards, *Hoel* launched a half-salvo of torpedoes, but *Kongo* avoided the four that her crew spotted by making a sharp turn to port. *Hoel* took more hits in her after boiler room and after turbine, knocking out three guns and the port engine, and jamming the rudder hard right. Before steering control was shifted aft, *Hoel* found herself coming straight at *Kongo*, firing her two remaining guns at the battleship until she miraculously steamed clear.

Despite the beating *Hoel* had taken, Desdiv 95's Commander Thomas was still determined to carry out his orders to divert major gun fire from the CVEs, and ordered torpedoes launched at the leader of another heavy cruiser column, *Haguro*. At 7.50, 'using manual train and selective aim with the torpedo officer in No. 2 mount due to the loss of communications with the torpedo mounts', another half-salvo was fired at 6,000 yards, at an angle of 50 degrees. The Americans claimed to have seen 'large columns of water rise from the cruiser at about the time scheduled for the torpedo run', but *Haguro*'s log stated that all the torpedoes had, in fact, missed.

At 7.42, Sprague ordered a second attack by his 'Wolves', as he code-named the destroyers. *Heermann*, which had been on the disengaged side of the escort carrier formation, had been too late to join *Johnston* and *Hoel* in their first attacks; now she raced forward to take part in the second one. Also lending their four sets of twin 5in guns and three torpedoes to the fight were Taffy 3's destroyer escorts, or 'Little Wolves'. During the first attack, Lieutenant Commander Robert W. Copeland, captain of the DE *Samuel B. Roberts*, had asked Commander Thomas: 'Do you want Little Wolves to go in with Wolves?' 'Negative,' Thomas had replied, but added, 'Little Wolves form up for second attack.' Now the time had come, but having been designed for anti-submarine duties, the DEs had no experience in 'forming up'. Because of the off-and-on visibility amid the smoke and squalls, *Heermann* almost collided with *Roberts* as she rushed to join *Hoel* for the second strike. Instead of locating her sisters, *Roberts* followed 3,000 yards astern of *Hoel* and *Heermann*.

At 7.50, just as Sprague ordered his second torpedo attack to get under way, *Johnston* emerged from a rain squall. 'GQ Johnny' had no torpedoes left, but as he passed the two destroyers and one escort, Commander Evans roared out: 'We'll go in with the destroyers and provide fire support!' *Johnston* then turned and took up the rearmost position in the column.

At 7.54, *Heermann* launched seven torpedoes at *Haguro*. They missed, as did the fifteen shells *Haguro* fired at her attacker. Even as her first torpedo salvo was being fired, *Heermann*'s gunnery officer, Lieutenant W. W. Meadows, spotted another column of large Japanese ships on the port bow – *Kongo*, followed by *Haruna* and, in the distance behind them, *Yamato* and *Nagato*. Climbing atop the fire control column, *Heermann*'s skipper, Commander Amos T. Hathaway, ordered a course change to 270 degrees and shifted 5in gunfire to *Kongo*'s pagoda-like bridge. Despite yellow dye-filled 14in shells that splashed around her with increasing accuracy, *Heermann* avoided being hit long enough to close to 4,400 yards of *Haruna*, at which point she fired her three remaining torpedoes at that ship before turning back to rejoin the carriers, pursued by more shells.

Thanks to some skilful smoke-laying, Taffy 3's destroyer escorts came within 4,000 yards of the Japanese heavy cruisers before launching their 'fish'. *Roberts* aimed all three of hers at an '*Aoba* class' cruiser, which was probably *Chokai*, but the Japanese ship evaded them – as did all the other enemy vessels at which the American destroyers launched their torpedoes. *Roberts* then retired while trading shots with one of the enemy cruisers, miraculously escaping unhit.

Of the other DEs, *John C, Butler* was trying to find the senior ship of her unit, *Dennis*, while Commander A. F. Beyer of the *Raymond*, hearing Sprague's torpedo attack order, automatically assumed that it applied to him and proceeded independently northwards until he encountered the lead Japanese ship, *Haguro*. At 7.55, *Haguro* turned her 8-inchers on *Raymond* and dropped a salvo 200 yards astern of her. A minute later, *Raymond* launched torpedoes at a range of 6,000 yards. Fate played *Raymond* false, however, for at that moment *Haguro* was beginning evasive action against other torpedoes – probably from American aircraft – in the process of which the Japanese reported seeing two of *Raymond*'s 'fish' pass close astern. *Raymond* then retired, pursued by more salvos from *Haguro*.

Meanwhile, *Dennis* had advanced independently and was a mile south-east of *Raymond* when she encountered *Haguro* and dodged some salvos from that cruiser between 7.52 and 7.55. *Dennis* launched an ambitious spread of three torpedoes at the second and third enemy cruisers in line – *Chokai* and *Tone* – before turning back at 8.02, trading gunfire with a Japanese cruiser that was also under air attack, before taking up formation with *Heermann*, *Johnston* and *Roberts*. *Dennis'* last-mentioned adversary may again have been *Haguro*, which had her No. 2 turret knocked out by a bomb hit at about 8.00. *Dennis* escaped unscathed.

The carriers, too, were getting involved in the gunplay. At 7.50, *Kalinin Bay* took the first of thirteen damaging 8in hits, but as the range closed to 10,000 yards, her 5in gun crew had the satisfaction of scoring a hit on the No. 2 turret of a Japanese cruiser. Sprague's flagship, *Fanshaw Bay*, took four 8in hits and two near misses, which killed three of her crew and wounded twenty. *White Plains* was grazed by a 6.1in salvo, while *Kitkun Bay* sustained shell fragment casualties from near misses. A 14- or 16in shell went through *Kalinin Bay* without exploding, the only direct hit scored by a battleship on any of the carriers. Although badly holed and suffering the loss of her main steering control, *Kalinin Bay* stayed in formation thanks to the Herculean efforts of her engineers and firemen, while quartermasters steered her by hand.

Throughout the running fight, aircraft hammered relentlessly at the Japanese, using torpedoes, 500-pound bombs and even 100-pound bombs, while fighters strafed them with machine-gun fire and under-wing rockets. When their ammunition ran out, many of the aircraft made 'dry runs' on the Japanese ships, hoping to bluff them into taking evasive action and thereby gain a little more time for the fleeing CVEs. Ten of the twenty strafing runs made by one Wildcat pilot, Lieutenant Paul B. Garrison, USNR, were made without ammunition. For two hours after using up the last of his ordnance, the leader of *Gambier Bay's* air group, Lieutenant Commander Edward J. Huxtable, repeatedly flew through enemy anti-aircraft fire to harass the Japanese cruisers, hoping to divert them from their course.

Many of the carrier aircraft that ran out of ammunition replenished aboard the carriers of Taffy 2 – *Natoma Bay*, *Manila Bay*, *Marcus Island*, *Kadashan Bay*, *Savo Island* and *Ommaney Bay*. Others flew 100 miles to refuel and re-arm at Tacloban Field, which the Army engineers had just rendered operational – in the nick of time, as it turned out.

Taffy 2's carriers were also lending their own aircraft to the fight, of course. Sending destroyers *Haggard*, *Hailey* and *Franks* astern to screen the rear of his task unit, Rear Admiral Stump launched a total of five air strikes. Twelve Avengers – including that of Ensign Hans Jensen – and eleven Wildcats from Taffy 2 were shot down by inaccurate but heavy Japanese anti-aircraft fire. Taffy 3's aircraft losses are not recorded, but were probably greater.

Given the fluctuating actions, smoke-screens and intermittent rain squalls, confusion reigned on both sides. As the 'Wolves' and 'Little Wolves' rejoined the jinking escort carriers, *Heermann* reported that she had to reverse her engines full to avoid a collision with *Fanshaw Bay*, which suddenly 'crossed our bow from port to starboard'. Five minutes later, *Heermann* had to repeat the emergency manoeuvre when she almost ran into *Johnston*, which 'was apparently having steering difficulty'.

Arguably the most critical act of confusion, in regard to the battle's outcome, occurred on the bridge of the battleship *Yamato*. At 7.54, she was in the act of pelting a burning destroyer – probably *Hoel*, which her crew had mistaken for a cruiser – with her 6.1in secondary armament, when torpedoes were spotted coming from 100 degrees to starboard. Kurita ordered *Yamato*'s captain, Rear-Admiral N. Morishita, to take evasive action, first on a 60-degree course, then due north. Vice-Admiral Matome Ugaki, who was also on *Yamato*'s bridge as commander of Battleship Division 1, later called the order 'highly unfortunate'. Straddled by two torpedo spreads – four to starboard, two to port – *Yamato* stayed on her northerly course for ten minutes, not daring to turn until the missiles had spent themselves. By the time she rejoined the chase, she was at the tail-end of the Japanese column. More important, Admiral Kurita had lost visual contact with the action.

Another ship that fell behind was the crippled *Hoel*, which had become boxed between *Kongo*, 8,000 yards to port, and a column of heavy cruisers 7,000 yards to starboard. With one engine out of commission, she was able to match the speed of the Japanese, but could not pull ahead. Fishtailing and chasing salvos, *Hoel* managed to dodge the enemy shells for an hour and five minutes, while her bow guns, the only two that remained, fired a total of 500 5in rounds at any target that presented itself. Finally, enemy shells began to score – 5in, 8in, even 16-inchers from the battleship *Nagato*. Most were armour-piercing shells that passed through her thin sides without exploding, but some were striking below the water-line and she took a total of 40 hits. At 8.30, an 8in shell disabled her remaining engine and generator. Five minutes later, as she lay dead in the water, her engineering spaces flooded and, with No. 1 magazine on fire, the order to abandon ship was finally passed. With shells still falling on her, *Hoel* went down at 8.55, taking 253 of her crew with her; fifteen survivors later died of their wounds. Although Commander Thomas was severely wounded, he was later rescued and recovered. Commander Kintberger also survived to write an epitaph for *Hoel*'s crew:

'Fully cognisant of the inevitable result of engaging such vastly superior forces, these men performed their assigned duties coolly and efficiently until their ship was shot from under them.'

Farther ahead, the wounded *Johnston* was still very much in the fight. Spotting *Kongo* moving up 7,000 yards off the port beam, Evans ordered the battleship engaged with radar-ranged gunfire, shooting off thirty rounds in forty seconds and claiming fifteen hits. 'As far as accomplishing anything decisive, it was like bouncing paper wads off a steel helmet,' said *Johnston's* gunnery officer, Lieutenant R. C. Hagen, 'but we did kill some Japs and knock out a few small guns. Then we ran back into our smoke. The battleship belched a few 14-inchers at us, but thank God, registered only clean misses.'

Tone and her sister *Chikuma* now took the lead, trying to cut the carriers off from the east. Sprague ordered the DEs on the starboard quarter of his flagship to deal with them, but at this juncture he received an ominous message: 'Screen reports all torpedoes expended.' A radioman in *White Plains* wryly remarked to the signal officer: 'The situation is getting a little tense, isn't it?'

One ship, in fact, still had some torpedoes – the *John C. Butler*, which joined *Dennis* and *Raymond* in attacking the enemy cruisers, firing their 5in guns at them at 17,000 yards. *Raymond* narrowed the range on *Tone* to 5,900 yards, causing the Japanese to shift fire from *Gambier Bay* to her for a few minutes, but scoring no hits. At 8.42, an air attack compelled *Chikuma* to turn a complete circle in an effort to dodge their bombs. This left *Tone* in the lead, paralleling the carriers and destroyer escorts, and blazing away at all of them. *Dennis* was the first to be struck, taking three hits before retiring behind *Butler's* smoke-screen with both her guns out of action. After near-missing the zig-zagging *Butler*, *Tone* turned her attention to *Fanshaw Bay* at 9.15. *Butler* was now running low on ammunition, but Sprague ordered her to dash ahead of his flagship, laying smoke to obscure her.

Elsewhere, *Roberts'* luck was running out. *Kongo's* lookout spotted what her log recorded as a '*Kuramben*' (*Craven*) class destroyer and she began firing on *Roberts*. At 8.51, a shell below the water-line took out *Roberts'* No. 1 boiler room, and a succession of hits followed until 9.00, when, according to Lieutenant Commander Copeland, 'a tremendous explosion took place'. This blast, believed to have been caused by two or three 14in shells, tore a 40 by 10-foot hole in the escort's side, wiped out No. 2 engine room, ruptured the after fuel oil tanks and started a fire in the stern.

Roberts' No. 2 gun, which had fired about 300 shells during the past hour, continued to bark defiance as its crew, commanded by Gunner's Mate Paul Henry Carr, loaded and fired six more rounds by hand – ignoring the hazards presented by the failure of the gun's gas ejection system. Indeed, while they attempted to fire a seventh shell, an internal explosion killed all but three of the crew outright. Lieutenant W. S. Burton described what followed:

'The first man to enter the mount after the explosion found the gun captain, Carr, on the deck of the mount holding in his hands the last projectile available to his gun. He was completely torn open and his intestines were splattered throughout the inside of the mount. Nevertheless, he held in his hand the 54-pound projectile, held it up above his head and begged the petty officer who had entered the mount to help him get that last round out ... The Petty Officer, who entered the mount, took the projectile from Carr and removed one of the other men, who was wounded and unconscious, to the main deck in order to give him first aid. When he returned to the mount, there was Gunner's Mate Carr again with the projectile in his hand, still attempting, though terribly wounded, to place the projectile on the loading tray ...'

Dragged from the gun mount, Carr died minutes later, as did another of his wounded crewmen. Only one of the crew, Samuel Blue, survived.

At 9.10, Copeland ordered Abandon Ship!, but insisted that the wounded be put on rafts first. At 10.05, the DE, which by now had been struck twenty times and was listing 80 degrees, turned over and went slowly down by the stern. Of the eight officers and 170 men aboard *Samuel B. Roberts*, three officers and 86 men died. Copeland was among the survivors and concluded his action report thus:

'To witness the conduct of the average enlisted man on board this vessel, newly inducted, unaccustomed to Navy ways and with an average of less than one year's service, would make any man proud to be an average American. The crew were informed over the loudspeaker system at the beginning of the action of the Commanding Officer's estimate of the situation, that is, a fight against overwhelming odds from which survival could not be expected, during which time we would do what damage we could.

'In the face of this knowledge the men zealously manned their stations wherever they might be, and fought and worked with such calmness, courage, and efficiency that no higher honor could be conceived than to command such a group of men.'

Thus far, the CVEs had avoided any crippling hits, but at 8.10 *Gambier Bay*'s battle report stated: 'First hit, after end of flight deck, starboard side, near Batt II [the ship's secondary control centre]. Fires started on flight and hangar deck. Personnel casualties small.'

It was only the beginning. *Chikuma* closed to 2,000 yards and began to deal punishing hits on the CVE with her 8-inchers. At 8.20 a hit on the water-line penetrated *Gambier Bay*'s forward port engine room. Despite efforts by damage-control crews to stave off flooding with two portable electric submersible pumps, in five minutes the engine room was past saving and had to be secured. Speed dropped to 11 knots and *Gambier Bay* began to fall behind.

While *Gambier Bay* was fighting her unequal battle with *Chikuma*, a cameraman aboard *Kitkun Bay* recorded the struggle, producing the only action photographs of the war in which an American and a Japanese warship appear in the same picture.

Chikuma was still firing away at the listing escort carrier at 8.30 when *Johnston* arrived and Commander Evans told his gunnery officer: 'Commence firing on the cruiser Hagen, draw her fire away from the *Gambier Bay*.' Hagen survived the action to describe what followed:

'We closed to 6,000 yards and scored five hits. Reacting with monumental stupidity, the Japanese commander ignored us completely and concentrated on sinking the *Gambier Bay*. He could have sunk us both. By permitting us to escape, he made it possible for us to interfere a few minutes later with a destroyer attack that might have annihilated our little carrier force.'

Johnston, however, was not the only destroyer engaging *Chikuma*. *Heermann*, still miraculously undamaged, came up on *Gambier Bay*'s disengaged side and at 8.41 started firing at *Chikuma* at a range of 12,000 yards. This time, the Japanese took notice – *Chikuma* turned in a tight circle and shifted some of her fire toward *Heermann*.

The heroic efforts of the two destroyers were not enough to save *Gambier Bay*. At 8.37, hits in the carrier's island knocked out steering control and, three minutes later, her radars went dead. At 8.42, water was flooding the aft engine room and, at 8.45 the last engine gave out, leaving the carrier dead in the water. At that point, too, the heavy cruisers *Haguro* and *Chokai*, together with the light cruiser *Noshiro* and a destroyer, added passing salvos to *Gambier Bay*'s misery. *Heermann* was also hit, a shell in the pilot-house killing three crewmen and mortally wounding a fourth. Commander Hathaway reported:

'During this period water from near-misses drenched the director and director platform deck from which station the commanding officer was conning, making him wish he had a periscope with which to see over the wall of water. Everything looked rosy, but only because the splashes were coloured red by the dye loads ... At 0902 the *Tone*-class cruiser turned sharply to port, and retired to the eastward. At this time a large fire was observed on her fantail.'

It was all too late for *Gambier Bay*, though. At 8.50, her skipper, Captain Walter V. R. Vieweg, had all classified material jettisoned, then ordered Abandon Ship! About 750 of the ship's 849 crewmen complied, but some of them were killed by shell fragments as two enemy heavy cruisers continued to fire on the doomed CVE. Those who made it into the water began lashing life-rafts, floater nets, sections of the flight deck and any other floating debris into seven or eight separate groups, at the same time struggling to get clear of the suction which their sinking ship would cause when she went down. *Gambier Bay* finally capsized and sank at 9.07. The survivors would not be rescued until 45 hours later, at which point the casualties stood at 23 known dead, 99 missing and 160 wounded.

Heermann almost shared *Gambier Bay*'s fate. One of *Chikuma*'s shells hit her on the water-line well forward, flooding the forward magazines. Heated by the explosion and swept aft by the destroyer's momentum, the water converted a nearby storage locker full of Navy beans into a warm paste and – with some comic irony – swept it over the supply officer who was standing nearby. On a more serious note, *Heermann* was down by the head, her anchors dragging in her own bow wave. Commander Hathaway had seen what stopping dead in the water had meant to *Hoel* and *Gambier Bay*, so he kept his ship going at full speed while firing with the four of his five main guns that were still able to function. Thanks to extra shoring timbers installed during her last call in port, *Heermann* managed to keep from running under bows-first as she steamed clear of her pursuers.

By now *Chikuma* was out of the fight. Struck by a torpedo from one of Taffy 2's TBMs during an attack at 8.53, she turned away for good at 9.02 – and then came under another air strike. The omnipresent Commander Fowler observed this attack and reported:

'The third plane hitting the stern sent the heavy cruiser into a sharp right turn. After pulling out of the dive, I observed the heavy cruiser go about 500 yards, blow up and sink within five minutes.'

Tone took up the chase and between 9.07 and 9.10 *Heermann* traded shots with her, until *Tone*, too, came under attack by aircraft from Taffy 2 and fell astern of *Haguro* and *Chokai* at 9.20. At this juncture, *Heermann* resumed laying smoke for the carriers.

While most of Kurita's ships chased Sprague's flotilla, Fowler noticed that *Kongo* and *Haruna* were veering off in the direction of Taffy 2, thirty miles away, and radioed Stump a warning to that effect. At 8.41 Japanese shells began to straddle *Haggard, Hailey* and *Franks*. After his rearguard destroyers had spent half an hour evading this unwelcome attention, Stump recalled them. At 9.24 the masts of the Japanese battlewagons were just visible from Stump's carriers and 14in shells began walking toward the CVEs.

At 905, Taffy 3 lay about thirty miles north-east of Asgad Point on Samar Island when *Haguro* and *Chokai* caught up with *White Plains*, closing the range to 11,700 yards. By skilful changes in course, the carrier avoided their salvos, while her single 5in gun gamely spat back. *White Plain's* action report noted: 'At least six hits were observed on a heavy cruiser, one of which appeared to decommission a forward turret.' 'Hold on a little longer boys,' yelled the chief gunner on one of the carrier's quad mounts, 'We're sucking them into 40mm range!'

Such bravado made for stirring press, but it was *White Plains'* aircraft that were causing *Chokai* the most harm. Four of her Avengers came out of a cirrus cloud with the sun at their backs and took the enemy cruiser completely by surprise, encountering no anti-aircraft fire at all. Their bombs scored five hits amidships, one hit and two near-misses astern and three hits in the bows. According to *Haguro's* combat report, *Chokai* was also hit repeatedly by American shells, which put one of her engines out of commission, then began a slow retirement. At 9.05, a torpedo from one of *Kitkun Bay's* TBMs stopped her dead in the water. Finally, destroyer *Fujinami* evacuated her crew and finished off the crippled cruiser with one of her own torpedoes at 9.30.

Despite the loss of *Gambier Bay*, the armour-piercing shells of the Japanese cruisers were doing a better job of puncturing Taffy 3's ships than demolishing them. As *Johnston* was disengaging with *Gambier Bay's* tormentors, however, she spotted a more serious threat coming up fast. Taking some personal initiative at 8.45, Admiral Kimura, flying his pennant in the light cruiser *Yahagi*, led four destroyers of Desron 10 – the veterans *Urakaze*, *Yukikaze*, *Isokaze* and *Hamakaze* – and sped forward to attack with their deadly Type 93 'Long Lance' torpedoes.

With *Hoel* and *Roberts in extremis* and the other escorts still harrying the cruisers, *Johnston* was all that stood in Kimura's way. Kimura reported what happened next: '0850 – Enemy destroyer plunged out of smoke-screen on our port bow and opened gunfire and torpedo attack on us. *Yahagi* executed right rudder, making wide evasive turn, at same time ordering destroyers to attack.'

At 9.05, before making her turn, *Yahagi* launched seven torpedoes and took about a dozen shell hits from *Johnston*, as well as a strafing run from a carrier aircraft that killed one of her officers and wounded several others. As *Yahagi* turned out of column to clear the way for her destroyers, *Johnston* fired on the leading destroyer as well. *Johnston* was attempting to cross the T on Desdiv 10 when all the Japanese ships turned 90 degrees to starboard and launched their torpedoes after the carriers. They had done so at too great a range to be effective, however – the nearest CVE, *Kalinin Bay*, was 10,500 yards away and fleeing at almost 18 knots. All the torpedoes eventually slowed down. An Avenger from *St. Lo*, piloted by Lieutenant Leonard Waldrop, USNR, strafed one of the Long Lances and blew it up. *St. Lo* herself managed to explode another with her 5in gun.

Aboard *Johnston*, a jubilant Evans strutted across the bridge, chortling: 'Now I've seen everything!' But with their torpedoes expended, Kimura's ships turned their guns on *Johnston*, toppling what was left of her radar mast. Even in this condition 'GQ Johnny' steered to port to resume harassing the Japanese cruisers, alternating her gunfire between them and the destroyers. Lieutenant Hagen wrote:

'At 0910 we had taken a hit which knocked out one forward gun and damaged the other. Fires had broken out. One of our 40mm ready-lockers was hit and the exploding shells were causing as much damage as the Japs. The bridge was rendered untenable by the fires and explosions, and Commander Evans had been forced at 0910 to shift his command to the fantail, where he yelled his steering orders through an open hatch at the men who were turning the rudder by hand ...

'We were now in a position where all the gallantry and guts in the world couldn't save us. There were two cruisers on our port, another dead ahead of us, and several destroyers on our starboard side; the battleships, well astern of us, fortunately had turned coy. We desperately traded shots first with one group and then the other.'

At 9.40, *Johnston*'s one remaining engine room and boiler room were demolished by a deluge of shells. All ship's communications broke down. Only the No. 4 gun was firing, and that by local control. With his ship dead in the water, Evans finally ordered Abandon Ship! at 9.45.

As *Johnston*'s crew went over the side, Kimura's destroyers circled the doomed ship, still shelling her. As one of the destroyers closed to finish her, a swimming survivor swore he saw her captain on the bridge, saluting *Johnston* as she went down.

Of *Johnston*'s crew of 327, about 50 were killed in the battle, but another 45 died of their injuries while on rafts awaiting rescue. Ninety-two others, including Commander Evans, were seen in the water, but were not found by the rescue ships. One man was killed by a shark. Another was bitten twice but unaccountably released, leaving him with a row of tooth marks on his right thigh to back up a future tale of having not been to a shark's taste. He would be one of *Johnston*'s 141 survivors.

While the sailors and airmen of Taffy 3 were fighting for their lives, Ozawa's decoy fleet was likewise conducting a fighting retreat with Halsey's Task Force 34 in hot pursuit. At 8.10, Halsey's aircraft made contact and began a series of strikes that would eventually sink all four Japanese carriers. At 8.22, the first plain-language message from Kincaid was handed to Halsey, which included the plea: 'Request Lee proceed top speed to cover Leyte; request immediate strike by fast carriers.' Kincaid thought that some of Halsey's fleet was still somewhere within striking range of San Bernardino Strait; in actuality they were attacking Ozawa's ships, with Lee's battle group out ahead as the vanguard.

More messages followed with a rising tone of urgency, but it was not until 10.00 that a message from the CINCPAC, Admiral Chester W. Nimitz, caught Halsey's attention. In an effort to encode the message, Nimitz's yeoman of signals sandwiched the sentence between two meaningless phrases, the latter of which was paraphrased from Lord Alfred Tennyson's poem *The Charge of the Light Brigade*, since October 25 marked the 90th anniversary of that event. As a result, the essence of the message, 'Where is, repeat, where is, Task Force 34?' became: 'Turkey trots to water. Where is, repeat, where is, Task Force 34, the world wonders.'

Believing the padding on the end to be a meaningful phrase, Halsey never forgave Nimitz for what he perceived as stinging criticism, but it did spur him to order Lee's battle line – including Halsey's flagship, *New Jersey* – and Bogan's Task Group 38.2 to reverse course at 11.15 and proceed at full speed to Samar.

By this time, however, it was too late for the Third Fleet to intervene on Sprague's behalf. While *Johnston* was making her last stand, *Haguro* and *Tone* came ever closer to Taffy 3's five remaining carriers and the escort vessels that had all but shot their bolt. Admiral Sprague described what happened next:

'At 0925 my mind was occupied with dodging torpedoes when near the bridge I heard one of the signalmen yell, "Goddamit, boys, they're getting away!" I could not believe my eyes, but it looked as if the whole Japanese Fleet was indeed retiring. However, it took a whole series of reports from circling planes to convince me. And I still could not get the fact to soak into my battle-numbed brain. At best, I had expected to be swimming by this time.'

Incredible though it seemed, *Haguro* had ceased fire at 9.12 and *Tone* at 9.17. Both turned and retired north – and with them, the rest of Kurita's First Striking Force.

Sprague later offered his own explanation of why his ships were still afloat and their crews still alive:

'The failure of the enemy body and encircling light forces to completely wipe out all vessels of this task unit can be attributed to our successful smoke-screen, our torpedo counter-attack, continuous harassment of enemy by bomb, torpedo and strafing air attacks, timely maneuvers, and the definite partiality of Almighty God.'

It was a fair assessment, but it left out one key factor: Kurita's order, issued at 9.11, to 'Rendezvous, my course north, speed 20.' His primary intention was to regroup, regain control of his scattered ships that he had lost more than an hour earlier, assess damage and then proceed into Leyte Gulf. But Kurita spent the next three hours manoeuvring off Samar, trying to decide – with rapidly declining enthusiasm – whether to resume his advance or not.

During that time, Kurita launched two seaplanes from *Yamato* to reconnoitre. They failed to return. A report came in – apocryphal, as it later turned out – of an American task force 113 miles north of Suluan Island, which Kurita suspected might be the main component of Halsey's Third Fleet. At 10.18, Kurita received a radio message from the destroyer *Shigure*, the sole survivor of Nishimura's Force C, updating him on what had happened in Surigao Strait: 'All ships except *Shigure* went down under gunfire and torpedo attack.' This, combined with Admiral Shima's earlier report that he was retiring from the Strait and a succession of radio transmissions picked up from the Americans, convinced Kurita that powerful enemy naval units were converging on Leyte Gulf. At 12.36 p.m. he sent a message to his superiors in Tokyo:

'First Striking Force has abandoned penetration of Leyte anchorage. Is proceeding north searching for enemy task force. Will engage decisively, then pass through San Bernardino Strait.'

Kurita never encountered the 'enemy task force' for which he claimed to be searching, but he kept going. And with the departure of his force, the last Japanese hope for a victory in Leyte Gulf evaporated.

In addition to the already sunken *Chikuma* and *Chokai*, Kurita lost a third heavy cruiser at Samar when the destroyer *Okinami* evacuated *Suzuya*'s crew and scuttled her. Another destroyer, *Nowaki*, stayed behind to rescue survivors from *Chikuma*, but she lingered too long, being caught and sunk by Halsey's vanguard surface force. One other ship would be sunk before Kurita's force got out of range of Halsey's avenging carrier aircraft – *Noshiro*, sunk off Batbatan Island at 9.10 on the morning of 26 October by aircraft from the carriers *Wasp* and *Hornet*.

Taffy 3's ordeal was not quite over, either. At 10.50, five Mitsubishi A6M5 Zero fighters from Mabalacat airfield, Luzon, were suddenly spotted approaching at low altitude – under the Americans' radar – and went for the carriers. One Zero climbed and then dived on *Kitkun Bay*, strafing the bridge, then crashed into the catwalk and fell in the sea. Its bomb exploded nearby, causing considerable damage. Two Zeros were shot down while trying to dive on *Fanshaw Bay*. Two more attacked *White Plains*. One of them circled the carrier, then crashed into her side between the port catwalk and the waterline, injuring eleven crewmen and showering the deck with debris and bits of the pilot. The last Zero, hit and smoking, turned and dived straight for *St. Lo*, crashing through her deck and starting a fire which touched off seven more explosions among her torpedoes and bombs. Ablaze and beyond saving, *St. Lo* sank at 11.25. During the next four hours, *Heermann*, *John C. Butler*, *Dennis* and *Raymond* fished 754 of her crew from the sea. *St. Lo* had been the first ship to be sunk by a new weapon, unleashed by a desperate enemy in lieu of naval and conventional air resources that had proven ineffective – the suicidal 'divine wind', or *Kamikaze*.

Although the Battle of Leyte Gulf was the greatest naval battle in history, there should have been no question as to its outcome. Instead, the Japanese came tantalisingly close to accomplishing their goal of reaching and destroying the American beachhead, leaving the conduct of both sides during the battle open to endless debate. Halsey's blunder has been widely attributed to his obsession with aircraft carriers, but it must be noted that he did not know that Ozawa's carriers had so few aircraft left, and the last time he heard anything about Kurita's First Striking Force, it was retiring.

The decision by which Kurita cancelled out Halsey's mistake has also been subject to frequent discussion, especially in the present-day Japanese navy, where a popular question among officers is: 'What would you have done, had you been in Kurita's place on the morning of 25 October 1944?' Hindsight is always 20-20, though, and it does not take much effort to realise that Kurita was just as ignorant about what he was up against as was Halsey. His confidence shaken by a series of calamities – the loss of his flagship *Atago* at the onset, and later of the mighty *Musashi* – Kurita was psychologically prepared to over-estimate the carrier unit he encountered off Samar, even claiming that the 'fleet carriers' were barrelling along at 30 knots, instead of 18 ('I knew you were scared, Ziggy,' an admiral quipped to Sprague on reading Kurita's report, 'but I didn't know you were *that* scared!').

Any hopes Kurita had of collecting accurate data on his opponents were dashed when *Yamato* reversed course to comb the American torpedoes launched at her. From then on, he was completely out of touch, and his ships, each concerned with its own individual fight, did little or nothing to enlighten him. Finally, convinced that he was engaging a powerful element of the Third Fleet, and that more units were converging on him, Kurita gave up.

The ultimate key to Kurita's loss of communications, and the disproportionate resistance that wore him down, lay in the canny fighting retreat improvised by Clifton Sprague, and in the peerless valour shown by the destroyermen, destroyer escort crews, and the airmen and crews of the 'Woolworth carriers'. Their sacrifice had been great – of the six major warships sunk by the Japanese in Leyte Gulf, five had been lost by Taffy 3. But the Japanese lost a total of 26 of their own ships, reducing their navy to little more than an auxiliary force. Even in a best-case scenario, the Japanese expected Operation '*Sho*-1' to be a sacrificial gesture. When that best-case scenario unexpectedly presented itself, Taffy 3 did the most to render that Japanese sacrifice a vain one.

References

Fletcher, Lieutenant Commander Leon, USNR. 'The Attack on Taffy Three' in *Sea Classics*, vol. 5, No. 6, November 1972, pp 55–62.

Hoyt, Edwin P. *MacArthur's Navy: The Seventh Fleet and the Battle for the Philippines*, Orion Books, New York, NY, 1989.

Morison, Samuel Eliot. *History of United States Naval Operations in World War II*, vol. XII, Leyte, June 1944–January 1945, Little, Brown & Co., Boston, 1958.

Roscoe, Theodore. *Tin Cans*, Bantam Books, New York, NY, 1968.

Vat, Dan van der. *The Pacific Campaign, World War II, The U.S.–Japanese Naval War 1941-1945*, Simon & Schuster, New York, NY, 1991.

CHAPTER 14

Almost Total Exclusion
ARA *San Luis* in the Falklands, May 1982

To General Leopoldo Galtieri, leader of the military Junta that was then in political control of Argentina, Operation 'Rosario', the invasion and occupation of the Falkland Islands on 2–3 April 1982, must have seemed a good idea at the time. When he had taken office in December 1981 he had sworn that the Argentine flag would fly over *los Islas Malvinas*, as they were known to the Argentineans, before the 150th anniversary of their annexation by Great Britain in 1833. Such a move, he reasoned, would give a great boost to national pride – and perhaps distract some public attention from Argentina's domestic problems.

So far as the possible consequences of the seizure were concerned, Galtieri and his colleagues believed that Britain would ultimately be compelled to accept it as a *fait accompli*. Since the Second World War, the British Empire had receded to all but non-existence and its armed forces were undergoing a rapid process of reduction. Within this scheme, the transition of the faraway Falklands from British to Argentinean stewardship seemed inevitable – and the Argentinean military had simply hastened the process.

In forcibly taking over the islands, however, the Junta made a gross miscalculation. The 1,813 English-speaking inhabitants of the Falklands had no desire to exchange an absentee constitutional monarchy for a military dictatorship. The islanders' plight, and the very fact that the Falklands had been taken by force rather than by negotiation, made all the difference to Prime Minister Margaret Thatcher, practically the whole of Parliament, and the British people themselves – a distant colonial embarrassment was transformed overnight into a matter of principle.

Had the Argentineans waited even one year longer before staging their invasion, the Royal Navy might have been too depleted to respond, but in April 1982 Britain was able – and certainly willing – to mobilise and dispatch sufficient forces to retake the islands. On 12 April, the British announced the establishment of a Total Exclusion Zone (TEZ) encompassing a 200-mile radius around the Falklands, asserting that any Argentine ship caught within that area would be sunk. On 20 April, Rear-Admiral John 'Sandy' Woodward arrived in the aircraft carrier *Hermes* to take command of the British Task Force bound for the Falklands.

In military terms, the South Atlantic War was the first major conflict to involve the full-scale operational use of electronic, guided weaponry, such as guided missiles and wire-guided torpedoes, as well as nuclear-powered submarines and vertical-take-off jet aircraft, in the form of the British Aerospace Harrier GR.3 and Sea Harrier FRS.1. Given such hardware, many advocates of high-tech warfare predicted a war in which the roles played by terrain, weather, and even such human factors as endurance, courage and conviction, would be greatly diminished in importance. In those suppositions, however, such pundits would be proven wrong.

On the part of the Royal Navy, consummate professionalism, rather than exceptional heroism, was the general rule. Referring to the performance of his men, Admiral Woodward stated afterwards: 'I suppose what surprised me was that they didn't surprise me. They did exactly what you would expect of a British sailor. Go in and get on with it. That's exactly what our guys did. While the technology may change, the people are as wonderful as they always were.'

The *Armada Republica Argentina* (ARA) was far less consistent in performance, largely due to lack of sound leadership, inadequate preparation and insufficient training. Unquestionably, the most spectacular showing was made by the aircrews of the *Comando Aviacion Naval Argentina* (CANA), operating from land bases alongside the equally professional airmen of the *Fuerza Aerea Argentina* (FAA). Of the major Argentinean warships, it may be argued that the most valour, if not success, was displayed by the crew of the submarine ARA *San Luis*, which operated deep in enemy-controlled waters for more than ten days.

San Luis (S32) and her sister, *Salta* (S31), were small diesel-powered vessels of the Type 209 class, designed by the West German IKL firm and built by Howaldtswerke at Kiel. Laid down on 1 October 1970, *San Luis* was launched on 3 April 1973 and delivered to the ARA on 24 May 1974. Powered by two 2,400hp diesels or by one electric motor driving a single shaft, she had a speed of 10 knots surfaced and 17 knots submerged.

The Type 209s were built in several models that differed in dimensions; the two Argentinean submarines were of the '56-metre' variant, with a length of 183.7 feet, a beam of 20.3 feet, a draft of 18 feet and a complement of 32 officers and men. Their normal operational diving depth was 300 metres (984 feet) and the maximum diving depth was 500 metres (1,640 feet). Displacement was 1,185 tons surfaced, 1,285 tons submerged.

The Type 209's armament consisted of fourteen 21in SST-4 wire-guided torpedoes which were launched through eight tubes. In addition to her guided torpedoes, *San Luis* differed from earlier-generation submarines in her more advanced electronics – one surface-search radar, one low-frequency bow sonar, one passive intercept sonar, a fire-control/action information system and an ESM (electronic surveillance measures) system.

Argentina possessed two other submarines when hostilities with Britain began, *Santa Fé* and *Santiago del Estero*. Both were Second World War vintage *Balao*-class submarines, updated with streamlined 'GUPPY III' hulls and conning towers, that had been acquired from the USA in 1971. In comparison with the ARA's undersea contingent, the British Task Force had three nuclear-powered attack submarines at its disposal – *Conqueror*, *Spartan* and *Splendid* – as well as the *Oberon*-class diesel submarine *Onyx*.

The Argentinean navy was not entirely prepared when it was ordered to carry out the occupation of the Malvinas, let alone oppose a counter-offensive by the Royal Navy. On 17 April, however, the ARA dispatched Task Force 79, under the command of *Contraalmirante* Gualter Allara, to confront the British fleet. On the 29th the task force split into three groups. Its main component, Task Group 79.1, including Allara's flagship, the aircraft carrier *Veinticinco de Mayo* (*25 May*), took up a station 270 nautical miles (nm) east of San Jorge Gulf. Task Group 79.4, a destroyer escort group, deployed to the north-east of the main force, while a third unit, TG.79.3, centred around the light cruiser *General Belgrano*, steamed east-southeast of Allara's group.

While the Argentinean surface units stayed discreetly outside the British-imposed TEZ for the time being, the ARA's two Type 209 submarines left their base at Mar del Plata with orders to enter the 'free-fire zone' just north of the Falklands, reconnoitring or attacking enemy shipping as circumstances should dictate. *Salta* was not long at sea, however, when her machinery began to make an intolerable noise which her crew were unable to remedy. Forced to abort her mission, *Salta* returned to Mar del Plata where she would remain for the rest of the war. *San Luis* suffered no such problem and soon was taking up her assigned patrol zone northeast of the Falklands, to await the arrival of the British.

Back at Mar del Plata, the elderly *Santiago del Estero* was found to be unable to submerge and was moved to Bahia Blanca and camouflaged. *Santa Fé*, on the other hand, was sent on a supply run to South Georgia Island, arriving at Grytviken Harbour on 23 April.

On the night of 24 April, *Santa Fé* left Grytviken as a British task group, commanded by Captain B. G. Young, approached South Georgia. At 8.55 in the morning of the 25th, her periscope was detected by the radar in 'Humphrey', a Westland Wessex helicopter from the destroyer *Antrim*, crewed by Lieutenant-Commander Ian Stanley (First pilot), Sub-Lieutenant Stewart Cooper (Second pilot), Lieutenant Chris Parry (observer) and Petty Officer Aircrewman David Fitzgerald (sonar operator). Closing to a distance of 5 nm to investigate, 'Humphrey' made positive visual identification and, seeing that *Santa Fé* was preparing to dive, attacked her with depth-charges. Damaged and unable to submerge, *Santa Fé* turned hard a-port and headed back for Grytviken, oil and smoke pouring from her hull.

A Westland Lynx from the frigate *Brilliant* next arrived on the scene, only to come under machine-gun fire from the submarine. The helicopter launched a Mark 46 torpedo at *Santa Fé*, but failed to score a hit, after which it fired back at the vessel with its own machine-guns until a Westland Wasp from the frigate *Plymouth* arrived and attacked the Argentineans with its AS.12 missiles. Another two Wasps from the ice patrol ship *Endurance* added their AS.12s to *Santa Fé*'s misery. Finally reaching Grytviken, the crew of the crippled submarine ran her aground and abandoned her.

At 2.45 that afternoon, HMS *Antrim*'s Wessex 'Humphrey' led *Brilliant*'s two Lynxes to land the first of 150 Royal Marines and Special Air Service troops on South Georgia. By the end of the day, the Argentinean garrison – including *Santa Fé*'s crew – had surrendered. Miraculously, *Santa Fé*'s only serious casualty was a machine-gunner wounded from an AS.12 missile hit, who consequently had to have a leg amputated by *Antrim*'s medical officer.

San Luis was now the only operational Argentine submarine in the South Atlantic, and *Santa Fé*'s fate served notice as to what might well happen to her if she had the temerity to take on any unit of the main British Task Force off the Falklands. Nevertheless, that was what her captain, *Capitan de Corbeta* (Lieutenant-Commander) Fernando Azcueta, had been sent to do, and he planned to do his best to carry out his orders.

Hostilities in the Falklands proper officially began on the morning of 1 May, when the airfield at Port Stanley was bombed, first by a single Avro Vulcan from 101 Squadron, Royal Air Force, then by Sea Harriers from the carriers *Hermes* and *Invincible*, which also attacked the smaller airstrip at Goose Green. At the same time, the destroyer *Glamorgan*, in company with the frigates *Alacrity* and *Arrow*, bombarded Argentinean positions around Stanley. As the warships withdrew, they were attacked by three Israel Aircraft Industries Daggers from *Grupo 6 de Caza*, FAA, whose bombs missed but whose 30mm cannon fire holed *Arrow*'s superstructure and wounded a young rating. A near-miss by a bomb caused *Alacrity* to take water, but she was quickly repaired.

Of the 35 Argentinean aircraft that reached the Falklands, the Daggers were the only ones to actually carry out anti-shipping attacks. In their first taste of air-to-air combat, Sea Harriers shot down a Dagger, an English Electric Canberra and two Dassault Mirage IIIEAs without loss, establishing a measure of air superiority over the Falklands that the Argentineans would not challenge again. Faced in any case with a 400-mile flight which stretched their striking range to the limit, the FAA and

CANA aircrews adopted tactics of flying straight in and out, striving to avoid the Sea Harriers, in an attempt to eliminate the British ships – especially the aircraft carriers.

The British, who already suspected *San Luis* to be in the area, had not left her out of their attack plan for 'softening up' resistance on and around the islands. Shortly after daybreak on 1 May, the frigates *Brilliant* and *Yarmouth* were detached to search for her north-east of East Falkland Island. On their way there, they were joined by three anti-submarine warfare (ASW) Westland Sea Kings of 826 Squadron from *Hermes*.

At 10 a.m., *San Luis* spotted a large surface warship looming in the morning mist, although visibility was too poor for Lieutenant-Commander Azcueta positively to identify just what kind it was. The one thing he could be sure of was that it was British, and he fired a spread of torpedoes at it. Much to the frustration of captain and crew, however, all the torpedoes missed the target. Sometime after the moment that his torpedoes were supposed to have struck, Azcueta heard an explosion, but he was never able to determine just what his torpedo had hit. One thing did become clear, however – there was a problem with the automatic computer that had been used to make the torpedo attack. Moreover, the wire guidance system had not been working – one wire was found to be broken, and the rest had clearly malfunctioned.

Although Azcueta never professed certainty as to the ship he had fired on, nor to the outcome of his attack, Argentinean propagandists were more than willing to speculate. Among the large Royal Navy ships that they regarded as likely candidates, the one most cited was the carrier *Invincible* – even though she was, in fact, lying to the east of the Falklands at the time, in anticipation of air attack. Another Argentinean claim was that *San Luis'* target had been the destroyer *Exeter*, although that ship was in the West Indies at the time and would not join the Task Force until 21 May.

Most likely, Azcueta had seen *Brilliant*, a new ship of the Type 22 *Broadsword* class which had acquired her 'frigate' designation primarily to avoid a refusal of funds for her construction. With a fully loaded displacement of 4,400 tons, a length of 430 feet and a hull with increased freeboard to allow operation in rough weather without significantly reducing speed, *Brilliant* presented a massive silhouette that would be relatively unfamiliar to the Argentineans – and readily subject to exaggeration.

Soon after having fired his torpedoes and hearing the belated explosion, Azcueta made the logical decision to take evasive measures against the British onslaught that would most surely follow. In the case of his small diesel-electric submarine, the best course of action was to dive to the bottom of the Falklands shelf, shut down engines and wait. Unknown to Azcueta, however, his torpedoes had run so wild that they had been not even been noticed by the British, who still had only the vaguest general idea of where *San Luis* might be.

While *Brilliant* and *Plymouth* continued to comb the area with their sonar, the accompanying trio of Sea Kings, led by Lieutenant-Commander A. J. M. Hogg, tried to locate the target using sonobuoys and dunking sonar. Each helicopter carried a spare 4-man crew who were disembarked aboard the frigates before the flight commenced a systematic sweep north-east of Port Stanley, about 180 miles from *Hermes*. In order to interrupt the operation as little as possible, helicopter in-flight refuelling (HIFR) was carried out for the first time under combat conditions. Each Sea King would hover over the stern of a frigate, lower a hook and pick up the fuel line. While this 15-minute operation was under way, the frigate continued her normal ASW manoeuvres while the helicopter matched her movements.

Just after darkness fell, the three helicopters returned to *Hermes*, having refuelled from the frigates a total of ten times, changed crews once each, and dropped six Mk II depth-charges and two Mk 46 torpedoes over a 10-hour period. One of the Sea Kings, XZ577, set a helicopter record for the time of 10 hours, 20 minutes spent in the air during an operational mission. The frigates continued the hunt for *San Luis* throughout the night.

For all the technical achievements going on above the waves, however, none of the ASW teams' efforts succeeded either in locating or damaging *San Luis*. Lieutenant-Commander Azcueta's strategy of heading for the bottom and waiting out his pursuers was as old as the submarine itself, but he was most effectively aided by the nature of the terrain, an irregular, rocky underwater shelf which managed to foil the most modern sonar. The crew's contribution to their ship's safety was simply to keep noise to an absolute minimum for the more than eighteen hours that she lay unmoving on that rocky shelf.

Nevertheless, after all the nerve-racking suspense was behind him and his men, Azcueta's combat report stated that while he heard the depth-charges detonating near his position, they never came close enough for him to feel that his ship was in serious danger. The depth-charges, he deduced, were probably intended less to destroy his ship so much as to disturb the acoustics of his own sonar, or simply to keep him down. And indeed, even if the British did not have a fix on him, Azcueta was not foolish enough to press his luck by leaving the ocean floor. Despite their lack of success in catching their quarry, the British frigate and helicopter crews could retrospectively find consolation in the fact that, as long as their random flailing kept *San Luis* lying low, she would not be able to threaten the Task Force.

While the British ASW team was searching for *San Luis*, TG.79.1, centred around *25 de Mayo*, was taking up a position just outside the TEZ, north-west of the Falklands. In mid-afternoon, Admiral Allara received information confirming the presence of a British task group, including the carrier *Invincible*, north of Port Stanley.

The stage was set for the first duel between aircraft carriers since the Battle of Leyte Gulf on 25 October 1944. But now fate took an unexpected twist. With more than 250 nautical miles between *25 de Mayo* and her British counterparts, her eight Douglas A-4Q Skyhawks were carrying a full combat load of fuel and 500lb Mk 82 Snake-eye retarded general-purpose bombs, for which the carrier's speed and her catapult would not be sufficient to launch the aircraft safely without the added boost of a wind factor of at least 25 knots. Normally, winds well in excess of that minimum required speed should not have been hard to come by in the stormy waters of the South Atlantic at this time of year, but on this particular day, the Argentineans found themselves in the middle of a high pressure zone. Wind velocity rarely surpassed 5 knots, rendering it impossible for the aircraft to launch. By 5.30, the attack had become unfeasible and a frustrated Admiral Allara decided to postpone the mission until dawn the next day.

Although *25 de Mayo*'s Skyhawks were not equipped for night operations, the six Grumman S-2E Trackers of her *Escuadrilla Antisubmarina* were. Just before midnight, one of the Trackers re-established contact with the British. Just after midnight, however, the Argentinean carrier group was in turn located by a Sea Harrier from *Invincible*.

On the morning of 2 May, Allara briefed his Skyhawk pilots to be ready for a renewed effort to strike at *Invincible* – only to postpone the mission again at about 9 a.m., after one of his Trackers reported that it was unable to relocate the British in the area where they had been earlier.

Thus far, despite growing Argentinean anxiety about the threat posed by the three British nuclear submarines known to be operating in the deep waters between the Falklands and the mainland, *25 de Mayo* had escaped their notice. *General Belgrano* and TG.79.3, however, were less fortunate, having been sighted by HMS *Conqueror* on the afternoon of 1 May and shadowed thereafter. On the morning of 2 May, a War Cabinet meeting was held in London to discuss whether the rules of engagement allowed an attack on the Argentine cruiser, which was approaching, but nevertheless still lay outside the TEZ. Prime Minister Thatcher decided in favour of an attack and the message reached Commander Christopher Louis Wreford-Brown in *Conqueror* at about noon.

Although his submarine carried modern, wire-guided Mark 24 Tigerfish torpedoes, Wreford-Brown opted instead for the Second World War vintage Mk 8 torpedoes because he could fire more of them at a time, and because their heavier warheads (750 pounds compared to the Tigerfish's 331 pounds) would be more likely to be effective against the cruiser's armoured hull. After spending more than two hours getting into a good striking position, at 3.57 p.m. *Conqueror* fired a spread of three torpedoes at the gently zigzagging cruiser and her two destroyer escorts from a distance of 1,400 yards. Forty-three seconds later, Wreford-Brown saw an orange fireball erupt from *Belgrano*, followed by a second. His third torpedo struck the destroyer *Hipolito Bouchard*, but failed to explode.

Shouting above the uproar of thirty cheering crewmen, Wreford-Brown ordered: 'Ten down, starboard thirty, half ahead, 130 revs.' A few minutes later, the detection of a burst of sonar, followed by the loud report of a depth-charge brought *Conqueror's* jubilant crew back to reality. 'There was silence throughout the boat,' one officer wrote. 'Suddenly it was no longer fun to be doing what we were. We were on the receiving end.'

Diving to 985 feet, *Conqueror* managed to evade the attentions of *Bouchard* and her sister, *Piedrabuena*. After showering the area where they thought the submarine should be with depth-charges and hedgehogs for about a quarter of an hour, the two Argentinean destroyers left the area, rather than risk being sunk themselves.

Left to her fate, *Belgrano* was *in extremis*. *Capitan de Navio* Hector Bonzo estimated that the two hits on his ship caused about 330 casualties among a crew largely made up of untrained conscripts, in addition to which all power, lights and electric pumps were put out of commission. Within twenty minutes, *Belgrano* had developed a 21-degree list and at 4.25, Bonzo ordered Abandon Ship!. At about 5.00, the cruiser went down. As the US Navy light cruiser *Phoenix*, she had survived the Japanese surprise attack on Pearl Harbor on 7 December 1941; now, she had the dubious distinction of being the last Pearl Harbor survivor to be lost in combat – at the hands of a former ally. *General Belgrano* was also the first victim of a nuclear-powered submarine, although the torpedoes which sank the cruiser were scarcely more modern in concept than she was.

Taking to about fifty brightly coloured rafts, the survivors huddled against 30mph winds in choppy seas and a wind-chill temperature of minus 20 degrees Celsius. After about 32 hours, during which time seven men in two rafts froze to death, the survivors were found and rescued. Of *General Belgrano's* 1,138 crewmen, 368 had died.

Shortly after *Belgrano* went down, word of her loss reached TF.79.1. The deaths of so many of their comrades was a profound blow to all ARA personnel, but for the Argentinean naval commanders the sinking confirmed the vulnerability of all their ships to submarine attack and forced them to re-appraise their priorities. Prior to the seizure of the Falklands, the ARA's primary adversary had been the smaller but none the less potent navy of Chile, with whom Argentina had frequent border disputes, and with whom the prospect of war was a constant possibility. Suddenly, in the eyes of the Argentinean admiralty, the risk of losing 25 *de Mayo* as well as *General Belgrano*, and thereby tilting the balance of naval power in Chile's favour, became an unacceptable price to pay for a handful of barren, windswept South Atlantic islands. Accordingly, *25 de Mayo* and the rest of TF.79 withdrew to coastal waters, the carrier returning to Puerto Belgrano on 4 May. The carrier's Skyhawks, Trackers and Sikorski S-61D-4 Sea King helicopters were transferred to land bases, from which they, together with the FAA units, would carry on the fight.

Also still operating was the submarine *San Luis*, which was now the sole major fighting ship of the ARA still at sea – and still lurking within the Total Exclusion Zone.

Ironically, the most intense British ASW activity would be carried out in reaction to an attack with which *San Luis* had nothing to do whatsoever. On 4 May, the CANA got its chance to avenge *General Belgrano* when an AM.39 Exocet missile fired from a Dassault-Breguet Super Etendard of the *2 Escuadrilla de Caza y Ataque* hit the destroyer HMS *Sheffield*. The missile failed to explode, but it fractured fuel lines, destroyed water main pumps, wrecked the ship's control room and came to rest in the damage control headquarters, where its own burning fuel started fires that could only be fought with fire extinguishers and buckets of water. Twenty-one of *Sheffield*'s crew were killed.

Confusion arose after the frigates *Arrow* and *Yarmouth* arrived to assist the crippled destroyer, accompanied by their helicopters. The fact that the Exocet – which, having been used for the first time in combat, had not yet been identified as such – had entered *Sheffield* at the waterline caused the British to think the ship might have been the victim of a torpedo. With that premise and the ASW activities of 1 May to fuel the imagination, one of the helicopter crews reported possible submarine activity in the vicinity.

Accordingly *Yarmouth* was diverted from her evacuation duties to assist in pin-pointing the contact, while *Arrow* remained alongside to help fight *Sheffield*'s fires and, when all was seen to be lost, evacuate 236 of her crew. Joining *Yarmouth* was her Wasp helicopter, as well as *Arrow*'s Lynx, which made several attacks with its Mk 46 torpedoes that produced no positive results. Five Sea Kings of *Invincible*'s 820 Squadron and several from *Hermes*' 826 Squadron also conducted ASW searches which continued next day.

The 'submarine activity' that had inspired those ASW efforts may have come from a whale or a patch of seaweed, but it certainly had not come from *San Luis*. For the time being, Azcueta was lying low to the north, resting his crew for a renewed effort and assessing his own disappointing attack of 1 May. Given the unreliable nature of the automatic computer and the wire guidance systems of *San Luis*' torpedoes, he concluded that his next strike would have to be carried out using manual calculations, at closer range.

On 9 May, *Yarmouth* took *Sheffield* in tow, in an attempt to move her to South Georgia. Next day, however, the weather deteriorated and *Sheffield* finally gave up the ghost and sank.

On the night of 10/11 May, the frigate *Alacrity*, commanded by Commander C. J. S. Craig, was steaming through Falkland Sound to locate shore defences or minefields when she encountered an unidentified ship that would not answer her challenges. *Alacrity* promptly engaged the vessel with rapid fire from her 4.5in gun and scored several hits, whereupon the ship exploded in a sheet of flame and quickly sank. She had been the 3,840-ton naval transport *Isla de los Estados*, which had been trying to run the British blockade to Fort Howard with a load of aviation fuel and other supplies for the garrison. Only two of her crew survived, to be rescued two days later.

Alacrity, in company with *Arrow*, went on to complete the sweep of the Sound, emerging through the north-east passage – where, unknown to them, *San Luis* had returned to resume her own deadly mission. According to Azcueta's report, he saw two surface ships, probably destroyers, enter his patrol area. Using sonar information and manual guidance, he got a fix on one of the vessels and, at 1.40 a.m. on 11 May, launched an SST-4 torpedo from a range of 5,000 yards.

Again, the results of the attack were inconclusive. From the Argentineans' viewpoint, the two British ships seemed to 'run outside the area at very high speed', but, significantly, there was no retaliation by ASW units as had been the case on 1 May.

For a time, *San Luis* continued her patrol, but later that same day Azcueta received orders to terminate his mission and return to his base at Mar del Plata. The ARA decided that Azcueta and his men had done their best, but that he had risked his ship and his men long enough with weaponry that seemed to be accomplishing nothing.

Later, HMS *Arrow*'s crew discovered that a torpedo decoy which they had been towing had been damaged. At first they attributed it to grounding, but it is more likely that the device had been struck by *San Luis*' torpedo – which, to cap off a cruise fraught with disappointments, had failed to explode.

The rest of the South Atlantic campaign is history. On 21 May the British landed at San Carlos and began a land offensive that would eventually lead to Port Stanley. While the soldiers and marines advanced, a desperate struggle took place at sea between the supporting Royal Naval units and the aircraft of the FAA and the CANA – beginning with the sinking of the frigate *Ardent* on the day of the landing. Two days later, the frigate *Antelope* was hit by two non-exploding 1,000lb bombs dropped by Skyhawks, one of which later detonated. Next day, *Antelope* broke in two, forming a final defiant 'V' shape before slipping beneath the waves.

The British were expecting fireworks on 25 May, the enemy's Independence Day, and the Argentineans did not disappoint them. The frigates *Broadsword* and *Argonaut* were hit by bombs, the latter seriously damaged, while the destroyer *Coventry* was bombed and sunk with the loss of seventeen men by A4P Skyhawks of *Grupo 5 de Caza*, FAA. Later, the Super Etendards of 2 *Escuadrilla de Caza y Ataque*, CANA struck again, two of their Exocets mortally damaging the 15,000-ton container ship *Atlantic Conveyer*.

On 30 May, the FAA and CANA shot their collective bolt in a last all-out effort to eliminate the British task force by means of widely scattered air attacks, meant to cause as much damage to as many ships as possible. Intermittent air attacks continued thereafter – one of which, by two Skyhawks of the FAA's *Grupo 5 de Caza* on 8 June, did such damage to the landing-ship *Sir Galahad* that she was sunk as a war grave twenty days later – but by that time, the Argentinean cause was lost. At midnight on 14 June, General Benjamin Menendez surrendered the last of his forces on the islands and the Islas Malvinas officially became the Falklands again.

Not long after the loss of the Malvinas, the discredited military Junta of General Leopoldo Galtieri collapsed, to be replaced by a democratic government.

The British servicemen who recovered the Falklands returned home to a heroes' welcome. Many received decorations, including a Distinguished Service Order for Commander Christopher Wreford-Brown of HMS *Conqueror*, and other medals for several members of his crew.

No such official recognition awaited the Argentinean fighting men upon their immediate return, although their airmen were soon to learn of the grudging praise expressed about them by their British adversaries. Several years later, however, the Argentinean National Congress issued three grades of recognition to those who had done their duty during the South Atlantic War – a campaign ribbon for all who served, about 80 ribbons of somewhat higher status for those who had distinguished themselves in combat, and two or three special medals for acts of extraordinary valour. One of the second-rank awards went to the captain of the submarine *San Luis*, with the simple legend: 'From the National Congress to Lieutenant-Commander Azcueta, combatant in Malvinas'.

Although the material damage *San Luis* caused to the British Task Force was practically nil, her presence caused considerable anxiety and generated a disproportionate amount of ASW activity – even when she was not on the scene. Her penetration of the Total Exclusion Zone, and her subsequent safe return gave a much-needed morale boost to the Argentinean fleet amid the bitterness of lost ships and a lost war.

San Luis was also the unwitting source of a mythical scrap of Falklands folklore. Although Azcueta made no positive claim to have hit anything, that did not prevent his homeland's propaganda machine from suggesting that *San Luis* had struck the carrier *Invincible* with a torpedo that failed to explode. Instead of checking the veracity of the claim, the British press generally 'ran' with the story – as, subsequently, did the British Atlantic Committee. Only later did *Invincible*'s crew learn that their ship had been 'torpedoed'. Consequently, on her return home the carrier was dry-docked and her hull subjected to a minute examination for impact damage. None was found, but by that time the story was 'common knowledge' and widely set down in print.

On a more serious level, *San Luis*' modest feat taught a sobering lesson to Britain and other members of the North Atlantic Treaty Organization in regard to what small diesel-electric submarines could do. She had, after all, penetrated the formidable defences of the Royal Navy, carried out two torpedo attacks and then given her pursuers the slip. Had her torpedoes functioned better – or her crew been better trained in their use – the lesson could have been far more bitter for the British.

But when it came to limitations in electronic warfare and high-tech weaponry, ARA *San Luis* was in good company during the South Atlantic War. Her more successful counterpart, HMS *Conqueror*, had used old-fashioned, conventional torpedoes to sink her victim, while state-of-the-art ASW equipment was not good enough to catch *San Luis*. Two British ships had been sunk by air-to-surface guided missiles, but four had been lost to iron bombs dropped by brave and skilful pilots, differing from their Second World War predecessors only in the speeds at which they flew. For every aspect of warfare that had changed in the Falklands, another had remained the same.

One of those ancient, seemingly unchangeable factors was courage – the courage of men on both sides to face a variety of death-dealing devices that now ranged from 7.62mm bullets to guided missiles.

There had been little to distinguish Lieutenant-Commander Azcueta and his crew from the men who had fought the submariners' lone fight in past wars, save for the more advanced technology they had to face. And the fact remains that they had violated waters that none of their countrymen had been able to enter – and came back to tell the tale.

References

Burden, Rodney, *et al*. *Falklands: The Air War*, London, Arms & Armour Press, 1986.

Critchley, Mike. *British Warships and Auxiliaries*, Liskeard, Cornwall, Maritime Books, 1986.

English, Adrian, and Watts, Anthony. *Battle for the Falklands (2): Naval Forces*, London, Osprey Men-at-Arms Series No. 134, 1982.

War Machine 95: Modern Diesel Submarines, London, Orbis Publications, 1985.

Postscript

The question of how anything as inherently mobile as a ship or naval force can find itself in desperate straits has several answers. The most obvious one lies in a popular military adjunct of Murphy's Law: No plan, however well laid, survives first contact intact. The raiding force of which Captain Richard Grenville's *Revenge* was part would not have let a Spanish battle fleet get near it, had it not been pre-occupied with sick crewmen at Flores. Captain Isaac Hull could not have let a British squadron approach so dangerously near to the frigate *Constitution*, had he not been expecting an American squadron to appear in the same vicinity. *Emden*'s Captain Karl Müller would not have dallied so long at Direction Island if he had known that HMAS *Sydney* was as close as she was – and if *Sydney*'s Captain John Glossep had not maintained his radio silence in order to keep Müller in the dark. Perhaps Vice-Admiral Takeo Kurita's First Striking Force would never have got anywhere near Leyte Gulf if he had not turned and fled after undergoing air attack in the Sibuyan Sea, while at about the same time his attacker, Admiral William F. Halsey, learned the whereabouts of Vice-Admiral Jisaburo Ozawa's decoy force to the north – and even then, if an American flying-boat had overflown San Bernardino Strait at another time, perhaps the Battle of Samar might have been averted. But in war, one must always be ready to expect the unexpected – as Rear-Admiral Raizo Tanaka's destroyermen proved to be at Tassafaronga.

Sometimes, the circumstances of an uneven engagement are created by the outmatched commanders themselves. In 1692, French Admiral Count Tourville could have avoided a direct confrontation with an Anglo-Dutch fleet more than twice the size of his own off Barfleur, but a direct order from his king, combined with a fighting man's sense of duty, left him no such option. Likewise, Admiral Sir John Jervis might have been excused from taking on a much larger Spanish fleet of Cape St. Vincent, but his sense of duty also transcended such a consideration since, as he put it, 'A victory is very essential to England at this moment.' Lieutenant Isaac Brown and the crew of the ironclad *Arkansas* would have been commendably prudent in balking at the idea of taking on 33

Federal vessels off Vicksburg, but their dedication to the Southern cause of states' rights left them only two alternatives: prevail or 'die game'. Similarly, the Japanese Samurai code of *Bushido* left only two choices for the two destroyers guarding the damaged troop ship *Sasago Maru* against two waves of Allied cruisers and destroyers in Badoeng Strait: victory or death.

For the captain and crew of the Argentinean submarine *San_Luis*, their inexperience in the use of sophisticated but untried and possibly unreliable weapons against more numerous, better-trained and technologically superior adversaries was weighed against duty to orders and probably an added motive that their British counterparts would understand – a strong unwillingness to 'let the side down'. It was doubtful that they could accomplish much, but, as crewmen of the sole major Argentinean warship in the Falkland Islands, they had to try – and try they did, with courage, if not success. Arguably, the ship's company who were the least duty-bound to fight were the mainly civilian crew of the Liberty ship *Stephen Hopkins* – but fight they did.

As is the case on land, however, many desperate sea actions were motivated by the simple instincts of self-preservation, or the preservation of others. Too slow to outrun the Japanese armed merchant cruisers *Aikoku Maru* and *Hokoku Maru*, the crewmen of the oiler *Ondina* and her escort, the sloop *Bengal*, were fighting for their lives from the moment they came under fire. Captain Edward Fegen of the AMC *Jervis Bay* knew how hopeless the odds were when he squared off with the German armoured ship *Admiral Scheer*, but he had to do what he could to save the cargo ships he was escorting, if only by gaining them time to disperse. Off Samar, Rear Admiral Clifton Sprague tried to accomplish both objectives: delay Kurita's advance on the American beachhead at Leyte, while somehow keeping his own escort carrier unit from being annihilated.

In several of the actions discussed in this book, the ability of a captain or commander to evaluate the situation and make a calculated risk, rather than commit an act of blind desperation, made the difference between survival and martyrdom. Like Themistocles at Salamis, Jervis had faith that the skill and experience of his captains and crews would prevail over Spanish numbers at Cape St. Vincent – and, like Themistocles, he proved to be right. Similar confidence in his modified submarine and, to a greater degree, in the crew that manned it, attended Lieutenant Commander Norman Holbrook's venture into the Dardanelles on 13 December 1914.

If the desperation of knowing one has no other choice – by circumstance or command decision – is the common thread that runs through this volume, so too is the team effort by which the embattled naval units rise to the desperate occasion. In the case of a ship, however, teamwork is an essential element to survival under any circumstances. When not contending with human enemies, ships and their crews are engaged in a perpetual struggle with the sea itself. And for a ship's crew, their vessel is more than just a fighting platform – it is home.

A good working rapport between a capable leader and his subordinates who know what needs to be done has always been the key to a good stout fight, if not outright victory. In some cases, this rapport is established quickly between like-minded professionals, as was the case with Tourville and his squadron commanders, with Jervis and Nelson, or between Isaac Hull and the crew he carefully selected for *Constitution*. More often, it is a long, well-developed relationship, like that between Tanaka and his destroyer captains.

Given the universal need for shipboard teamwork, it may be noted that élitism appears to be less of a factor behind great sea actions than in their land-based equivalents. By 1797, the Royal Navy had established a general sense of *élan* and tradition that permeated all ranks, but more often the ships and units did not represent any special branch of their service. In many cases, the commanders and crews were motivated to some degree by a desire to 'prove something' to their superiors. In 1812, the fact that the US Navy was dismissed by the British – and the other European powers – as too small to constitute any kind of threat, motivated American seamen to do whatever they could to change that notion. During the Second World War, the *Deutches Kriegsmarine* was eager to erase the stigma of its general inactivity during the previous war. Going beyond their inherent devotion to duty, Japan's destroyermen derived a defiant, private pride in their self-perception as stepchildren of the Imperial Navy, forced to take on both the menial and the dangerous tasks in waters where more powerful ships feared to go. Members of the Confederate Navy like Isaac Brown and the crew of *Arkansas* were keen to emulate the exploits of their soldiers and, despite the greater odds they faced on the water, they did not want to be accused of failing to give their all in support of the Army and the Cause.

The greatest motivator – survival – can make even the most ordinary ship's crew rise to the occasion, as *Stier* learned when she attacked *Stephen Hopkins*, crewed by a motley collection of naval reservists and merchant seamen. Taffy 3, too, was hardly among the fighting élite of the US Navy, but when faced with a battle fleet comprising some of the most illustrious warships in the Japanese Navy off Samar, its predominantly reservist crews added names like *Hoel*, *Johnston* and *Samuel B. Roberts* to history's pantheon of hero-ships. Alas, less recognition has been afforded to the equally deserving officers and men of HMIS *Bengal* and the oiler *Ondina*.

If there is any general conclusion to be drawn from the intentionally eclectic compendium presented, it is that courage is a universal human trait. And, as my father imparted to me from his experiences during the Pacific War, 'One really cannot predict when, where or from whom heroism will emerge in combat – the emergency arises, and often some least-likely individual emerges to deal with it.'

Index